Leo Strauss

ON MODERN DEMOCRACY, TECHNOLOGY, AND LIBERAL EDUCATION

SUNY series in the Thought and Legacy of Leo Strauss

Kenneth Hart Green, editor

Leo Strauss

ON MODERN DEMOCRACY, TECHNOLOGY, AND LIBERAL EDUCATION

Timothy W. Burns

Cover image of the Churchill funeral; used by permission of British Pathé.

Published by State University of New York Press, Albany

For information, contact State University of New York Press, Albany, NY
www.sunypress.edu

Library of Congress Cataloging-in-Publication Data

Name: Burns, Timothy W., author.
Title: Leo Strauss on modern democracy, technology, and liberal education /
    Timothy W. Burns.
Description: Albany : State University of New York Press, [2021] | Series:
    SUNY series in the Thought and Legacy of Leo Strauss | Includes
    bibliographical references and index.
Identifiers: ISBN 9781438486130 (hardcover : alk. paper) | ISBN 9781438486154
    (ebook) | ISBN 9781438486147 (pbk. : alk. paper)
Further information is available at the Library of Congress.

10 9 8 7 6 5 4 3 2 1

To the memory of my parents, Tom and Liz Burns

Contents

Acknowledgments

I'd like to thank Peter Ahrensdorf, Thomas L. Pangle, and Devin Stauffer for their very valuable comments on an earlier draft of this study.

I'd also wish to thank Brill Verlag for permission to republish sections of chapter 4 of this study, which originally appeared as "Leo Strauss' 'The Liberalism of Classical Political Philosophy,'" in *Brill's Companion to Leo Strauss' Writings on Classical Political Thought* (Brill Academic Publishing, 2015), and British Pathé for permission to use the image from Churchill's funeral that appears on the cover. Finally, I'd like to thank the Roman and Littlefield Publishing Group for permission to republish sections of chapters 1 and 2, which appeared in chapter 25 of *Democracy and the History of Political Thought* (2021).

Introduction

L eo Strauss is famous for his recovery of classical political philosophy. This does not initially bespeak a friend of democracy. As he himself succinctly puts it, "To speak first of the classics' attitude toward democracy, the premises: 'the classics are good' and 'democracy is good' do not validate the conclusion 'hence the classics were good democrats.' It would be silly to deny that the classics rejected democracy as an inferior kind of regime. They were not blind to its advantages. . . . [But] the classics rejected democracy because they thought that the aim of human life, and hence of social life, is not freedom but virtue."[1] There are to be sure, as he frequently noted, differences between classical democracy, which was, owing to economic scarcity, inevitably the rule of the poor and hence the uneducated, and modern democracy, which has far more abundance and which is structured toward greater abundance. Yet modern democracy, which Strauss considered the most decent of the available modern regimes, suffers from a new malady: it is "mass democracy," and as such stands in need of an education that "broadens and deepens" the soul—the very type of education that its dynamic economy of plenty threatens to destroy.

Strauss disagreed, moreover, with a number of his prominent contemporaries, some of them friends—Krüger, Löwith, Voegelin—on the secularization thesis, according to which modern democracy embodied the historically disclosed "truth" of Christianity, the secular manifestation of an advanced moral consciousness, first expressed within Christianity, of the equal dignity of each individual. He argued that modern democracy emerged, rather, through the modern philosophic-scientific project, and has therefore within

---

1. Strauss, "What Is Political Philosophy?," in *What Is Political Philosophy? and Other Studies* (New York: Free Press, 1959), 36.

1

it the very serious threat to humanity that is posed by technology. In fact, he goes on to argue, after the passage I have quoted, that "the difference between the classics and us with regard to democracy consists *exclusively* in a different estimate of the virtues of technology." The classics foresaw that "the emancipation of technology, of the arts, from moral and political control . . . would lead to disaster or to the dehumanization of man."[2] It is this concern that predominates in Strauss's analysis of modern democracy.

Modern Political Thought as Technological Thought

Yet students of Strauss may well be surprised by his claim that the fundamental difference between the ancients and the moderns on democracy rests on the difference in their respective assessments of technology. Given Strauss's attention to *political* philosophy, one may even be (fairly) inclined to consider that statement (or even to dismiss it) as an exaggeration. In fact, however, Strauss not only made similar and corroborative statements throughout his work—from his earliest to his latest—but understood technological thinking to be at the very core of modern political philosophy: in its stand toward nature as something to be "conquered" by the increase of human "power," and its shift in human attention away from the political-moral question of the right end or ends of human life to the means to *any* desired end; in its enlisting of modern science and its attention to efficient causality in the project of conquering nature, including human nature; in its consequent and important obfuscation of the radical difference between the theoretical and practical/political/moral life; and in its promulgation of democratic and liberal political teachings.

That Strauss understood modern science as technological science is clear. In the Hobbes chapter of his first book, *Spinoza's Critique of Religion*, he identifies the spirit of modern "physics" with "technology": the very title of the book's first subsection is "The Spirit of Physics (Technology) and Religion."[3] And, as this section of the work makes clear, he identifies technology with the goal of the conquest of nature. It is a distinctively modern goal, not found in the classics. (Since recent scholarship has presented the recovery of Lucretian Epicureanism as playing a decisive role in the

---

2. "What Is Political Philosophy?," 37 (emphasis added).

3. Strauss, *Spinoza's Critique of Religion*, trans. Elsa M. Sinclair (New York: Schocken, 1965), 88.

birth of modernity,[4] it is worth noting that, as Strauss later made clear, he included Lucretius among the classics and hence as quite distinct from the modern, technological thinkers: "For Lucretius, happiness can be achieved only through contentment with the satisfaction of the natural pleasures, no rushing out, no conquest of nature, glory, domination, power, or even charitable technology—technology inspired by the desire to improve the human lot. There is a very radical difference."[5])

That Strauss saw the moderns' disposition toward technology as decisive for at least one modern political regime is also clear. Readers of Strauss are bound to be familiar with his statements concerning technology's effect on the prospects, not indeed of democracy, but of modern tyranny. In his "Restatement on Xenophon's *Hiero*," for example, he states:

> Present-day tyranny, in contradistinction to classical tyranny, is based on the unlimited progress in the "conquest of nature" which is made possible by modern science, as well as on the popularization or diffusion of philosophic or scientific knowledge. Both possibilities—the possibility of a science that issues in the conquest of nature and the possibility of the popularization of philosophy or science—were known to the classics. (Compare Xenophon, *Memorabilia* 1.1.15 with Empedocles, fr. 111; Plato, *Theaetetus* 180c7–d5.) But the classics rejected them as "unnatural," i.e., as destructive of humanity.[6]

Seven years later, in *Natural Right and History*, one finds the same focus, in the difference between the ancients and the moderns, on technology's effect on the prospects of universal tyranny:

> The world state presupposes such a development of technology as Aristotle could never have dreamed of. That technological development, in its turn, required that science be regarded as essentially in the service of the "conquest of nature" and

4. See Steven Greenblatt, *The Swerve: How the World Became Modern* (New York: W. W. Norton, 2011).

5. Strauss, in Rasoul Namazi, ed., "Leo Strauss on Thomas Hobbes and Plato: Two Previously Unpublished Lectures," *Perspectives on Political Science* 47, no. 4 (2018), 16.

6. Strauss, "Restatement on Xenophon's *Hiero*," in *On Tyranny*, ed. Victor Gourevitch and Michael S. Roth, rev. and exp. ed. (New York: Free Press, 1991), 178. See also 208.

that technology be emancipated from any moral and political supervision. Aristotle did not conceive of a world state because he was absolutely certain that science is essentially theoretical and that the liberation of technology from moral and political control would lead to disastrous consequences: the fusion of science and the arts together with the unlimited or uncontrolled progress of technology has made universal and perpetual tyranny a serious possibility.[7]

Both statements speak to the dark prospect of universal and perpetual tyranny, made possible by technology—a prospect that is, to say the least, as real as ever. What is less often observed are both Strauss's highlighting, in these statements, of the ancients' awareness of the possibility of technology, and their rejection of it on the ground that the use and dissemination of "essentially theoretical" science would be destructive of humanity. And the fundament, according to Strauss, of the ancients' humane stand against both technological science and its dissemination ("enlightenment") is the certainty that "science is essentially theoretical," and hence the gulf between the theoretical life and the life of praxis.

But this gulf obtains, necessarily, in considerations of the desirability of modern democracy no less than of modern tyranny. That this is so—and that the "destruction of humanity" is a term that encompasses not only our physical destruction—is perhaps no more clearly stated than in the original Walgreen lectures that became *Thoughts on Machiavelli*.[8] Here Strauss again makes explicit that a different disposition toward technology is the decisive difference between the ancients and us on the choice for or against democracy. He presents it as emerging from an "estrangement" or alienation from the fundamental "human situation" of "acting man," that is, of attempted discernment of our end or ends in the world of human action. And he distinguishes his attention to this estranging shift from the alternative tendency to attribute the rise of modernity to a newfound and better understanding of justice. In its stead, he proposes a different assessment of, or disposition toward, technology:

---

7. Strauss, *Natural Right and History* (Chicago: University of Chicago Press, 1953), 23. *Natural Right and History* is hereafter referred to as *NRH*.

8. Published in Anthony Vecchio and J. A. Colen, eds., "The 'Modern Principle': The Second Walgreen Lectures by Leo Strauss (1954)," *Interpretation* 47, no. 1 (Fall 2020), 43–117.

The shift from the perspective of the founder to the intellectual situation of the founder, i.e. the shift from the direct apprehension of the end to the reflection on the efficient cause implies an estrangement from the primary issue, and therewith an estrangement from the human situation, from the situation of acting man. This estrangement is connected with the assumption that chance can be conquered and therefore that the founder of society has not merely to accept the materials of his art, just like the smith and the carpenter, but that his material is almost infinitely malleable. . . . We cannot leave it then at applauding Machiavelli as a fore-runner of modern democracy, but most consider the reason why the tradition which Machiavelli attacked was not democratic. Plato and Aristotle did not lack social justice or a sense of it. They knew as well as we can know them the true principles of justice, the beautiful principles of justice. They saw therefore, as well as we do, that a society ruled by a privileged group is of questionable justice, since social superiority and natural superiority do not necessarily coincide. But it is not hard to see that only men who are truly educated, who are experienced in things noble and beautiful, ought to rule, that average men cannot fulfill this condition, if they are not well-bred from the moment they are born, that such good breeding requires leisure on the part of both the parents and the children, that such leisure requires a reasonable degree of wealth, and that having or lacking wealth is not necessarily proportionate to deserts. The classics accepted this element of arbitrariness, and therefore of injustice, because there was only one alternative to the social scheme they espoused, that alternative being perpetual revolution, which means perpetual chaos. They did not consider another alternative, namely, that all members of society should receive the same good breeding. They did not consider this alternative because they took for granted an economy of scarcity. Not a different understanding of justice, but a different notion of whether an economy of scarcity could or should be replaced by an economy of plenty, separated modern man from the classical thinkers. The problem of scarcity or plenty is however connected with the problem of [whether] the mechanical and other arts should be emancipated from moral and political control, and whether or not theoretical science should lend its supports to the increase of productivity. But increase of productivity means necessarily also increase of destructivity. What separates modern man from the classics is not a different notion of justice, but a different attitude toward technology. We are no longer so certain as we were a short while ago that we have made a decisive progress beyond the classics by taking here a different stand, or that we have chosen wisely.[9]

What here comes again into clear relief is Strauss's understanding of technology as entailing the introduction of theoretical science, and its attention to efficient causation, into the arts. The radical disjunct between theoretical and practical life—which, as we will see, is finally denied by Martin Heidegger—is a crucial part of Strauss's understanding of technology and hence of the difference between the ancients and the moderns, including their different assessments of democracy.

As Strauss next makes clear in the same talk, he did not consider the move to technology to have been necessary or impelled by a correction of an alleged weakness in philosophic thinking begun by the ancients that found its fuller elaboration or fate in the moderns: "But can we speak here of a choice? Must we not speak rather of a fateful dispensation?" (The implicit confrontation with Heidegger, who viewed technological thinking as the mysterious or fateful dispensation of Being in the West, continues here.) Strauss first, to be sure, makes the case that there was indeed a weakness to classical political philosophy that moved Machiavelli to correct the ancients by introducing an embrace of technology, or conquest of nature:

> As I see it, there was only one fundamental difficulty in the political philosophy which Machiavelli attacked. The classics were what is now called conservative, which means fearful of change, distrustful of change. But they knew that one cannot oppose social change without also opposing what is now called technological change as well. Therefore, they did not favor the encouraging of invention, except half-ironically in tyranny. Still, they were forced to make one crucial exception: they had to admit the necessity of encouraging technological invention as regards the art of war. They bowed to the inescapable requirements of defense. By accepting this principle, they might seem to be driven eventually to the acceptance of the hydrogen bomb. This

9. Strauss, in Vecchio and Colen, "Modern Principle," 107–10.

is the only difficulty which could be thought to be an entering wedge for the modern criticism of classical political philosophy, and therefore indirectly also for Machiavelli's criticism. This difficulty might be thought to imply the admission of the primacy of foreign policy.

But as he goes on to argue, it was the strictly speaking unnecessary, unfated enlistment of theoretical science in the artful conquest of nature that was decisive:

> It seems to me, however, that the real difficulty arises, not from the admission of the necessity of military invention, but from the use of *science* for this purpose. Therefore the fundamental issue concerns the character and the function of science. If we were to consider this fundamental issue, I believe we would realize that the classical position is not only thoroughly consistent, but as irrefutable as it has always been.[10]

As this statement suggests, Strauss—again, contra Heidegger—understands technology not as originating with Plato but with Machiavelli; he sees it as born not of a "fateful disposition" of Da-Sein in the West but (as he goes on to argue) of anti-theological ire;[11] as something to be distinguished sharply from the *techne* of the smith or carpenter and his tools (to which Heidegger frequently appeals early in *Being and Time* to elucidate heedful being together with the "world," or our association in and with the surrounding world);[12] as "an *estrangement* from the situation of acting man," and as consisting not of thinking essentially directed to a "standing reserve of energy," as does Heidegger, but most essentially as the deployment of theoretical science in the conquest of nature.

As the following statement from the (published) *Thoughts on Machiavelli* makes clear, Strauss did not alter his position on this matter. To the

---

10. Strauss, in Vecchio and Colen, "Modern Principle," 110 (emphasis added).

11. "I would then suggest that the narrowing of horizons which Machiavelli affected, was *caused by an anti-theological ire,* a passion which has produced and is still producing a stronger blindness in otherwise free minds, than any other passion of which I know." Strauss, in Vecchio and Colen, "Modern Principle," 111.

12. Martin Heidegger, *Being and Time*, trans. Joan Stambaugh (Albany: State University of New York Press, 1996), secs. 15–16 (*Sein und Zeit*, pp. 66–76); see also sec. 69a, pp. 322–26 (*Sein und Zeit*, pp. 352–56).

contrary: the original Walgreen lectures help us the better to understand the import of what he says in that published work:

> The classics were for almost all practical purposes what now are called conservatives. In contradistinction to many present-day conservatives however, they knew that one cannot be distrustful of political or social change without being distrustful of technological change. Therefore they did not favor the encouragement of inventions, except perhaps in tyrannies, i.e., in regimes the change of which is manifestly desirable. They demanded the strict moral-political supervision of inventions; the good and wise city will determine which inventions are to be made use of and which are to be suppressed. . . . The difficulty implied in the admission that inventions pertaining to the art of war must be encouraged is the only one which supplies a basis for Machiavelli's criticism of classical political philosophy. One could say however that it is not inventions as such but *the use of science for such inventions* which renders impossible the good city in the classical sense. From the point of view of the classics, such use of science is excluded by *the nature of science as a theoretical pursuit*. Besides, the opinion that there occur periodic cataclysms in fact took care of any apprehension regarding an excessive development of technology or regarding the danger that man's inventions might become his masters and his destroyers. Viewed in this light, the natural cataclysms appear as a manifestation of the beneficence of nature.[13]

As the founder of the technological project of putting theoretical science in the service of the political goal of the conquest of nature, Machiavelli, in Strauss's reading, launched modernity and its move toward democratic politics.

We will attempt in subsequent chapters to spell out more fully how, according to Strauss, both the promise and the threat of technology is not limited to modern tyranny but is posed likewise by modern, liberal democracy, and how the "destruction of humanity" that he has in mind involves not only its material annihilation. For now, we will note that Strauss attributes technological thinking to "our present-day orientation" broadly, and to the political doctrine and practice of liberalism—of which he considered Hobbes the founder—more particularly.

---

13. Strauss, *Thoughts on Machiavelli* (Glencoe, IL: Free Press, 1958), 298–99 (emphasis added).

He does so most explicitly in two lectures, on Hobbes and on Plato, given in 1954.[14] As these lectures make clear, what he had identified as the Machiavellian technological shift toward efficient causality was expressed broadly in Hobbes as the technological shift toward "power," that is, toward the *means* to whatever ends we happen to desire—a shift, again, away from the consideration of the right ends of human life. This shift Strauss understands to inform the political distinction between the state and society that is so crucial to modern, liberal democracy:

> The Hobbesian concept of power implies a certain indifference to the end for which the power is used. The power is, in a way, independent of the end for which it is used or to be used. This means that the concept of power as developed first by Hobbes, implies a shift in orientation from the end to the means, and this had infinite consequences. One of them, the distinction between state and society, is one of the basic principles of our present-day orientation.

As he goes on to say:

> One further point about the concept of power: Hobbes also said that science is for the sake of power. Thus, the whole theoretical, philosophic enterprise is subordinated by Hobbes to the concern with power. There is nothing said about the use of that power. We all are the heirs to this situation.

The primary *political* doctrine of modern liberalism—the distinction between the state, on one hand, and society, on the other—is thus traced by Strauss to the technological disposition (and hopes) of the moderns.[15]

---

14. "Leo Strauss on Thomas Hobbes and Plato," 13.

15. Consider also the very Cartesian reading that Strauss gives to Hobbes's work in his first (incomplete and left-unpublished) book on Hobbes, *Hobbes' Critique of Religion*, trans. Gabriel Bartlett and Svetozar Minkov (Chicago: University of Chicago Press, 2011). See Timothy W. Burns, "Leo Strauss on the Origins of Hobbes's Natural Science," *Review of Metaphysics* 64, no. 4 (June 2011), 823–55. On the composition of the German original, see Heinrich Meier, introduction to *Hobbes's politische Wissenschaft und zugehörige Schrifte—Briefe* (2001), Band 3 of *Gesammelte Schriften*, ed. Heinrich Meier (Stuttgart: J. B. Metzler, 2008), ix–xii.

But we cannot leave off this initial account of Strauss's presentation of the technological orientation of modern, liberal political philosophy, and therewith of modern man, without briefly noting that, according to Strauss, a crucial incoherence defines it from the outset. He attributes Hobbes's novel argument concerning our pursuit of "power" to Hobbes's account of a natural (innocent) desire, shared with other animals, to find the best means to any desired ends. But he ascribes Hobbes's argument about "right"—the *just* use of that power—to Hobbes's (quite incompatible) argument concerning our distinctively *human*, nonmaterial capacity to conceive of "effects imagined," to our thinking about things with regard to something other than their immediately intended utility, and thereby to our becoming aware of our power, of our powerfulness, and hence to our becoming vainglorious—to our no longer *innocently* pursuing power like animals but instead our becoming capable of consumingly and *wrongfully* proud of our ability to acquire many powerful means to our ends.

The former (the pursuit of power) informs Hobbes's account of the sovereign as the person or persons who, upon calculation, we must always obey, in pursuit of our power, regardless of his or their justice, lest we revert to the dangerous state of nature. This is a strictly materialist argument. "When Hobbes says that there are no criteria of judgment independent of positive law he implies there is nothing but natural bodies and political bodies. In no moral or political matter can you ever go behind the body politic, ultimately the will of the sovereign."[16] The latter (the distinctively human pursuit of vainglory), on the other hand, informs Hobbes's *moral* argument concerning the sovereign as a person or persons whom we must obey because his or their rule is *just*—kingly rather than tyrannical. For the human tendency to vainglory rather than to fearful, rational self-preservation is what opens up in Hobbes the possibility of naturally unjust (not self-preserving but vainglorious) action, in the sovereign or in anyone. Hobbes, that is, *attempts* to make his argument concerning "right" something grounded in our material, animal nature—with our reason as having not two ends, social and rational, but only one, rational (self-preservation), since he denies that we are beneficently social by nature. But Hobbes's attention to justice, to what (he and other) citizens or subjects believe when they distinguish between a tyrant and a just ruler, leads him, inconsistently, to abandon his naturalist-materialist account while still presenting it as a materialist account—an account allegedly consistent with, but certainly meant to bring

16. "Leo Strauss on Thomas Hobbes and Plato," 14–15.

about, the transformation of human life, by means of the new technological science, the reorientation of man away from any nonmaterial happiness that this would entail. It allows for the establishment of government that

> should make possible for the citizen to enjoy all sorts of innocent delectations and surely an air conditioner and a refrigerator are innocent delectations. In other words, Hobbes would have been very enthusiastic about the full development of the productive forces of the society and with a deep understanding of the profit motive.[17]

We will have occasion later on to spell out how this inconsistency is not, for Strauss, merely problematic, but helps to account for the continued, sustained role of a nonhistoricist, commonsense moral reasoning, and even greatness, in modern, liberal regimes. For now, we must turn to a brief, preliminary sketch of Strauss's account of how the modern technological transformation of modern politics became fully democratic.

Technology and Democracy

If the classics foresaw that "the emancipation of technology, of the arts, from moral and political control . . . would lead to disaster or to the dehumanization of man,"[18] and if it is this concern that predominates in Strauss's analysis of modern democracy, how, specifically, according to Strauss did the modern, essentially technological thought of modernity come to be democratic?

Strauss's account of how it did so begins to become clear in a sketch of the evolution of modern liberal democracy, in its resemblance to and its difference from the classical mixed regime, that Strauss draws in "Liberal Education and Responsibility." The sketch begins as follows:

> The modern doctrine starts from the natural equality of all men, and it leads therefore to the assertion that sovereignty belongs to the people; yet it understands that sovereignty in such a way

---

17. Ibid., 15. See also *What Is Political Philosophy*, 175n.

18. "What Is Political Philosophy?," 37 (emphasis added). See also "Restatement on Xenophon's *Hiero*," 178.

as to guarantee the natural rights of each; it achieves this result by distinguishing between the sovereign and the government and by demanding that the fundamental governmental powers be separated from one another. The spring of this regime was held to be the desire of each to improve his material conditions. Accordingly the commercial and industrial elite, rather than the landed gentry, predominated.

The fully developed doctrine required that one man have one vote, that the voting be secret, and that the right to vote be not abridged on account of poverty, religion, or race.[19]

Few would find fault with this brief description of the modern doctrine of (liberal or constitutional) democracy. But even as Strauss found "unhesitating loyalty to a decent constitution and even to the cause of constitutionalism," as he says later in the same essay, to be a requirement of political "wisdom," he found liberal democracy to be highly problematic. As he continues:

> Governmental actions, on the other hand, are to be open to public inspection to the highest degree possible, for government is only the representative of the people and responsible to the people. The responsibility of the people, of the electors, does not permit of legal definition and is therefore the most obvious crux of modern republicanism.[20]

Especially in light of the fact that he begins the same essay by explaining that "responsibility" is the contemporary (and degraded) substitute for "virtue," the "crux" to which he refers here initially comes to sight as the problem of the maintenance, in modern liberal regimes, of public-spiritedness or sense of duty in the people, who exercise sovereignty in liberal democracy—under the dominant activities of its new "commercial and industrial elite." But Strauss does not simply or for long identify the maintenance of public spiritedness among the people as the crux of the problem. Rather, he initially presents that as the crux of the problem as it was perceived at a certain period (the

---

19. "Liberal Education and Responsibility" in Strauss, *Liberalism Ancient and Modern* (New York: Basic Books, 1968), 9–25. The quotation is from 15. *Liberalism Ancient and Modern* is hereafter referred to as *LAM*.

20. *LAM* 155.

late eighteenth and early nineteenth century) by friends of the modern democracy that had come into being. The *deeper* (and earlier) problem, as he subsequently suggests, is tied up with the original, anti-biblical intention of the founders of the modern technological-scientific enterprise and its goal of "enlightenment" of the people. Owing to developments within the "stupendous enterprise" of modern philosophy-science, which, Strauss will argue, was from the start *behind* modern democratization, a "race" to "enlighten" the people before it came into its sovereignty replaced what had appeared, subsequently, to some to be the problem of educating the people in public-spirited virtue. The late, open admission of modern science that it is (and ever was) incapable of providing any moral guidance to anyone, but (however increasingly efficient and specialized) is in fact "value-free," has finally had the result that what most characterizes our present situation is "hardly more than the interplay of mass taste with high grade but strictly speaking unprincipled efficiency."[21] Technology, in its anti-theological end, causes democracy to emerge out of modern philosophy, and has resulted in the highly problematic, deeply degraded contemporary situation in which we find ourselves.

We have alluded to Strauss's implicit disagreement with Heidegger on the source of technology and the best disposition towards it. The more we examine Strauss's presentation of liberal democracy and technology, the more Strauss's debt to Heidegger and break with Heidegger will come into focus. We note for now that, in a talk titled "Existentialism," Strauss indicates that his concern about the degradation of humanity posed by technology is one that he had in common with Heidegger.[22] And in a letter to Heidegger student Hans-Georg Gadamer, Strauss goes so far as to express his agreement with Heidegger's characterization of our present situation as that of "the world night":

> It is strange that there should be a difference between us where you take a stand against Heidegger and I stand for him. I shall

---

21. Strauss first uses this phrase in this essay (at *LAM* 19) with reference to what is taught in contemporary political science, but he later speaks of it as emerging from modern science simply (*LAM* 22–23), on which contemporary political science attempts to model itself.

22. "Existentialism," a talk originally given at Hillel House, University of Chicago, in 1956, published in David Bolotin, Christopher Bruell, Thomas L. Pangle, eds., "Two Lectures by Leo Strauss," *Interpretation* 22, no. 3 (Spring 1995), 303–20.

state this difference in a way which probably does not do full justice to you. I believe that you will have to admit that there is a fundamental difference between your post-historicist hermeneutics and prehistoricist (traditional) hermeneutics; it suffices to refer to your teaching regarding the work of art and language which at least as you present it is not in any way a traditional teaching; this being so, it is necessary to reflect on the situation which demands the new hermeneutics, i.e. on our situation; this reflection will necessarily bring to light a radical crisis, an unprecedented crisis and this is what Heidegger means by the approach of the world night. Or do you deny the necessity and the possibility of such a reflection?[23]

That Strauss's work is everywhere a "stand toward" Heidegger, and therefore deeply informed by the work of Heidegger, is clear from the introductory remark that he makes prior to one of his rare published confrontations with that work (and even a possible invitation to dialogue with it): "As far as I can see," says Strauss, "[Heidegger] is of the opinion that none of his critics and none of his followers has understood him adequately. I believe that he is right, for is the same not also true, more or less, of all outstanding thinkers? This does not dispense us, however, from taking a stand toward him, for we do this at any rate implicitly; in doing it explicitly, we run no greater risk than exposing ourselves to ridicule and perhaps receiving some needed instruction."[24]

---

23. Strauss, letter to Gadamer, May 14, 1961, in "Correspondence with Hans-Georg Gadamer concerning *Wahrheit und Methode*," *Independent Journal of Philosophy* 2 (1978), 11. On "the world night," see Martin Heidegger, *Introduction to Metaphysics*, trans. Gregory Fried and Richard Polt (New Haven, CT: Yale University Press, 2000), 40–41 (*Einführung in die Metaphysik* [Tübingen: Max Niemeyer Verlag, 1953], 29): "For the darkening of the world, the flight of the gods, the destruction of the earth, the reduction of human beings to a mass, the hatred and mistrust of everything creative and free has already reached such proportions throughout the whole earth that such childish categories as pessimism and optimism have long become laughable." See also 47 (34 of the German): "The essential happenings in this darkening are: the flight of the gods, the destruction of the earth, the reduction of human beings to a mass, the preeminence of the mediocre."

24. Strauss, "Philosophy as a Rigorous Science and Political Philosophy," in *Studies in Platonic Political Philosophy*, ed. Thomas L. Pangle (Chicago: University of Chicago Press, 1983), 30.

But unlike Heidegger, who likewise identifies the problem of technology and utilitarian thinking as a great threat to humanity,[25] Strauss does not call for a "new thinking," characterized above all by an authentic and resolute, angst-induced attunement to one's true, "thrown" situation as disclosed in full awareness of death, to replace or directionally supplement the technological thinking that, Heidegger alleges, became more dominant in modern philosophy but has its roots in Plato's alleged failure to grasp the "ontological difference" and the need, in the light of it, to become attuned to an angst that makes possible an authentic life of being-toward-death. Strauss instead finds Plato and the other ancient political philosophers unflinchingly aware of their mortality and the passing away of all human things and of its significance, and for that very reason as drawing a sharp distinction between philosophy and political-moral thinking, with religion and ancestral tradition having an important and admirable role in the latter and serving as both a bulwark for human excellence and a crucial interlocutor with philosophy. And unlike the nihilists, both of Germany in the 1930s and of today, whose repulsion at what they saw as the immoral and amoral character of modern society led them to will the destruction of liberal democracy, he saw political-moral thinking and action, and even greatness, as manifestly still possible in modern democratic regimes—with the example of Winston Churchill being most important. The modest political recommendation that Strauss offers for our time, a time dominated by the technology of modern science, is faithful adherence to a liberal democratic constitutionalism whose tone and direction may be provided by a subpolitical "aristocracy within democracy," one whose thinking is informed by both serious religious education in one's ancestral traditions and study of the Great Books.

The four writings in which Strauss most directly addressed these matters are "What Is Liberal Education?," "German Nihilism," "Liberal Education and Responsibility," and "The Liberalism of Classical Political Philosophy." Looking first at the two works on liberal education and then at "German Nihilism" will enable us to understand the meaning of an "aristocracy within democracy" that Strass intended as the best means to sustaining and improving the regime of which he considered himself not a flatterer but a friend and ally, and the recovery of the nonhistoricist political reasoning that

---

25. See Martin Heidegger, *Gelassenheit* (Pfullingen, Ger.: Günther Neske, 1959), 24–25; *Discourse on Thinking*, trans. John M. Anderson and E. Hans Freund (New York: Harper and Row, 1966), 55–56.

would make this possible. Having examined these works, we will turn to the fourth, Strauss's extended review of Eric Havelock's *The Liberal Temper in Greek Politics*. Havelock attempted in his work to find in the classics—in Plato's work and in the pre-Socratics—a buried ground for contemporary liberalism and technology, over and against the "moral absolutism," begun by Plato, that he saw as a threat to these. By examining the classical works on which Havelock's study relies, Strauss brings to light the reason for the ancients' stand against the autonomy of technology, for their support for healthy ancestral traditions, and for the art of writing that was required by their insight into the true character of moral-political life, in its opposition to the philosophic life. In the course of doing so, he extends his critique of Heidegger and his project, which he had begun in its explicit form in *Natural Right and History*, even as he indicates some limited agreement with him on the matter of "rootedness."

Before approaching these writings, I offer the following caveat. Among the thinkers whose words Strauss examines in these essays is John Stuart Mill, who likewise devoted attention to the problem of education within modern democracy, and who likewise suggested the reading of the classics as part of liberal education. Mill did so in part because the works of the classics, unlike most works written in modern democracy, were, in his words, "not written in haste," but rather with each word carefully chosen. The *seventeen-page* essay of Strauss in which this quotation from Mill is given was written in response to a request for an elaboration on *two sentences* from "What Is Liberal Education?" It thus permits us to see, among other things, how weighted is Strauss's own writing, and so to see the careful reading that is needed to understand such careful writing. While what follows can claim to be no more than a preliminary study of these four works, I invite readers—friends and foes alike of Strauss—to join me in this preliminary effort with this need in mind.

CHAPTER ONE

Democracy and Liberal Education

In "What Is Liberal Education?"[1] Strauss makes a case for liberal education by explaining the need for it in a "modern democracy," explicitly raising the question "What is modern democracy?" He begins his answer by turning to something "once said," not indeed about modern democracy but about democracy: it "is the regime that stands or falls by virtue: a democracy is a regime in which all or most adults are men of virtue," and, he adds, "since virtue seems to require wisdom, a regime in which all or most adults are virtuous and wise, or the society in which all or most adults have developed their reason to a high degree, or *the* rational society" (*LAM* 4). He appears to have in mind the argument of Protagoras in Plato's *Protagoras* (319c–323b), as his words in subsequent chapters of this collection of essays indicate.[2]

This remarkably elevated characterization of democracy is then summarized as follows: "Democracy, in a word, is meant to be an aristocracy

---

1. Originally delivered as a commencement address; republished, without the first paragraph, in *LAM* 3–8.

2. See *LAM* 12–13, and especially 48: Strauss notes that according to Protagoras, who presents himself as the teacher of the political art, "all men must partake of reverence or right. . . . The Platonic Protagoras' assertion that there is a fundamental difference between the arts and 'man's moral sense' is meant to be the basis of democracy: all men are equal as regards that knowledge by which civil society stands or falls," that is, knowledge of the "virtue" of justice.

that has broadened into a universal aristocracy." Not surprisingly, given the actual rarity of virtue, Strauss then states that "prior to the emergence of modern democracy, theorists of democracy" felt doubts about whether such a regime is possible. For as Strauss brings out in the subsequent references to Protagoras to which we have alluded, Protagoras, claiming to teach the political art, had made his argument not in seriousness, but, prompted by Socrates, as evidence of his awareness of the need of rhetorical protection against the Athenian *demos*, who understood themselves to have already been in possession of that art or to have "divined" it. Protagoras's teaching of his (to say the least) nondemocratic civic art only to wealthy Athenians (as opposed to Socrates's desire to engage only those with good natures) needed to avoid the wrath that might well have arisen from the rest of the Athenians. Accordingly, Protagoras offered a rather severe if subdued or quietly stated "qualification of democracy" in the sequel.[3]

But this subsequent denigration of democracy by Protagoras is omitted from "What Is Liberal Education?" In its stead Strauss quotes from "one of the two greatest minds among the theorists of democracy," who also had doubts about its possibility: "If there were a people consisting of gods, it would rule itself democratically. A government of such perfection is not suitable for human beings." The (again unreferenced) quotation is from Rousseau's *Social Contract* (3.4), and offers a high-minded and even piously expressed doubt about the possibility—but not the desirability—of democracy so understood, while at the same time quietly transitioning the argument to modern political thinkers. It thereby serves Strauss's immediate purpose of condemning contemporary gainsayers of this aristocratic democracy: "This still and small voice has by now become a high-powered loudspeaker." Given Strauss's association of loudspeakers with mass parties and even totalitarian tyranny,[4] one might suspect that he is referring to Nazi and Communist practices. And he may well be. But he turns his sights instead on a different target: contemporary political scientists.

Their lack of support for the high, aspirational aristocratic democracy that Strauss has brought to his listeners' ears comes by way of their claims about the truth of democracy: it is elites who really run things. The political scientists' intent in broadcasting this claim has nothing to do with the health

---

3. *LAM* 12–13, 47, 55–56. That the people are said by Protagoras to "divine" what virtue is indicates what he takes to be the central issue dividing him from them.

4. See, e.g., "Restatement on Xenophon's *Hiero*," 195: "Much as we loathe the snobbish silence or whispering of the sect, we loathe even more the savage noise of the loudspeakers of the mass party."

of liberal democracy, much less with elevating it to a broadened aristocracy. Rather, the social science behavioralism that they practice wishes to present democracy "as it is" in contrast to its original, elevated vision; following the natural sciences, it wishes to be "value free" in its findings. Strauss highlights the oddity of our situation vis-à-vis this practice of contemporary political scientists by calling theirs an "extreme view," while noting that it is, at the same time, "the predominant view in the profession" (*LAM* 5). He reiterates this point in his concluding paragraph (8), where he suggests that political scientists' view of democracy is both the extreme and the "average" or vulgar opinion: against it, he speaks of "the boldness implied in the resolve to regard the accepted views as mere opinions, or to regard the average opinions as extreme opinions which are at least as likely to be wrong as the most strange or the least popular opinions. Liberal education is liberation from vulgarity." Contemporary political scientists, in short, ostensibly "value-free" in their studies of democracy, actually pride themselves on tearing down the elevated opinion about democracy, loudly broadcasting its allegedly real or true character, in order to disenchant their readers; they are in fact trapped in contemporary, vulgar opinion. They fail to see that precisely those with an elevated opinion of what democracy might be saw through to what it is in practice but were—and had unnoticed reasons to be—reticent about it. The remainder of the essay can therefore be seen as Strauss's case for taking seriously, as the older theorists of democracy did, the need both to see and somehow to pursue the elevation of it, even with the quiet awareness held by the older theorists of its typical character.

Contemporary political scientists, Strauss continues, describe what is necessary to the "smooth working" of democracy, and in this make their only reference to a "virtue": "electoral apathy, viz., lack of public spirit" (*LAM* 5). "Not indeed the salt of the earth but the salt of modern democracy are those citizens who read nothing but the sports page and the comics section." But this stinging rebuke of contemporary political scientists and what their writings actually promote—which, incidentally, contains an implicit contrast between what the Christian Scriptures call for and what modern democracy allegedly needs—allows Strauss to now highlight an important, and indeed defining, characteristic of liberal democracy: its distinction between a public realm, on one hand, and a private realm, society, the realm of "culture," on the other—which had been the opening theme of the talk.

"Democracy is indeed then not mass rule but mass culture," Strauss states, drawing out the conclusion to which contemporary political scientists lead one, and then adds bluntly, "A mass culture is a culture which can be appropriated by the meanest capacities without any intellectual and moral effort whatsoever and at a very low monetary price." Yet even from the viewpoint of societal need as understood by contemporary political science, Strauss argues, mass culture cannot sustain democracy. "But democracy, even if it is only regarded as the hard shell which protects the soft mass culture, requires in the long run qualities of an entirely different kind: qualities of dedication, of concentration, of breadth and of depth." And it is this need of democracy on which Strauss makes his case for liberal education, a case that does not indeed promise to fulfill the "ideal" of democracy derided by political scientists, that is, democracy "broadened into universal aristocracy." For as his other writings and talks make clear, he was aware of the fact that *liberal* democracy "stands or falls" by the distinction between the state and society,[5] and was therefore deeply wary of the government scrutiny that would result from the attempt of thinkers like John Dewey to ensure, by social engineering, that the capacities of everyone, regardless of "race, sex, class, or economic status," become "released."[6] He instead uses the distinction

---

5. See, e.g., the preface to *Spinoza's Critique of Religion*, 8: "Liberalism stands or falls by the distinction between state and society, or by the recognition of a private sphere, protected by the law but impervious to the law, with the understanding that, above all, religion as particular religion belongs to the private sphere." The distinction follows, Strauss argues, from Hobbes's redefinition of "power," and is thus part of—the political part of—the modern technological project. See also "Leo Strauss on Thomas Hobbes and Plato," 13. See also *What Is Political Philosophy*, 175n.

6. As Strauss puts it, quoting John Dewey (*Reconstruction in Philosophy* [New York: Holt], 186), " 'Government, business, art, religion, all social institutions have a meaning, a purpose. That purpose is to set free and to develop the capacities of human individuals without respect to race, sex, class or economic status.' '. . . the supreme test of the political institutions and industrial arrangements shall be the contribution they make to the all-around growth of every member of society.' " Strauss continues, "Like utilitarianism, *the theory subjects every form of organization to continual scrutiny and criticism.* But instead of leading us to ask what it does in the way of causing pains and pleasures to individuals already in existence, it inquires what is done to release specific capacities and co-ordinate them into working powers." " 'Sociology of Knowledge' in Pragmatism," lecture 3 [on Dewey] of "Philosophy and Sociology of Knowledge," lectures delivered in the summer of 1941 at the New School for Social Research, box 6, folder 9, Leo Strauss Papers, Special Collections Research Center, University of Chicago Library. (Series of sheets written with a pen, with the general titles "Philosophy and Sociology of Knowledge I" and "Philosophy and Sociology of Knowledge II," without clear division between these two.) My copy is from Emmanuel Patard, ed. and intro., "Leo Strauss at the New School for Social Research (1938–1948): Essays, Lectures, and Courses on Ancient and Modern Political Philosophy" (doctoral diss., Université Paris I Panthéon-Sorbonne, 2013), 490–91 (emphasis added). This work, hereafter cited as "Patard," is an unpublished English translation of a doctoral

within modern democracy between the state and society (or "culture")[7] to open up the possibility of founding "an aristocracy within democratic mass society":

> Thus we understand most easily what liberal education means here and now. Liberal education is the counter-poison to mass culture, to the corroding effects of mass culture, to its inherent tendency to produce nothing but "specialists without spirit or vision and voluptuaries without heart." Liberal education is the ladder by which we try to ascend from mass democracy to democracy as originally meant. Liberal education is the necessary endeavor to found an aristocracy within democratic mass society.

---

dissertation. It has been for me an invaluable source of meticulously edited writings and lectures of Strauss composed while he was teaching at the New School for Social Research. Since the work remains unpublished, I have when possible provided in all references to Strauss's texts the box, folder, and page numbers of the original documents as they appear in the Leo Strauss Papers, as supplied by Patard.

7. In presenting "culture" in this way Strauss may be said to move toward or appeal to a Kantian notion of "society" as "the voluntary" realm, or that part of the modern state/society dichotomy that not only permits the free economic competition meant to unleash the "full productive forces" of society through the "profit motive" and thus produce "innocent delectations," or comfortable self-preservation, but the voluntary, uncoerced, high moral life. See *The City and Man* (Chicago: University of Chicago Press, 1964), 33:

> The actions of the market are as such voluntary, whereas the state coerces. Yet voluntariness is not a preserve of the market; it is above all of the essence of genuine, as distinguished from merely utilitarian, virtue. From this it was inferred in modern times that since virtue cannot be brought about by coercion, the promotion of virtue cannot be the purpose of the state; not because virtue is unimportant but because it is lofty and sublime, the state must be indifferent to virtue and vice as such, as distinguished from transgressions of the state's laws which have no other function than the protection of the life, liberty, and property of each citizen. We note in passing that this reasoning does not pay sufficient attention to the importance of habituation or education for the acquisition of virtue. This reasoning leads to the consequence that virtue, and religion, must become private, or else that society, as distinguished from the state, is the sphere less of the private than of the voluntary. Society embraces then not only the sub-political but the supra-political (morality, art, science) as well. Society thus understood is no longer properly called society, nor even civilization, but culture.

> Liberal education reminds those members of a mass democracy who have ears to hear, of human greatness.

With a quotation of Max Weber,[8] Strauss indicates how even this defender of the fact-value distinction had long-standing, grave concerns about the degradation that Strauss is identifying in modern society. And, far from intending to lead a takeover of democracy by a new "elite," Strauss calls for the founding of an aristocracy within the subpolitical, "cultural" sphere of democracy, for the sake of cultivating habits of mind and heart needed by democracy, which cannot, as he sees it, sustain itself on the thin, commercial gruel of mass culture. The education of that aristocracy within democracy will be characterized above all by reminders of "human greatness."

What Strauss stated in one of his own seminars at the University of Chicago, on the day after Winston Churchill's death, permits us to begin to see what he had in mind by the need for reminders "of human greatness," over and against contemporary political science's approach to democracy:

> The death of Churchill is a healthy reminder to academic students of political science of their limitations, the limitations of their craft.
>
> The tyrant stood at the pinnacle of his power. The contrast between the indomitable and magnanimous statesman and the insane tyrant—this spectacle in its clear simplicity was one of the greatest lessons which men can learn, at any time.
>
> No less enlightening is the lesson conveyed by Churchill's failure, which is too great to be called tragedy. I mean the fact

---

8. Max Weber, *The Protestant Ethic and the Spirit of Capitalism*, translated by Talcott Parsons (New York: Scribner's, 1958), 182. "Specialists without spirit, sensualists without heart; this nullity imagines that it has attained a level of civilization never before achieved." Weber had defended both specialization in the German universities and the fact-value distinction. See his 1918 Munich University address, "Science as a Vocation" ("Wissenschaft als Beruf"), in *From Max Weber: Essays in Sociology*, trans. and ed. H. H. Gerth and C. Wright Mills (New York: Oxford University Press, 1977), 129–56. Weber stood against the existing, dilettantish *Bildung* (criticized by Nietzsche's Zarathustra in his description of the last man) and in favor of *Unterricht*, in the post–World War I battle over the future of the German university. (My thanks to Thomas Pangle for pointing this out.)

that Churchill's heroic action on behalf of human freedom against Hitler only contributed, through no fault of Churchill's, to increase the threat to freedom which is posed by Stalin or his successors. Churchill did the utmost that a man could do to counter that threat—publicly and most visibly in Greece and in Fulton, Missouri.

Not a whit less important than his deeds and speeches are his writings, above all his Marlborough—the greatest historical work written in our century, an inexhaustible mine of political wisdom and understanding, which should be required reading for every student of political science.

The death of Churchill reminds us of the limitations of our craft, and therewith of our duty. We have no higher duty, and no more pressing duty, than to remind ourselves and our students, of political greatness, human greatness, of the peaks of human excellence. For we are supposed to train ourselves and others in seeing things as they are, and this means above all in seeing their greatness and their misery, their excellence and their vileness, their nobility and their triumphs, and therefore never to mistake mediocrity, however brilliant, for true greatness. In our age this duty demands of us in the first place that we liberate ourselves from the supposition that value statements cannot be factual statements.[9]

The flesh-and-blood manifestation, in the modern world, of someone Strauss does not hesitate to call a magnanimous statesman, and his deeds—which, we note, were undertaken not on behalf of virtue but only on behalf of its necessary condition, freedom—should be called to the attention of students, as a reminder of greatness and thereby an antidote to the powerful tendency of value-free social science, precisely in pursuit of an understanding of things in liberal democracy "as they are." The reminder is unlikely to have any effect on behavioral political scientists. Its appeal is, rather, intended for youth who, reared in the fact-value distinction, need and already long to see examples of greatness—to liberate them from the artificial stifling of, or estrangement from, their moral perception by positivist, value-free social science.

9. Strauss, "Leo Strauss on Churchill," Churchill Project, Hillsdale College, https://winstonchurchill.hillsdale.edu/leo-strauss-on-churchill/.

Yet, strikingly, though he mentions freedom in this tribute, Strauss makes no appeal to "natural rights," nor to any of the other principles of liberal democracy; the contrast he draws is simply between tyranny and genuine greatness manifest on behalf of freedom. And so we must wonder: Do reminders of Churchillian greatness truly act to the benefit of liberal democracy? Is not the greatness, the high or noble rather than vulgar use of freedom, and not the freedom that is its mere condition, what we are being asked to admire? One can readily see how greatness belongs to aristocracy and hence could support the founding of an aristocracy within democratic society, but might such an aristocratic counterweight to democracy's mass culture eventually prove detrimental, precisely as it develops the strength it needs to sustain itself, to democracy and its attention to equality in freedom?

Students of Strauss may be tempted to answer this question—to explain Strauss's appeal to greatness, and to the related appeal to founding an aristocracy within a democracy—by comparison of it with the efforts of Tocqueville, another friend of democracy, and in particular to Tocqueville's attempt to cultivate practices and institutions that would put the brakes on the overwhelmingly leveling, mass tendencies of modern democracy. And there are indeed important similarities between the two thinkers, especially in their respective analyses of the reorientation of individual action by the cultural forces of mass democracy. Moreover, there is considerable agreement concerning one major threat to democracy: its temptation in the direction of egalitarian despotism: the "soft" despotism against which Tocqueville warned had taken a hard or brutally tyrannical form in the person of Stalin. In fact, Strauss here presents, as the failure of Churchill, "too great to be called tragic," the failure to defeat Stalin and his successors. Not only that: "Churchill's heroic action on behalf of human freedom against Hitler only contributed, through no fault of Churchill's, *to increase* the threat to freedom which is posed by Stalin or his successors." Now this threat was, to be sure, military and geopolitical. But it did not arise out of thin air: it included many "popular fronts" in Western Europe, and, in the United States, had from time to time in its ranks such deeply thoughtful and conscientious men as Whittaker Chambers.[10] More generally, Strauss knew

---

10. To speak of Strauss's own respectful engagement with thoughtful Marxists: students of his work are aware of his public exchange and extended correspondence with Alexandre Kojève and of his appreciative review of C. B. Macpherson's *The Theory of Possessive Individualism*. But Strauss's serious study of Marxists extends much further. He was taking seriously in the 1920s, for example, the work of Karl Korsch (*Marxismus und Philosophie*, 1923) and Georg Lukács (*Geschichte und Klassenbewusstsein*, 1923). See

that communism arose in the West, in moral reaction against the modern liberal state as outlined by Hegel, out of the perceived *failures* of that state—and not merely its perceived economic failures.[11] (As recent political events have shown, despite the fall of the Soviet Union, that threat remains with us.) Liberal democracy thus appears inherently unstable—even more so than Tocqueville saw—owing not only to a desire for material comfort but to the moral dissatisfaction with it of some of its most conscientious inhabitants and some of its more penetrating thinkers.

But there are more striking (and more fruitfully noticed) differences between Strauss and Tocqueville. To speak only of the most important: Strauss means to present through the example of Churchill the greatness of a *contemporary* statesman, *within* a liberal democracy, while Tocqueville points almost exclusively to the past for examples of greatness, and counsels contemporary *democratic* solutions—such as the doctrine of self-interest rightly understood, voluntary associations even of the most prosaic kind, and the democratic family—to "tyranny of the majority" and "individualism."

"Philosophy and Sociology of Knowledge," box 6, folder 9, Leo Strauss Papers (Patard, 498). And he referred to Lukács, in 1969, with reference to his critique of Heidegger's presentation of *Sein*, as "the most intelligent of the Western Marxists." Strauss, "The Problem of Socrates," *Interpretation* 22, no. 3 (Spring 1995), 330.

11. See, e.g., "Existentialism," in "Two Lectures by Leo Strauss," 314, where Strauss delineates the reaction to Hegel:

> The owl of Minerva commences its flight at the beginning of dusk. The completion of history is the beginning of the decline of Europe, of the west and therewith, since all other cultures have been absorbed into the west, the beginning of the decline of mankind. There is no future for mankind. Almost everyone rebelled against Hegel's conclusion, no one more powerfully than Marx. He pointed out the untenable character of the post-revolutionary settlement and the problem of the working class with all its implications. There arose the vision of a world society which presupposed and established forever the complete victory of the town over the country, of the Occident over the Orient; which would make possible the full potentialities of each, on the basis of man having become completely collectivized.

See also Strauss, "Philosophy as a Rigorous Science and Political Philosophy," in *The Rebirth of Classical Political Rationalism*, ed. Thomas L. Pangle (Chicago: University of Chicago Press, 1983), 32. And consider also Strauss's argument that anyone coming after Hegel who desired a meaningful, moral life, a life "which has a *significant* and undetermined future" (*NRH* 320; emphasis added), had to reject what was now called "theory" or philosophy in the name of "life."

Not only that (but in keeping with it): Tocqueville, who was convinced of the Christian origin of the modern movement toward liberal equality, encouraged his aristocratic readers (who, as his introduction suggests, are his primary European audience) to bow to "a force superior to man" that he saw carrying us along toward modern democracy, to *abandon* their attachment to aristocracy and the possibilities of human greatness that it made possible—and which, as he presents it, democracy must foreclose.[12] This represents more than a difference of degree between Tocqueville and Strauss. It is a difference traceable to the fact that Strauss did not subscribe to what came to be called the Whig notion of democracy's development—a variant of the secularization thesis—that lay behind Tocqueville's judgment and counsel.[13] Strauss's understanding of the modern development is closer

---

12. In his most succinct presentation of the differences between the aims of aristocratic and democratic government and society, Tocqueville addresses those who seek the promotion of loftiness of spirit, contempt for material goods, profound convictions, great devotions, elevated mores, heroic virtues, brilliance, great actions, promise of national glory, and great individual undertakings, over and against democracy's turn to the necessities of individuals, material life, prosperity and well-being, peaceful habits, and vices rather than crimes. After encouraging such readers to bow to "a force superior to man" that carries us along toward democracy, he bids them "seek at least to derive from it all the good that it can do; and knowing its good instincts as well as its evil penchants, strive to restrict the effects of the latter and develop the former." Alexis de Tocqueville, *Democracy in America*, trans. Harvey C. Mansfield and Delba Winthrop (Chicago: University of Chicago Press, 2000), vol. 1, pt. 2, ch. 6, conclusion.

13. The most important of these in France was Arthur de Gobineau, author (among many other works) of *Histoire générale de la civilisation en Europe* (1828); in the United States the most important was George Bancroft, author of the magisterial *History of the United States, from the Discovery of the American Continent*, the first volume of which appeared in 1834, though his (unattributed) work, *A History of the Political System of Europe and Its Colonies, from the Discovery of America to the Independence of the Continent* (New York: G. and C. Carvill), appeared in 1829. It is worth noting that Bancroft studied in Germany from 1817 to 1820, receiving his doctorate (under Arnold Heeren) from the University of Göttingen in 1820, having studied also at Heidelberg and Berlin. Bancroft sought out, among others, Goethe, von Humboldt, Schleiermacher, Hegel, Byron, Savigny, Constant, Guizot, Lafayette, Macaulay, and Manzoni. For more on the Whig historians, see Herbert Butterfield, *The Whig Interpretation of History* (1931; New York: W. W. Norton, 1965), which implicitly attacked Macaulay, William Stubbs, and G. M. Trevelyan as exemplars of this historical tradition. Its practitioners presented history as a struggle between the allies and enemies of progress, "of which the Protestants and whigs have been the perennial allies." Bancroft's work made it widely ascribed to especially by New Englanders in the 1830s, especially the providential role in the historical "progress"

to that of Tocqueville's friend Gobineau (from whom Strauss differed in many other respects).[14] And this means that, for all of Tocqueville's pre-

---

toward religious and political liberty. See, by contrast, e.g., Strauss's letter to Karl Löwith of August 20, 1946: "Now, around 1750 the structure of mechanistic physics and the politics resting on it is completed: the consciousness of its problematic comes into the foreground, Hume and above all Rousseau. One sees that the promise of enlightened politics (Hobbes, Encyclopedia) to create the just order through the propagation of mechanistic physics and anthropology cannot be kept; one sees it (one that is, Rousseau) because one learns to see again from Plato the problem 'science-politics' (it had never been entirely forgotten: Spinoza, also Leibniz); society needs 'religion.' A generation after Rousseau one sees that one cannot 'make' religion, as Robespierre wanted to: therefore Christianity or something like Christianity. From this reaction to the Enlightenment, the Enlightenment itself is interpreted as Christianity motivated, and this succeeds because the Enlightenment had always accommodated itself, for political reasons, to Christianity. The thus created *fable convenue* is the basis of the view ruling today."

14. See Tocqueville's letter to Gobineau, September 5, 1843: "But the most notable innovation of the moderns in morality seems to me to consist in the immense development of and the new form given in our day to two ideas that Christianity had already brought very much to the fore; that is, the equal right of all men to the goods of this world and the duty of those who have more to come to the aid of those who have less." He owns that "great and unexpected developments" in "the principle of equality" are traceable to the Enlightenment, while "Christianity had still situated rather in the immaterial sphere than in the realm of visible facts." Tocqueville notes the secularization of the Christian principle of equality, substituting as he does so "fortune" or chance for God: "Christianity had made benevolence, or, as it was called, charity, a private virtue. We make it more and more a social duty, a political obligation, a public virtue. The great number of people in need of assistance, the variety of needs that one believes oneself obliged to provide for, and the disappearance of great individuals to whom one could have recourse in order to meet such obligations, have caused everyone to look toward governments. We have imposed on them a strict obligation to redress certain inequalities, to remedy certain misfortunes, to give a hand to all the weak and all the unfortunate." Gobineau replies (September 8, 1843) with a contrast, first, between the centrality of fidelity to religious doctrine and the modern securing of religious liberty; and second, between Christian charity, for the salvation of one's soul, and the modern doctrine of "humanity," for the actual relief of, and end to, suffering: "In a word, it was no longer a question of feeling compassion for men; the only concern was for humanity. From this point of view, suffering is no longer holy. Like the plague or like scourges it must be eliminated. I will no longer take pity on the unfortunate so as to bring him momentary aid; rather, I, as subject, will give the government the means to destroy poverty, and to return the worker, who as a human being must not remain inactive, to social utility." Gobineau adds as novelties of the new morality the right to work and earn one's living versus the Christian doctrine that all are compelled to work, and the new doctrine, consistent with enlightenment, that the poor have a right to an education; a concern for rehabilitating prisoners, grounded in the will "to improve the earthly situation

scient analysis of democracy's drift toward equality of material comforts, entertainment, and security, and hence toward the soft despotism that promises to satisfy them, Strauss is more keenly insistent—and not only because of the increased progression in his century of democracy toward mass democracy—on the repulsiveness, to certain individuals (and not only French aristocrats), of the mass culture that exists even in the more or less free liberal democracies, and hence of the deep need to respond to it with *contemporary* examples of greatness. But then the comparison of Strauss's effort with that of Tocqueville only sharpens our question: Is the appeal to greatness, and to the founding of an aristocracy within democracy, not bound to be at odds, in the long run, with democracy?

We cannot answer this question without examining a prior appeal by Strauss to Churchillian greatness made by Strauss in the context of his account, in "German Nihilism," of the thinking that moved intelligent but badly directed German youth to support National Socialism, over and against liberal democracy. We will undertake such an examination in chapter 3. The remainder of "What Is Liberal Education?," together with the elaboration on the need for and the meaning of an "aristocracy within democracy" that

---

of humanity." "The rights of the guilty! Now there is surely an altogether modern application of the word 'rights.'" Elaborating on this appeal of modernity to the self-interest of the individual, he states, "Christianity banished the passions with severity; contemporary morality is seen to be indulgent towards them and does not give up on reconciling them with morality, because it thinks that many of them are useful. Thus the love of luxury and of material pleasures is no longer an evil." The modern moral order is one "that is now more indulgent to [every man's] natural inclinations." He adds, as a cautionary note, that "clearly ancient religions had a ready means to ennoble morality by putting it under the aegis of divinity. Now it has been brought down to earth, and it is not yet clear what it derives from." Tocqueville responds (October 2, 1843) first by confessing that he is not a believer, and then by distinguishing Christianity "in itself" from how it has come down to us, namely, as "a weapon in the hands of kings and priests." He admits that "when heavenly pleasures are lost to view, one obviously concentrates increasingly on the only remaining goods, those of this world," but denies that this means that modern doctrines do not have their source in Christianity. He doubts that the modern "rehabilitation of the flesh," over and against the Christian glorification of the spirit "to extremes," is traceable to modern philosophers: "The flesh would have rehabilitated itself just fine without the help of philosophers." He concedes "that charity, which was private, has become social." He adds that "most of the things that you take to be innovations in morality seem to me to be the natural and necessary effects of the weakening of religious faith and of doubt concerning the other world." He fails to consider the possibility, raised by Strauss, that this weakening was the practical and theoretical goal of modernity. Hence he remains convinced that "Christianity is the great source of modern morality." (Translation by Ralph Hancock, for a Liberty Fund conference, Burlington, VT, June 2002).

Strauss provides in "Liberal Education and Responsibility," will prepare us to fully understand that work.

Contemporary Nihilists, Ancestral Traditions, and Liberal Education

Having stated that liberal education entails reminders of greatness that are much needed in modern mass democracy, Strauss's argument in "What Is Liberal Education?" now takes (at the bottom of *LAM* 5) a somewhat surprising turn. We may say that Strauss here presents, and invites us to a sympathetic consideration of, a contemporary (kinder, gentler) version of the argument that we will see presented by the German nihilists of the 1920s and 1930s. He here presents an objector who finds the argument he has made for liberal education in modern, mass democracy to be "merely political." It fails, it would seem to this objector, to realize the depth of the problem faced by "the whole of modern society"; it "dogmatically assumes the goodness of modern democracy." Like the German nihilists, the objector raises a moral outcry against, and expresses a moral desire to wipe out, modernity and its technology, and "return" to a better, primitive past: an image of pristine nature, prior to its destruction and death for human purposes, informs his question: "Can we not return to nature? To the life of preliterate tribes? Are we not crushed, nauseated, degraded by the mass of printed material, the graveyards of so many beautiful and majestic forests?"

We might well associate the objector with a member of the deep ecology movement that was to arise soon after Strauss's words were written: someone who is disgusted with technology, morally repulsed that beautiful or magnificent trees, there by nature and (or when) beheld by man uncorrupted by or freed from technology, are turned into pulp for books. "It is not sufficient," Strauss warns his listeners, "to say that this is mere romanticism, that we today cannot return to nature." For the very power unleashed by technology makes the vision informing the objector's otherwise futile moral longing a serious possibility: a cataclysmic thermonuclear war could *compel* future generations "to live in illiterate tribes." Strauss's admonition appears to be a response to Heidegger, whose work did in fact come to inform that of leaders of the deep ecology movement.[15]

---

15. For an account of that influence that is both sympathetic and critical, see Michael E. Zimmerman, "Re-thinking the Heidegger–Deep Ecology Relationship," *Environmental Ethics* 15, no. 3 (1993):195–224. —Strauss presents the two "prospects" of living in

The objector's "longing for a return to nature" that is made "intelligible" by "the horrors of mass culture"[16] is answered by Strauss as follows. He first notes that "an illiterate society at its best is a society ruled by age-old ancestral custom." What it is like at its worst—perhaps for millennia—Strauss, following Aristotle (*Politics* 1253a29), leaves largely to his listeners or readers to imagine.[17] For at its best—which is how the objector imagines it—it must entail already "ancestral custom"; law, divine law, in the beginning of its problematic status, emerges in this prephilosophic state of reasoning, in a way that the nature-revering Heideggerian objector, in his deprecation of what is merely "political," appears to have overlooked. A preliterate people ruled by "age-old ancestral custom" will trace this custom "to original founders, gods, or sons of gods or pupils of gods" (for reasons we will elaborate in chapter 3). But "since there are no letters in such a society, the late heirs cannot be in direct

---

illiterate tribes or enduring "the horrors of mass culture" as coming to "affect our thoughts concerning thermonuclear war." Contrast Heidegger's *Gelassenheit*, 24–25; *Discourse on Thinking*, trans. John M. Anderson and E. Hans Freund, trans. (New York: Harper and Row, 1966), "Memorial Address," 55–56, where Heidegger argues that "a far greater danger threatens" than "the complete annihilation of humanity and the destruction of the earth" that would result from an atomic world war, "precisely when the danger of a third world war has been removed." He describes that danger as follows: "The approaching tide of technological revolution in the atomic age could so captivate, bewitch, dazzle, and beguile man that calculative thinking may someday come to be accepted and practiced as the only way of thinking. What great danger then might move upon us? Then there might go hand in hand with the greatest ingenuity in calculative planning and inventing indifference toward meditative thinking, total thoughtlessness. And then? Then man would have denied and thrown away his own special nature—that he is a meditative being. Therefore, the issue is the saving of man's essential nature. Therefore, the issue is keeping meditative thinking alive." And he presents that thinking as available to all: "Yet anyone can follow the path of meditative thinking in his own manner and within his own limits" (47).

16. Strauss includes "guided tours of integer nature" (*LAM* 6) among what the objector will consider horrors. Compare Martin Heidegger, "The Question Concerning Technology," in *The Question Concerning Technology and Other Essays*, trans. with intro. William Lovitt (New York: Harper and Row, 1977), 16: "Let us ponder for a moment the contrast that speaks out of the two titles, 'The Rhine' as dammed up into the power works, and 'The Rhine' as uttered out of the art work, in Hölderlin's hymn by that name. But, it will be replied, the Rhine is still a river in the landscape, is it not? Perhaps. But how? In no other way than as an object on call for inspection by a tour group ordered there by the vacation industry." Heidegger also uses the example of the felling of trees and their use in the forestry industry for cellulose used for paper, as an example of how humans become swept up in the results of authoritative technology (18).

17. Consider, by contrast, *The City and Man*, 126.

contact with the original founders; they cannot know whether the fathers or grandfathers have not deviated from what the original founders meant, or have not defaced the divine message by merely human additions or subtractions." A moment's reflection tells us that this argument contains a quiet acknowledgment that *all* ancestral guidance must be to peoples who were, at one time in their past, preliterate tribes, and hence that *all* claims to knowledge of what was told to remote ancestors is necessarily questionable and so will result in questions. "Hence," says Strauss, "an illiterate society cannot consistently act on its principle that the best is the oldest." If it is sufficiently thoughtful, such a society will begin to attempt then to understand what is best simply, or understand what the gods in question must have said,[18] on the basis of their judging, reasoned perception of the world. Strauss does not draw this conclusion, confining himself to the much narrower point that "only letters that have come down from the founders can make it possible for the founders to speak directly to the latest heirs," and thus that it is "self-contradictory to wish to return to illiteracy." Yet even this limited reply, by speaking of "the latest heirs," echoes the problem of the ancestral in light of what appears best, since these "heirs" necessarily belong to what, at least hitherto, had long been an illiterate society. "Letters," in other words, arrive late, and arrive when or as the problematic status of the divine ancestral law has already begun to emerge. These writings may—in the rare case—take something akin to the biblical route of turning away from the incipient philosophic reasoning that moves away from the ancestral, while deepening the ancestral insight that justifies such turning away; or they may follow a poetic or mythical route, which takes up the problematic even as it pays deference to the ancestral.[19] In any event, those writings are not immune to the kind of rational scrutiny to which, as Strauss suggests next, Socrates and his companions subjected them, in light of the distinction between the great or noble, on one hand, and what is useful to happiness, on the other, that characterizes Socrates's investigation of old books as well as his dialogues with young men.[20]

But the "perfect gentlemanship" that Strauss describes as emerging from a Socratic education in old books is made immediately ambiguous: only a rare few, and not "we," are likely to become philosophers, in the serious and ancient sense of seekers of wisdom, though we can, he argues, through

18. Compare Strauss, *The Argument and Action of Plato's "Laws"* (Chicago: University of Chicago Press, 1975), 7, 8, 11, 21, 146, 166, 169–70.

19. See chapter 3, p. 106, note 59, chapter 4, pp. 141–42, note 33, and chapter 5, p. 181, note 21.

20. *LAM* 6.

the perfect gentlemanship that education brings about and that welcomes examples of human greatness, be open to the philosophic life as the best candidate for the best life, and even "try to philosophize" by listening to the conflicting arguments of the greatest minds.[21] But, as he makes clear, this education will not strictly speaking be philosophic, even if, in rare cases, it results in the emergence of a philosopher. It faces, moreover, the need to overcome the contemporary "facile delusion" of perspectivalism of "comprehensive views," brought about by the Enlightenment's attempt to found a rational society. (Just how the attempt to form a rational society brought this about Strauss does not here say, and we need to be attentive to indications of it in the next chapter.) Such perspectivalism hides from us, Strauss asserts, our "awesome situation."

He presents—perhaps surprisingly, in light of his stress on the *philosophic* part of the needed education—that situation as one in which "we have lost all simply authoritative traditions in which we could trust," a situation caused by the fact that "our immediate teachers and teachers' teachers believed in the possibility of a simply rational society." Liberal education, he thereby implies, was once education in *authoritative traditions*, though one that developed, at some point, a relation with a Socratic examination of the "old books" in which ancestral divine law was elaborated and explored. With the loss of authoritative traditions, we face a novel situation: "Each of us here is compelled to find his bearings by his own powers, however defective they may be." And he warns that "we have no comfort other than that inherent in this activity. Philosophy, we have learned, must be on its guard against the wish to be edifying—philosophy can only be intrinsically edifying."[22] Strauss does not offer philosophy as providing to nonphilosophers any morally edifying guidance to political life in our present, "awesome" situation.

An implicit contrast is thus drawn by Strauss between the (non-edifying) classical, Socratic philosophy to which he here points, and the

---

21. *LAM* 7–8.

22. By philosophy's "wish to be edifying" Strauss appears here again to have Heidegger in mind above all. See Martin Heidegger, "The Self-assertion of the German University and The Rectorate 1933/34: Facts and Thoughts," trans. with intro. Karsten Harries, *Review of Metaphysics* 38, no. 3 (1985): 467–502. Heidegger presents the science or knowing of Germans (and, through them, all humans) as taking place in a new situation, one quite different from that of "the Greeks": we must now engage in science in light of the finding of Nietzsche, "that passionate seeker of God," that "God is dead," and hence "face up to the forsakenness of modern man in the midst of what is" (474). See below, chapter 4, pp. 135–139.

modern political philosophy that has brought about the destruction of all traditions and hence our present situation. Socratic political philosophy was, it seems—perhaps in awareness of the rarity of genuine philosophizing and its intrinsic edification—much friendlier toward, more attentive to the preserving of, those authoritative traditions than was modern philosophy, even as it engaged, for its own private purposes (with "friends"), in a questioning of those traditions. We recall that, with regard to democracy, the difference between the two rests in their respective stance toward the liberation of technology,[23] which the classics rejected on the ground that it would lead to the "dehumanization of man." Modern philosophy was actively destructive of traditions, above all of the biblical tradition, which Strauss now alludes to, in his final paragraph, by speaking of the "evils" which "may well break our hearts in the spirit of good citizens of the City of God," and of realization of the "dignity of man" resting on awareness of "the dignity of the mind," the mind as "created" by that God. (He implicitly contrasts with this the philosophic disposition whose "understanding of understanding," "so high, pure, noble an experience that Aristotle could ascribe it to his God," leads one to "the realization that all evils are in a sense necessary if there is to be understanding, to "accept all evils," and to realize that the "dignity of man" rests on awareness of "the dignity of the mind," the mind as "uncreated.") The modern embrace of technology "for the relief of man's estate" has led to the loss of this rich, ennobling biblical tradition. While Strauss sometimes indicated that that embrace had a certain indirect biblical root, in the (heartbreaking) disappointment with Providence and the determination to replace it with human providence,[24] he argued, as we will see in the next

---

23. Again, according to Strauss, "The difference between the classics and us with regard to democracy consists *exclusively* in a different estimate of the virtues of technology." *What Is Political Philosophy?*, 37 (emphasis added).

24. In *The City and Man* (41–43), Strauss makes an extended argument concerning Aristotle's principle that there exists a life affording man a happiness that is according to nature. The moderns' attack on Aristotle's principle does not rest, according to Strauss, on their rejection of final causes. It instead begins in thoughtful agreement with a conclusion that Aristotle himself suggests when he declares that our nature is enslaved in many ways, that is, that nature is a harsh step-mother, or that "the true mother of man is not nature" (42). Modern thought alone draws from this common conclusion "the consequent resolve to liberate man from that enslavement by his own sustained effort." This new resolve shows itself in the "demand for the 'conquest' of nature: nature is understood and treated as an enemy who must be subjugated" by a humble and charitable science "devoted to the relief of man's estate" [a statement from Bacon], a science that would provide means to achieve the natural end of "comfortable self-preservation"

(42). While the modern resolve to liberate man from nature appears, to the moderns themselves, to be less naive than Aristotle's position, it might, Strauss here suggests, be better understood as a failure of resignation, a disappointed hope in the existence of a caring God and a consequent, confused sense of a "right to rebel" (41), in order to do for humanity what such a God would have done.

Consider also the following statement concerning Hobbes's and other modern philosophers' disposition toward nature, from a 1947 lecture at the New School, "The Origin of Modern Political Thought," typed manuscript, 50 pages, box 14, folder 11, Leo Strauss Papers (Patard, 311–53, at 352):

> Nature is, however, felt as a menace not because man has now discovered natural evils either in the world or in himself, which were unknown to classical philosophy, but because man had been accustomed by a tradition of almost two thousand years to believe himself or to be protected by Providence. When this belief became shattered, he could not immediately cease to hope for Providence, to expect help from it. Denial of Providence was thus from now on related not to serene and detached philosophizing, but rather to disappointed hope in Providence. What was in earlier times nothing more than the complaint of suffering, not yet enlightened, Job, became now, as it were, the keystone of philosophy. No classical philosopher could have said what Voltaire put into verses on the occasion of the earthquake of Lisbon.

On the Platonic-Aristotelean alternative, resignation toward our "enslavement" to nature, or our being "playthings of the gods," see also *NRH* 177: "No Scipionic dream illuminated by a true vision of the whole reminds [Hobbes's] readers of the ultimate futility of all that men can do." Not only in the Epicurean tradition but likewise in what Strauss has been calling, in *Natural Right and History*, the classical "idealistic" tradition of political philosophy, one finds a resignation to man's ultimate destruction. On this point, and the resigned moderation that results from such a vision of the whole, see also "The Problem of Socrates," second lecture, in *The Rebirth of Classical Political Rationalism*, ed. Thomas L. Pangle (Chicago: University of Chicago Press, 1989), 133, where Strauss addresses the "false estimate of human things" as a "fundamental and primary error." See also the subsequent discussion of spiritedness in the fourth lecture (167). Consider also the following statement from Strauss's "The Three Waves of Modernity," in *Political Philosophy, Six Essays*, ed. Hilail Gildin (Indianapolis: Bobbs-Merrill, 1975): "Man has a place within the whole: man's power is limited; man cannot overcome the limitations of his nature. Our nature is enslaved in many ways (Aristotle) or we are the playthings of the gods (Plato). This limitation shows itself in particular in the ineluctable power of chance. The good life is the life according to nature, which means to stay within certain limits; virtue is essentially moderation. There is no difference in this respect between classical political philosophy and classical hedonism which is unpolitical: not the maximum of pleasures but the purest pleasures are desirable; happiness depends decisively on the limitation of our desires" (84–85). The Plato statement can be found at *Laws* 709a1–3; compare *Laws* 644d7–e4 and 803c4–5. In his commentary on the passage in the *Laws* (*The Argument and Action of Plato's "Laws,"* 105–6), Strauss says the following:

chapter, that the attribution of the rise of both technology and democracy to Christianity was a deliberate misunderstanding, perpetrated by the Enlightenment and its science, to hide its true intention, which from the start was to bring about the disenchantment of human life. And what Strauss will point to emphatically in his analysis of the dangers of contemporary mass democracy is its *failure* to produce, as its philosophic progenitors had expected, a society that is genuinely satisfying to those who desire a fully human life. We note here only that in his celebrated exchange with Alexander Kojève, Strauss includes an extended statement concerning the negating activity of modern technological science, the fact-value distinction to which it (inevitably) gave rise, and the dehumanization of man that results from it.[25] It is with this failure in mind that we will begin to understand why he thought the appeal to contemporary, Churchillian greatness is so crucial with regard to the future of liberal democracy. In his "German Nihilism" talk, both the significance of that appeal for liberal democracy, and the humane, moral reasoning that Strauss wished to engender on its basis, becomes more apparent. Before turning to it, however, we will take advantage of the great opportunity supplied by "Liberal Education and Responsibility" to learn what Strauss means by "an aristocracy within democracy" and how, through the rise of technology and democracy, it came to be needed.

> We must never forget however that men are in the main puppets, partaking of the truth only in some small points (cf. 889d1–2). Megillos, the Spartan, is thoroughly displeased with this depreciation of the human race. The Athenian apologizes, therefore, excusing his statement by the fact that he had looked away toward the god and had therefore been affected in the way he was. We recall that the goal of education is the perfect human being (653a9). But if there is no perfect human being, if no human being is simply wise but in the best case a lover of wisdom (*philosophos*), one cannot help looking away toward the simply wise being, the god. The dissension between Megillos and the Athenian is the dissension between the political man who necessarily takes the human things very seriously, and the philosopher.

25. "Restatement on Xenophon's *Hiero*," 208–9: In the universal and homogeneous world state, "work in the strict sense, namely the conquest or domestication of nature, is completed. . . . Kojève in fact confirms the classical view that unlimited technological progress and its accompaniment, which are indispensable conditions of the universal and homogeneous state, are destructive of humanity. . . . Yet there is no reason for despair as long as human nature has not been conquered completely, i.e., as long as sun and man still generate man. There will always be men (*andres*) who will revolt against a state which is destructive of humanity or in which there is no longer a possibility of noble action and of great deeds."

CHAPTER TWO

An Aristocracy within a Democracy

"Liberal Education and Responsibility"

As noted in our introductory chapter, Strauss elaborates, in this seventeen-page response to a group dedicated to adult education, just what he means by the claim that liberal education entails the founding of an aristocracy within democracy. In the midst of doing so he notes the reigning alternative understanding, to his, of the origin and purpose of modernity—of modern natural science and of modern democracy—and articulates his own understanding of their origin and purpose and thereby of the current situation of democracy, to which his proposed education offers a modest corrective.

Since he had proposed, in his earlier talk, a liberal education that combines what is needed for "perfect gentlemanship" with the study of philosophy, Strauss first clarifies the original understanding of the relation of gentlemen and their regime, aristocracy, to philosophy, and clarifies the uneasy relation between them, or the limited "support" that philosophy offered to their education. He first provides a sketch of the original education of the gentleman, which was "liberal" in a sense "almost the opposite of its present political meaning": it was an education becoming a free man and the leisure that his wealth made available to him; it was a youthful preparation for the most serious or "earnest" things, the "most weighty matters," the "only things that deserve to be taken seriously for their own sake," namely, "the good order of the soul and of the city." It was an education "above all in the formation of character and taste," and "its fountain was the poets" (*LAM* 11). It also involved or was supplemented by the acquisition of "skills" needed to "administer nobly the affairs of his household and the affairs of his city by deed and by speech." The latter were acquired through "familiar intercourse with older and more experienced gentlemen, preferably with elder statesmen," by paid instructors in speaking, reading histories and books of travel, and "meditating on the works of the poets." While the "experience" of the statesmen in question would undoubtedly include acquisition of such useful skills, the stress is on contact with elders, and the heart of the education was clearly "the poets." There was no "philosophy" in this education.

To fully exercise their way of life, the gentlemen must rule, and Strauss next provides a presentation of the public aims of the ruling gentlemen (the aristocratic rulers), that is, the justifications they made for their rule, and he describes these in dialectical fashion (*LAM* 11–12). Perhaps especially with a view to the modern development that he will go on to describe, Strauss includes the economic justification made by the gentlemanly aristocrats. To be just, their rule has to be with a view to "the interests of the whole of society, and not merely a part"; their rule must be shown to themselves and everyone to be "best for everyone or for the city as a whole." And since they cannot reasonably be said to be unequal to the poor by birth but only by dint of an education unavailable to the poor, their rule appears unjust. The reply of the aristocrats is that equality in education will produce no more than "equality in drabness," founded on a demand of justice motivated by "the ignoble passion of envy," instead of "a structure which from a broad base of drabness rises to a narrow plateau of distinction and grace and therefore gives some grace and some distinction to its very base." Yet as helpful as this is in showing what it would mean for aristocratic gentlemen, who are guided by the noble, to set the tone of a whole society, it does not, Strauss indicates, answer the democrats' question of why, given the scarcity of resources, this family should be condemned to drabness and that one elevated to distinction. "The selection seems to be arbitrary, to say the least," especially when one recognizes that the aristocrats' wealth may "have its origins in crime." The next claim Strauss makes on the gentleman's behalf, that it is "more noble to believe, and probably also truer" that the "old families are the descendants from the first settlers and from leaders in war or counsel," a belief that should prompt a just gratitude from the people, can hardly be said to meet the issue. Little wonder that the ancient philosophers, as Strauss puts it a bit later, had "no delusions about the possibility of a perfect aristocracy ever becoming actual" (17; see also 21). Finally, the gentlemen cannot rule by popular election or be "responsible to the people" because the distance between themselves, who "regard virtue as choiceworthy for its own sake," and the demos or "vulgar," who regard virtue as "a means to acquiring wealth and honor," made it impossible for there to be "genuinely common deliberations" between the two: "The gentlemen cannot possibly give a sufficient or intelligible account of their way of life to the others" (12).

In light of this rule of gentlemen, democracy appears to be majority rule "of the uneducated" poor. "The principle of democracy is therefore not virtue but freedom as the right of every citizen to live as he likes."[1] Strauss adds to this simple statement of the principle of classical democracy that the attempt of the sophist Protagoras to teach the political art to the wealthy in a democratic city must be preceded by his disingenuous claim that it is an art already possessed by all "as a divine gift." Despite its apparent easy-goingness, the regime of the people is, this may remind us, even more than aristocracy, the home of piety.[2]

It is then the education of the gentlemen of the aristocratic regime, an education that "fosters civic responsibility and is even required for the exercise of civic responsibility," and whose liberally educated gentlemen "set the tone" by "ruling in broad daylight," into which "philosophy" suddenly enters. Repeating that "the pursuits becoming a gentleman are said to be politics and philosophy," Strauss suggests that the gentlemen were induced to see philosophy as the proper activity of their leisure, which even politics

---

1. *LAM* 12, bottom. Cf. *Republic* 557a–562c. It is striking that both here and in the section of his commentary in *The City and Man* that interprets the passages on democracy in book 8 of the *Republic*, Strauss uses the term "right" and even the plural "rights" in the modern sense of justified claims. *The City and Man* (on 131) states, "Democracy comes into being when the poor, having become aware of their superiority to the rich and perhaps led by some drones who act as traitors to their class and possess skills which ordinarily only members of a ruling class possess, at an opportune moment make themselves masters of the city by defeating the rich, killing and exiling some of them and permitting the rest to live with them in possession of full citizen rights. Democracy itself is characterized by freedom which includes the right to say and do whatever one wishes: everyone can follow the way of life which pleases him most."

2. The mention of "the sophist Protagoras" just before the introduction of "philosophy" in the discussion of the liberal education of the gentleman, and of how that education is transformed or "takes on a new meaning" thereby (*LAM* 13), might also signal a path to the introduction of philosophizing into a city that might otherwise be hostile to it. Consider its introduction, for example, in book 10 of Plato's *Laws*, as a means of combatting the atheistic doctrines of the sophists' account of the whole.

could not simply be said to be.[3] But the commonality of ends of the two is ambiguous. The gentleman pursues "decent political ends," while the philosopher engages in a "quest for truth about the most weighty matters" or "for the comprehensive truth" or "for truth about the whole" or "for the science of the whole" (*LAM* 13). These related but different alternative ends of the philosophic life, set off (as is often the case in Strauss's writings) by the disjunctive "or," differ in all cases from the ends of political life in that the latter are not investigated but instead "clearly presupposed by politics," and yet are said to "surely transcend politics." A genuine but limited commonality of the two ways of life is thus suggested; what affords a commonality is concern for "weighty matters" and the human soul: "For everything that comes into being through human action," Strauss states, explaining the transcending of politics of the ends that it presupposes, "and is therefore perishable or corruptible presupposes incorruptible and unchanging things—for instance, the natural order of the human soul—with a view to which we can distinguish between right and wrong actions" (13).

If this argument begins to suggest why the gentleman might be interested in philosophy, it does not yet tell us why a philosopher would be interested in gentlemen and their politics. Or rather, it only suggests it. If the philosopher's "dominating passion is the desire for truth, i.e., for knowledge of the eternal order, or the eternal cause or causes of the whole,"[4]

---

3. Strauss suggests this in the following way. Following Aristotle (*Politics* 1254a14–17 with 1255b37), he initially states that the free human being who is the master of his own time engaged in "the pursuits becoming him: politics and philosophy" (*LAM* 10, bottom). He then presents the gentleman, whose wealth and delegation of supervision of his country estate afford him leisure, as moving to the city and engaging in rule because he is compelled to "secure" his way of life from the rule of non-gentlemen (11). The virtue of the noble activity of politics has, this suggests, a strong element of the useful, or its virtue could well appear to be a means rather than the end that the gentleman claims and wishes it to be. (See also Aristotle, *Nichomachean Ethics* 1177b4–24.) The gentleman will then be on the lookout for a "noble" activity for his leisure that is genuinely an end in itself and hence becoming of him as a free man, and hence he will be not undisposed to philosophy as a possible candidate for that activity, especially if (as is the case with a Socratic political philosophy) that activity concerns the serious matter of "the good order of the soul" or what the philosopher calls "the nature of the human soul" (*LAM* 11, 13).

4. *On Tyranny*, 197–98; see also 212: "quest for the eternal order or for the eternal cause or causes of all things." See *NRH* 89–90, which contains no reference to "eternal order":

this entails, in any genuine philosophizing, a disposition or attitude toward causes—permanent necessities—that is at odds with that of political life. For the possibility of a genuine "*science* of the whole" requires that the whole be governed by the "necessities" to which Strauss alludes with his example of the soul.[5] Science requires that such necessities be genuine necessities, not only

---

"The philosophic quest for first things presupposes not merely that there are first things but that the first things are always and that things which are always or are imperishable are more truly beings than the things which are not always. These presuppositions follow from the fundamental premise that no being emerges without a cause or that it is impossible that 'at first Chaos came to be,' i.e., that the first things jumped into being out of nothing and through nothing. In other words, the manifest changes would be impossible if there did not exist something permanent or eternal, or the manifest contingent beings require the existence of something necessary and therefore eternal. . . . One may express the same fundamental premise also by saying that "omnipotence" means power limited by knowledge of "natures," that is to say, of unchangeable and knowable necessity; all freedom and indeterminacy presuppose a more fundamental necessity." In On *Tyranny* (200–201), when speaking of potential philosophers, whose souls "reflect the eternal order" by being "well-ordered souls," Strauss admits that this argument (which he had already indicated was made in a "popular and hence unorthodox manner") is defective: it cannot explain, for example, the souls of the pre-Socratic philosophers or of modern philosophers, who certainly did not think the whole well ordered.
Consider also Strauss, "The Mutual Influence of Theology and Philosophy," *Independent Journal of Philosophy* 3 (1979), 114.

> Classical philosophy is said to be based on the unwarranted belief that the whole is intelligible. Now this is a very long question. Permit me here to limit myself to say that the prototype of the philosopher in the classical sense was Socrates, who knew that he knew nothing, therewith admitted that the whole is not intelligible, who merely wondered whether by saying that the whole is not intelligible we do not admit we have some understanding of the whole. For of something of which we know absolutely nothing, we could of course not say anything, and that is the meaning, it seems to me, of what is so erroneously translated by the intelligible, that man as man necessarily has an awareness of the whole. Let me only conclude this point. As far as I know, the present-day arguments in favor of revelation against philosophy are based on an inadequate understanding of classical philosophy.

5. That is, his reference to the "*natural* order of the human soul," the study of which, unlike "human things," belongs *not* to political philosophy but to physics. See *The City*

in the soul but in "the whole." These very necessities are, moreover—if they exist—precisely what would dictate that "everything that comes into being through human action" is "perishable or corruptible," and, as Strauss makes clear elsewhere, not only things that come into being by human action, or "History," but *all* of what has come into being.[6] Yet precisely those engaged

---

and Man, 13: "'The human things' are not 'the nature of man'; the study of the nature of man is part of the study of nature." See also "Note on 'Some Critical Remarks on Man's Science of Man,'" (New School, 1945), box 14, folder 9, Leo Strauss Papers; José A. Colen and Svetozar Minkov, eds., "Leo Strauss on Social and Natural Science: Two Previously Unpublished Papers," *Review of Politics* 76 (2014): 619–633, at 632–33 (emphasis added):

> According to Aristotle, the study of human nature is a part of natural philosophy, whereas according to Bacon that study is a part of human philosophy; to say nothing of the fact that the Aristotelian distinction is equivalent to the distinction between theoretical and practical philosophy, whereas for Bacon the distinction between theoretical and practical philosophy ceases to be fundamental. . . . To understand the fact that the philosophic tradition split up the study of man among two main branches of inquiry—among the study of *human nature* which was considered a part of natural science, and the study of *human things* which was practically identical with political philosophy in the broad sense of the term—it suffices perhaps to understand a passage of the *Nicomachean Ethics* (1141a22–24). Aristotle says: "'healthy' and 'good' are different when applied to men or to fish, but 'white' and 'straight' are the same always." If we call something healthy or good, we imply that it is healthy or good *for man*. But if we say that a body is white or that a line is straight, we do not imply that the body is white for man only or that the line is straight for man only. There are things that are what they are simply and there are things that are what they are only for man as man, to say nothing of other things that are what they are only for man belonging to specific groups. This fundamental distinction is at the bottom of the distinction between theoretical and practical philosophy, and in particular of the distinction between the study of human nature and the study of human things, i.e., of the things that are what they are only for man.

6. *On Tyranny*, 200: the philosopher "fully realizes the limits set to all human action and all human planning (for what has come into being must perish again)." See again *NRH* 175–76, on the crackings of the *monia mundi*. That Strauss does not mean here

in political life—whose understanding accords with and is shaped by the poets—are radically *disinclined* to accept that this is so.[7] Their longings,

---

merely the earth, or what is of concern to political men, but everything that has come into being, is indicated both by his citing of Lucretius, *De rerum natura*, and by the two quotations, in German, that he provides toward the end of this section (176n10), which address the (wholly inadequate) responses of two contemporary exponents of historical progress to the findings of modern natural science concerning the "end of the world."

7. See *On Tyranny*, 197–98:

> The difference between the philosopher and the political man will then be a difference with respect to happiness. The philosopher's dominating passion is the desire for truth, i.e., for knowledge of the eternal order, or the eternal cause or causes of the whole. As he looks up in search for the eternal order, all human things and all human concerns reveal themselves to him in all clarity as paltry and ephemeral, and no one can find solid happiness in what he knows to be paltry and ephemeral. He has then the same experience regarding all human things, nay, regarding man himself, which the man of high ambition has regarding the low and narrow goals, or the cheap happiness, of the general run of men. The philosopher being the man of the largest views, is the only man who can be properly described as possessing *megaloprepeia* (which is commonly rendered by "magnificence") (Plato, *Republic* 486a). Or, as Xenophon indicates, the philosopher is the only man who is truly ambitious. Chiefly concerned with eternal beings, or the "ideas," and hence also with the "idea" of man, he is as unconcerned as possible with individual and perishable human beings and hence also with his own "individuality," or his body, as well as with the sum total of all individual human beings and their "historical" procession. He knows as little as possible about the way to the market place, to say nothing of the market place itself, and he almost as little knows whether his very neighbor is a human being or some other animal (Plato, *Theaetetus* 173c8–d1, 174b1–6). The political man must reject this way altogether. He cannot tolerate this radical depreciation of man and of all human things (Plato, *Laws* 804b5–c1). He could not devote himself to his work with all his heart or without reservation if he did not attach absolute importance to man and to human things. He must "care" for human beings as such. He is essentially attached to human beings. This attachment is at the bottom of his desire to rule human beings, or of his ambition. But to rule human beings means to serve them. Certainly an attachment to beings which prompts one to serve them may well be called

hopes, attachments, and education would instead incline them to hold that the world is the work of a mysterious but providential eternal god or gods, who overturn such necessities in their attention to justice. And since access to the fundamental sources of all things is unavailable to the philosopher, the necessities or "natures" that he seeks to uncover are "not self-evident," even and precisely if they "follow from the fundamental premise that no being emerges without a cause."[8]

By paraphrasing next a passage from Xenophon's *Oeconomicus*,[9] one in which Socrates offers an ironic and therefore quiet dialectical critique of the gentleman's virtue, Strauss signals both the source of this change in liberal education—*Socratic* philosophy, in its turn to the human things—and what it offered the philosopher: a dialectical examination of the understanding of virtue that vindicated the possibility of the philosophic life, and its "virtue," over and against that of the perfect gentleman.[10] Socrates's grasp of the problem posed by our lack of access to the underlying, ultimate causes of things had led to his "second sailing," that is, to an unprecedented attempt to ground the life of reason by means of a preliminary, dialectical investigation of political-moral questions. It led him to found political philosophy, as a liberal education that is a necessary "preparation," as Strauss here puts it, for *philosophy*.

Bearing this in mind, we can better understand the puzzles that attend the final two arguments of this section, in which Strauss is man-

---

love of them. Attachment to human beings is not peculiar to the ruler; it is characteristic of all men as mere men.

Consider also Strauss's commentary on a passage in Plato's *Laws* (681d7–682c8) in which the third stage of human development or regimes after a telluric cataclysm is described: "Oblivion of the cataclysms is indispensable in the third stage, in which men must be certain that what they live in and live for lasts forever, for otherwise it would be hard for them to dedicate themselves fully to their cities; oblivion of the initial (and final) terror is necessary for political felicity, for one cannot act on a grand scale without hope." *The Argument and Action of Plato's "Laws,"* 41.

8. *NRH* 89–90.

9. *Oeconomicus* 11.3–6. See also Strauss, *Xenophon's Socratic Discourse* (Ithaca, NY: Cornell University Press, 1970), 159–161. The investigation of "virtue" conducted by Socrates is in defense or justification of his life as a scientist—of one who, in the words of Aristophanes that Socrates quotes, "is an idle talker and measurer of the air." And it is a justification before the law (*LAM* 14: "lawful"; *Oeconomicus* 11.6: θεμιτὸν, allowed by divine law).

10. *LAM* 13, bottom.

ifestly holding things back.[11] Since the gentleman's virtue may be said to be "a political reflection" of the philosopher's virtue and hence to be "the ultimate justification of the rule of the gentleman" (*LAM* 14), one is led to wonder why the gentlemen, rather than the philosopher, should rule; the philosopher is after all said to be "best by nature and best by education." Strauss's response appears at first to be that what he has called the "higher rank" activity of philosophy (13) is such that the philosophers are too busy to rule: their "quest for wisdom" is such that the knowledge they seek, the "highest kind of knowledge that a man may seek," takes up all of their time: it "can never be simply at a man's disposal as other kinds of knowledge can; it is in constant need of being acquired again and again from the start" (14). A full engagement in the high activity of philosophizing means that "the rule of the philosopher proves to be impossible," and the philosopher allows himself to be ruled by gentleman.

But this reading overlooks the fact that Strauss is referring here not to the philosopher's activity as a philosopher, or "his own work" (which he will do subsequently—at *LAM* 15), or the "quest for the science of the whole" (13). He is referring to the philosopher's preparatory "education" in the "most weighty" matters, and the "most weighty matters" in question belong not only to the philosopher but also to the gentleman; they are not the preserve of philosophy as philosophy, but are addressed in that new liberal education that joins the gentleman's education and transforms it into a *preparation* for philosophy. And these weighty matters come, paradoxically, to be addressed "playfully" by the philosopher, that is, without a view to ever commencing the serious activities of the gentleman; the liberal education in the "most weighty matters" that leads to and informs the "public-spiritedness" of the gentleman takes a significant turn, then, away from public-spiritedness; its end has ceased to be the noble deeds of the gentlemen. What justifies this lack of public-spiritedness?

When addressing, as he does next, the "difficulty" of the gentleman's rule over the philosopher as the rule of inferiors over superiors—that is, the justice of the philosopher's allowing this arrangement—Strauss addresses a variant of this question. He argues that the philosophers are "not as such constituent parts of the city," or live only "side by side with the city" or political life, which appears to them as a "cave" in which the philosopher would have to be compelled to engage in political activity; the philosopher

---

11. Cf. "to say nothing of other things" and "for this reason alone, to say nothing of others" (14).

owes nothing to the city for his "highest gift of human origin," that is, for his liberal education; the philosopher "passively" obeys even unjust laws at the behest of the city"; only by "doing his *own* work, by his *own* well-being," does the philosopher contribute to the well-being of the city, through the "humanizing and civilizing" effect of that work; only in a "diluted form" can philosophy meet the need that the city has for it (*LAM* 15). The philosopher contributes to the city only indirectly and in diluted form. But this serves only to sharpen our questions: What justifies his lack of public-spiritedness? How can the philosopher's life be *known* to be "best by nature and best by education" if the philosopher's liberal education, which is supposed to establish this, is endless? In what way is the philosopher's ever-needful return to reacquiring from the start this knowledge, which he needs to be "at his disposal," more important, more serious than the pursuit of justice and noble deeds on his city's behalf? What, in short, is the content of this dialectically acquired and ever reacquired knowledge?

Two important points that Strauss makes in his account of the justice of the philosopher's disposition help us to answer this question. Just as, according to Strauss, "the gentlemen cannot possibly give a sufficient or intelligible account of their way of life to the others" and hence cannot have "genuinely common deliberations" (*LAM* 12), so (he now says) "the gentleman and the philosopher cannot have genuinely common deliberations" (14). The problem lies not, then, as the gentleman wishes to think and as we might have been led to think, simply in the deficiencies of the people's understanding (which may be quite real), but rather also in his own; the gentleman is as incapable of giving the philosopher a coherent account of his understanding of his noble life, which he considers good in itself, as he is of giving it to the people.[12] The very incoherence of the gentlemen's claims to rule is, after all, visible to the philosophers, who can see fatal problems with the justifications that the gentlemen make for their noble ruling, or see what could appear, through modern eyes, to be "hypocrisy" (21).

Second, the dialectic that yields this result takes place with gentlemen who, we recall, are guided in their education by "poets." And after stating that "the philosophers are not as such a constituent element of the city," Strauss adds the reason: "The only teachers who are as such a constituent

---

12. See e.g., *On Tyranny*, 204: "The philosopher, trying to remedy the deficiency of 'subjective certainty' [Kojève's term] engages in conversation with others and observes again and again that his interlocutors, as they themselves are forced to admit, involve themselves in self-contradictions or are unable to give any account of their questionable contentions."

element of the city are priests."[13] The noble and just rule of the poetically educated gentleman is fully compatible with, and assisted by, the office of the priesthood and its "care of the divine," whose view of the whole the priesthood and the poets sustain, and with it, both the gentleman's and the people's belief in the great significance and durability of public-spirited human deeds.

As his previous reference to the ultimate destruction of all human accomplishments (*LAM* 13) suggests, and as we will see in the next chapter,[14] attention to the most serious or "most weighty matters" to which Strauss refers—shared by the gentleman and the philosopher—includes a confrontation with our mortality, as individuals and as members of a political community. While the Socratic political philosopher's own confrontation with it results, as Strauss repeatedly states, in serene if sad resignation to it as a necessity of nature,[15] a deep and serious alternative response, that

---

13. *LAM*, 14. Here again, Strauss's radical disagreement with Heidegger, who takes Plato to be engaged in a rationalist attempt to guide the city, is visible. In the chapter that follows "Liberal Education and Responsibility" in *LAM*, Strauss presents "existentialism's" charge against classical political philosophy as "irreligious" as including the example of Aristotle placing the concern with the divine in "fifth and first" place; "only the citizens who are too old for political activity are to become priests." "On the Liberalism of Classical Political Philosophy," *LAM* 27; cf. Aristotle, *Politics* 1328b2–13: "fifth, and indeed first, the caring for the divine, which they call the priesthood . . . without which there cannot be a city." See also *The City and Man*, 33–34.

14. See chapter 3, pp. 94–98.

15. This serenity, the lack of desire to rule that accompanies it, and the distinction between what is by nature and what is by convention on which it rests, are overlooked by Heidegger in his various accounts of the cave allegory and his attempt to present liberation from it, rather than life outside of it, as most important for understanding *existenz*. See Strauss, *The City and Man*, 124–25:

> Why are the philosophers unwilling to rule? Being dominated by the desire, the eros, for knowledge as the one thing needful, or knowing that philosophy is the most pleasant and blessed possession, the philosophers have no leisure for looking down at human affairs, let alone for taking care of them. They believe that while still alive they are already settled far away from their cities in the "Islands of the Blessed." Hence only compulsion could induce them to take part in public life in the just city, i.e. in the city which regards the proper upbringing of the philosophers as its most important task. Having perceived the truly grand, the philosophers regard the human things as paltry. Their very justice—their abstaining from wronging their fellow human beings—flows from contempt for the things

of the "gentleman," presents an awareness, shared with and guided by the poets, of an alternative, moral-religious response that the philosopher, in his lack of access to primary, causal necessities, cannot ignore, in his desire to understand the causes of the whole. This alternative response, by its claims to moral-religious experiences of divine intervention in human affairs, presents the genuine philosopher with a challenge to his entire scientific disposition: the world may be such that what appear to be causes are not causes, that is, "natural" necessities, but rather the work of gods or a God who intervene(s) in human affairs on behalf of the virtuous. It is to this challenge, to repeat, that classical political philosophy addressed itself, in an effort to ground the philosophic-rational life, by means of dialectical engagement, on the prephilosophic level of common sense, or the "world view" of the gentleman. It did not aim at any scientific-philosophic trans-formation of society or of politics. Moreover, through its careful, friendly, and often abortive dialectical refutation of the opinions of the gentleman, it was able to recognize, simultaneously, the depth of the opinions it refuted (or backed off from refuting) in private conversations. It recognized that the moral life of sacrificial devotion to noble deeds and to justice entailed

---

for which the non-philosophers hotly contest. They know that the life not dedicated to philosophy and therefore even political life at its best is like life in a cave, so much so that the city can be identified with the Cave. [References to *Republic* 485b, 486a–b: 496c6, 499c1, 501d1–5, 517c7–9, 519c2–d7, 539e.]

On this serenity, consider also Strauss, "Restatement on Xenophon's *Hiero*," in *On Tyranny*, 197–98 (and compare Plato, *Laws* 967a); "An Untitled Lecture on Plato's *Euthphron*," ed. David Bolotin, Christopher Bruell, and Thomas L. Pangle, *Interpretation* 24, no. 1 (Fall 1996), 4–23, at 20–21; "Progress or Return?," in *The Rebirth of Classical Political Rationalism*, ed. Thomas L. Pangle (Chicago: University of Chicago Press, 1989), 251; *What Is Political Philosophy? and Other Studies*, 28; "Thucydides: The Meaning of Political History," in *The Rebirth of Classical Political Rationalism*, 97, 101, 103; "Reason and Revelation" [1948], published as an appendix in Heinrich Meier, *Leo Strauss and the Theologico-Political Problem*, trans. Marcus Brainard (Cambridge: Cambridge University Press, 2006), 161; "The Mutual Influence of Theology and Philosophy," 17. Heidegger's brief mention, by contrast of the "mood" of "equanimity" (*Gleichmut*) that characterizes authentic *Dasein* (in contradistinction to the "indifference" of inauthentic *Dasein*), appears to present it as a *step* toward authentic action: "*This* mood arises from the resoluteness that, in the Moment, has its view to the possible situations of the potentiality-of-being-a-whole disclosed in the anticipation of death." Heidegger, *Being and Time*, Stambaugh trans., 317; *Sein und Zeit*, sec. 67b, p. 345, end.

a deep and necessary attachment to the particular, "ancestral" way of life or account of the whole in which those deeds took place.

This understanding of the relation of philosophy and politics as understood by Socrates and Plato has a direct bearing on the alternative understanding of philosophy that came to predominate in modern democracy; on the widely influential, contemporary, alternative understanding of classical philosophy; and on the prescription for a radical new thinking about Being, initiated by Heidegger. We are therefore compelled, before moving to Strauss's account of the rise of modern democracy and of our current situation, to spell out what Strauss has in mind. Contra Heidegger, the political philosopher's engagement with the (prescientific, or commonsense) opinions of his political community is *not* intended to lead to a rational ethics, the spelling out of an "objective," scientific morality for the guidance of political life and "correct" education of citizens through "correspondence" of their opinions with the "ideas,"[16] but instead to the justification of a rare way

---

16. See especially Martin Heidegger, "Plato's Doctrine of Truth," trans. Thomas Sheehan, in *Pathmarks* [translation of *Wegmarken*], ed. Thomas McNeil (Cambridge: Cambridge University Press, 1998), 155–82. (This work, which was completed in 1931/32, published in 1940, contains the most direct and sustained account of the alleged problem of Western metaphysics, as it emerges from the thought of Plato. *Being and Time* itself treats this issue only through a brief critique of Aristotle's account of time. It was expected that the third part of *Being and Time* [which itself was only to be part 1 of two parts] would elaborate on this critique. This article thus serves as the closest writing of Heidegger that we have to the promised *destruktion* of the tradition that was simultaneously to be a recovery of the original understanding of Being.)

> This same interpretation of being as ἰδέα, which owes its primacy to a change in the essence of ἀλήθεια, requires that viewing the ideas be accorded high distinction. Corresponding to this distinction is παίδεια, the "education" of human beings, concern with human being and with the position of humans amidst beings entirely dominates metaphysics. The beginning of metaphysics in the thought of Plato is at the same time the beginning of "humanism." Here the word must be thought in its essence and therefore in its broadest sense. In that regard "humanism" means the process that is implicated in the beginning, in the unfolding, and in the end of metaphysics, whereby human beings, in differing respects but always deliberately, move into a central place among beings, of course without thereby being the highest being. Here "human being" sometimes means humanity or humankind, sometimes the individual or the community, and sometimes the people (*das Volk*) or a group of peoples. What is always at

of life, one in which the citizen who acts in a morally serious way, with a sense of his or her moral significance as a member of a morally significant community, has no part. What is more, Strauss considers *the turning away* from the crucial philosophic awareness of the perishing of all human things to belong not only to the thought of the pre- or nonphilosophic citizen. He considers it to have been an essential part of the thought of even the greatest of modern thinkers, from Hobbes and his "illustrious contemporar-

---

stake is this: to take "human beings," who within the sphere of a fundamental, metaphysically established system of beings are defined as *animal rationale*, and to lead them, within that sphere, to the liberation of their possibilities, to the certitude of their destiny, and to the securing of their "life." This takes place as the shaping of their "moral" behavior, as the salvation of their immortal souls, as the unfolding of their creative powers, as the development of their reason, as the nourishing of their personalities, as the awakening of their civic sense, as the cultivation of their bodies, or as an appropriate combination of some or all of these "humanisms." (181)

Heidegger justifies his peculiar reading of Plato, that is, as one that shows something of which Plato might not have been aware, as "made necessary from out of a future need" (167)—the need being to show the source of the path taken by Western metaphysics that has resulted in oblivion of Being.

See also Heidegger, "The Problem of the Ontological Difference," part 2, chapter 1, of *Basic Problems of Phenomenology*, trans. Albert Hofstadter (Bloomington: Indiana University Press, 1982), 227–330, a course given by Heidegger in 1927 that offers a more detailed reading of Aristotle's treatment of time in the *Physics* than is offered in *Being and Time*. Here too Heidegger looks at the allegory of the cave, and suggests that the Idea of the Good is actually the demiurge of the most beautiful objects in the heavens, alluded to by Socrates at *Republic* 530a4:

It appears as though our thesis that ancient philosophy interprets being in the horizon of production in the broadest sense would have no connection at all with what Plato notes as [a] condition of possibility of the understanding of being. Our interpretation of ancient ontology and its guiding clue seems to be arbitrary. What could the idea of the good have to do with production? Without entering further into this matter, we offer only the hint that the *idea agathou* is nothing but the *demiourgos*, the producer pure and simple. This lets us see already how the *idea agathou* is connected with *poiein, praxis, techne* in the broadest sense. (286)

See also Heidegger, *Being and Time*, Stambaugh trans., 388; *Sein und Zeit*, 423 (and note 10).

ies" to Hegel, and, finally, to Heidegger, as he argues in *Natural Right and History*.[17] Not a genuine encounter with mortality and the destruction of all that has come into being, and the establishment of it as a necessity, on the basis of the dialectically demonstrated incoherence of those who claim the existence of miracle-working gods, but a *flight* from this encounter, characterizes modern thought, including Heidegger's "new thinking." The temptation toward the enhancement of the status of man that characterizes the gentleman's encounter with mortality, a temptation that necessitated the Socratic political philosopher's return "again and again" to the beginnings of the "knowledge" dialectics afforded him, so that this knowledge was ever "at his disposal," was powerful enough that it was not resisted by the greatest of modern thinkers. Those included thinkers from Hobbes—who helped to launch what Strauss will call the "stupendous" political-scientific project, including its allegedly rational morality founded in nature—to Hegel, who sought to confirm the new modern consciousness as the product of the unplanned workings of History, to Heidegger, who attempted to ground, ontologically, the modern, atheistic thinking and its "Call" of conscience, while rejecting the utilitarian, rationalist thinking, in its turn away from the potentially morally electrifying encounter with death, that the moderns had begun and that Heidegger mistakenly traced to Plato. The new thinking, to which Heidegger invites everyone, entails an *enhancing* of the status of man and his works no less than does that of the gentleman.[18]

---

17. *NRH* 175–76. As Strauss there argues, Hobbes's activist efforts towards the reconstruction of the world, toward a "City of Man to be erected on the ruins of the City of God," a world in which man would "find a home," required the erection of "walls" against this crucial awareness, which was possessed clearly by the ancients (including Lucretius), and those walls—"enhancing the status of man and of his 'world' by making him oblivious of the whole or eternity"—were not torn down but replaced by incorporation of the "unplanned workings of "History" into the thought of the modern idealists, and finally by *Dasein* as the "highest principle" and the "mysterious ground of 'History,'" one that "has no relation to any possible cause or causes of the whole." In the footnote to this passage (176, note 10), Strauss cites as evidence of the turn away from the modern scientific findings concerning the ultimate destruction of the earth and its inhabitants, and of the effect that they should have had upon their political prescriptions, statements from "authors who belong to opposed camps but to the same spiritual family," Frederick Engels and J. J. Bachofen. See also "Progress or Return?," 237–38.

18. While there are obvious differences between Heidegger's resolute authentic *Da-sein* and the thoughts and deeds of the gentleman, it is worth noting the attention Heidegger gave to book 6 of Aristotle's *Nicomachean Ethics*, including its attention to *kairos* in

The Rise of Modern Science and the Evolution to Modern Democracy

The discrepancy between the truth and the justification of the classical gentlemen's rule meant that the Socratic philosophers "had no delusions" about "the probability of a genuine aristocracy ever becoming actual," and they settled for a "mixed regime" of gentlemen and people (which was not, of course, free from the problems inherent in the justifications of rule made by each part). While he notes that "the modern notion of the mixed regime and modern republicanism" have a "direct connection" with this classical notion, Strauss immediately emphasizes the difference between them: the modern "doctrine" understands the sovereignty of the people to be based on equality of "rights," to make the government responsible to this sovereign, and to have as its "spring" "the desire of each to improve his material conditions" (*LAM* 15). Not the landed gentry but "the commercial and industrial elite" dominated.[19] While the "fountain" of the education to public-spiritedness of both fundamental parts of the ancient city, the rich and the poor, was the work of the poets, and was publicly sustained by priestly attention to the divine, the new elite had its "spring" in the desire for material improvement. As Strauss will now suggest, the new, liberal, commercial, technological society aims precisely at the overthrow of all such religious authorities that guided both parts of the ancient mixed regime.

He does so through two short historical accounts of the modern development that start with the brief statement on the full development of liberal

---

treating time, over and against Aristotle's investigation of time in the *Physics*, which looks only at the "now" (*nun*) rather than at the "moment" or "instant" of humanly "significant" time. See his 1924 course called "Grundbegriffe der aristotelischen Philosophie," which appeared as volume 18 of Martin Heidegger, *Gesamtausgabe*, ed. M. Michalski (Frankfurt: V. Klostermann, 2002). See also "Introductory Part," chapters 1 and 3, of the 1924–1925 Marburg winter semester course on Plato's *Sophist*, published in German as *Platon: Sophistes* (Frankfurt: V. Klostermann, 1992); translated as *Plato's Sophist* by Richard Rojcewicz and Andre Schuwer (Bloomington, IN: Indiana University Press, 1997), 94–97. And see "The Problem of the Ontological Difference," part 2, chapter 1, of *Basic Problems of Phenomenology*, 288: "Aristotle already saw the phenomenon of the instant, the *kairos*, and he defined it in the sixth book of his *Nichomachean Ethics*; but, again, he did it in such a way that he failed to bring the specific time character of the *kairos* into connection with what he otherwise knows as time (*nun*)."

19. The past tense is in Strauss's essay, and seems to signal the eventual demise of this elite, at least as a distinct moral force.

democracy with which we began in our introductory chapter, looking at the new philosophic-scientific project as it relates to the two major political camps, rulers and people, which characterized that project. "Enlightenment," as the example of Locke—the originator of the doctrine of popular sovereignty based on equal rights—indicates, was "at first" to be of the rulers, with the moral education of the people remaining a largely religious, biblical education, so that they continued to hold themselves responsible to God and his judgment. A "rational ethics" rooted in "natural rights, the foundations of society, and the duties resulting from them," was to be made available to the nobility, "including countesses and dutchesses," by reading Pufendorff, and they were to be prepared for their public "calling" by the reading of ancient Roman and Greek works, for the sake of (in Locke's words) "good breeding." The Roman and Greek works were considered useful, we note, in their presentations of men engaged in political life and hence by moving their readers with accounts of the deeds of men educated in the ancient liberal education, whose moral disposition was to be blended with the (new, allegedly rational) duties that followed from the new doctrine of rights. The modern nobles certainly were not reading these "pagan" authors (see *LAM* 20, top) with any belief in the gods worshipped in the ancient cities in which their deeds took place, nor, a fortiori, with a view to the activity of Socratic dialectics that occurred in any of them.

But as Strauss then suggests, this early arrangement was espied by Locke's followers in America to be temporary. To be sure, in their awareness of the need to sustain a public-spiritedness in the people's representatives that was not needed in commerce or industry, they maintained the Lockean connection with the classics; *The Federalist Papers* were written by "Publius." But the "eminently sober" reasoning behind the commercial "republic" laid out by the Lockean Hamilton in the *Federalist Papers* turned to the emerging economic classes to ensure the desired social arrangement that would produce public-spirited representatives. It was an arrangement whereby men of virtue and public-spiritedness—men of the "learned professions," above all the lawyers, with a broader public interest than the landed classes or the merchant classes—would be the likely arbiters between the other two major interests and their representatives.[20] Strauss's immediately subsequent

---

20. *LAM* 16. That Strauss's fundamental argument in this first short historical account of the development of the new science and democracy is the mortal fate of religious education explains his selection of quotations from the *Federalist Papers* (and their subsequent critique in Burke's arguments), quotations that concentrate on how the new

quotations from Edmund Burke concerning lawyers brings to the surface the overlooked religious education that would actually have to continue to inform the virtue of the people's representatives: "God forbid," Strauss quotes Burke saying, "I should say anything derogatory to that profession, which is another priesthood, administering sacred justice," yet (Burke continues) "speaking legally and constitutionally" its function is not the same as exercising the "prudence" of statesmen, which, in Burke's understanding, relies on the older (duty-imparting) natural law (*LAM* 17, top).

Turning then to a second thinker from this period, Strauss sketches J. S. Mill's two efforts to correct for the deficiencies of legislators and civil servants, the "representatives of the people," in liberal democracy. Mill's two proposals were for a proportional representation that would ensure the election of liberally educated representatives, and (later) for appointments of liberally educated members of the civil service. He worried that the people's representatives increasingly lacked the liberal education in classics that lays what he called "an admirable foundation for ethical and philosophic culture," or what Strauss himself calls the "public-spirited intelligence" of "a liberally educated man whose liberal education affects him decisively in the performance of his duties" (*LAM* 17–18). Strauss's presentation of the fatal flaw of such thinking comes out not by way of a direct criticism of Mill but rather by a gently stated critique of the aim of the adult liberal education

commercial American republic, "Hamilton's republic," will meet the need for virtue and public spiritedness in the people's representatives, with no mention of a biblical education of the people. A number of Anti-Federalists had argued—sometimes with reference to the preservation of serious religious devotion—against the new constitution on the ground that it was a path for the unchecked ascent of the ambitious "aristocratical class" and would lead to insufficient representation of the "virtuous" democratic class. For they had come to see the new constitution through the lens of John Adams's *Constitutions of the United States*, which makes the case for the existence of three permanent classes of men throughout recorded history (the third being the "monarchic"); Adams understood recognition of the need to "balance" them in a republic as the singular development of modern political science. That is, Adams's book had taught the Anti-Federalists to view the newly proposed American constitution as an attempt at a version of a classical mixed regime, with modern checks, and to fault its deficiencies on these grounds. (Adams had written his book in response to the Montesquieuan Turgot.) Strauss hones in on the passages in which Hamilton implicitly counters the claims concerning these three allegedly permanent classes, and hence brings out the fundamentally commercial character of the new regime. See Timothy W. Burns, "Turgot, Adams, and the New Science of Politics," in *Classical Rationalism and the Politics of Europe*, ed. Ann Ward (Cambridge, UK: Cambridge Scholars, 2017), 197–229.

practiced by those who had invited Strauss to speak: Mill's education was intended for a representative elite, but as "representatives of the people," that elite came from the people and were responsible to them in their governing. Strauss suggests that, unlike Burke, Mill assumed that the public-spiritedness or sense of duty could be found in the intellectual training of the elite, in the absence of religion,[21] in the reading of the classics:

> In the light of the original conception of modern republicanism, our present predicament appears to be caused by the decay of religious education of the people and by the decay of liberal education of the representatives of the people. By the decay of religious education, I mean more than the fact that a very large part of the people no longer receives any religious education, although it is not necessary on the present occasion to think beyond that fact. The question as to whether religious education can be restored to its pristine power by the means at our disposal is beyond the scope of this year's Arden House Institute. Still, I cannot help stating to you these questions: Is our present concern with liberal education of adults, our present expectation from such liberal education, not due to the void created by the decay

---

21. In *On Liberty*, in fact, Mill goes out of his way to argue that genuine human virtues that present themselves as Christian virtues are actually the virtues of a godless Stoicism. From his theological writings, it is clear that his embrace of the modern understanding of consciousness of mortality lies behind this: "It seems to me not only possible but probable, that in a higher, and, above all, a happier condition of human life, not annihilation but immortality may be the burdensome idea." "Utility of Religion," in *Nature, The Utility of Religion, and Theism*, 4th ed. (London: Longmans, 1875), 128. Consider also the following remarks in the same work: "We are in an age of weak beliefs, and in which such belief as men have is much more determined by their wish to believe than by any mental appreciation of evidence" (70). "The tendency to disbelieve [credentials of allegedly divine messages] appears to grow with the growth of scientific knowledge and critical discrimination" (115). "I cannot but think that as the condition of mankind becomes improved, as they grow happier in their lives, and more capable of deriving happiness from unselfish sources, they will care less and less for this flattering expectation [of an individual life after death]" (118). "When mankind ceases to need a future existence as a consolation for the sufferings of the present, it will have lost its chief value to them, for themselves" (119). "The mere cessation of existence is no evil to anyone" (120). "The idea [of annihilation] is not really or naturally terrible . . . not philosophers only, but the common order of mankind, can easily reconcile themselves to it, and even consider it as a good . . . (121–22).

of religious education? Is such liberal education meant to perform
the function once performed by religious education? Can liberal
education perform that function? It is certainly easier to discuss
the other side of our predicament—the predicament caused by
the liberal education of the governors. (*LAM* 19)

What Strauss here declines to take up—in a sudden burst to the surface of
a direct argument concerning the close relation of religious education and
sense of duty or public-spiritedness—is quietly taken up in his subsequent
description of the evolution of modern democracy and the education of
the people that it required.

After a brief mention of the need for the "reform" of American liberal
education, and of his own efforts at "modest" reform within political science
departments and law schools, away from "narrow and unprincipled efficiency"
that characterizes their current state (*LAM* 19), Strauss turns, by way of
explaining how that state came about, to providing a second brief historical
account of the modern scientific enterprise and its relation to democracy, one
that touches directly on what he has just declined to take up: the dynamic
of modernity, of enlightenment, which includes its successful pretense of
union with Christianity even as it sought to defeat it (19–20). This second
historical description, which addresses the two sides of Mill's proposal and
the two sides of the classical justification for aristocracy—also includes an
account of the rise of modern "mass" democracy out of that dynamic.

The strong support that classical philosophy gave to the rule of gentlemen (aristocracy) was rooted in the perception by the gentlemen that
there is an activity that is "good in itself." After reminding us of both this
"support" for liberal education that classical philosophers offered and of the
important fact that "the end of the philosopher is radically different from
the end or ends actually pursued by the non-philosophers," Strauss now
takes a step back, to spell out the dramatic *change* in this relation that had
taken place in modern philosophy, which conceived of its end as "the relief
of man's estate" (Bacon): the end of the philosophers was now understood
as subservient to the end of the nonphilosophers.[22] "In *this* respect, the

---

22. Cf. *The City and Man*, 3–4: "According to the modern project, philosophy or science
was no longer to be understood as essentially contemplative and proud but as active and
charitable; it was to be in the service of the relief of man's estate; it was to be cultivated
for the sake of human power; it was to enable man to become the master and owner of
nature through the intellectual conquest of nature. Philosophy or science should make

modern conception of philosophy is fundamentally democratic" (*LAM* 19; emphasis added). Here, then, is a primary source of modern democracy, in the new end of philosophy. While that new end could be presented "with some plausibility as inspired by biblical charity" (20), Strauss suggests that this presentation was dubious and even insincere. The description that he then gives to clarify the modern understanding presents it initially as an effort to bring about life that is "longer, healthier, and more abundant," through the increase in human power and an "economy of plenty" to replace the "economy of scarcity" (20).

The political means to that goal came, Strauss now argues, in two important steps. He notes that this "stupendous enterprise" is one that "in its original conception" was to be in the control of "the philosopher-scientists"[23]—to be for, but not by, the people. Hence, he will go on to argue, it originally involved "working through the princes," but eventually, the direct enlightenment of the people (21). At the beginning of this description of this political path (at 20), however, he offers a tantalizing anti-biblical *motivation* to the new science, by referring to the need of the philosophers to open the people up to the gifts philosophy was now bringing them: "For the people were, to begin with, deeply distrustful of the new gifts from the new sort of sorcerers, for they remembered the command-ment, 'Thou shalt not suffer a sorcerer to live'" (see Exodus 22:18). What Strauss is indicating is that the people, having received a biblical education, were led by that stern education to reject in no uncertain terms the magic that had characterized the rule of Pharaoh, or, more generally, reliance on human arts instead of on God.[24] The people, and not only the "countesses

---

progress toward ever greater prosperity; it thus should enable everyone to share in all the advantages of society or life and therewith give full effect to everyone's natural right to comfortable self-preservation and all that that right entails or to everyone's natural right to develop all his faculties fully in concert with everyone else's doing the same."

23. For what Strauss may have in mind, see Francis Bacon's *The New Atlantis*, and see Timothy W. Burns, "Bacon's *New Atlantis* and the Goals of Modernity," in *Socrates and Dionysus: Philosophy and Art in Dialogue*, ed. Ann Ward (Cambridge, UK: Cambridge Scholars, 2013), 74–103.

24. See "Jerusalem and Athens: Some Preliminary Reflections," in *Jewish Philosophy and the Crisis of Modernity*, ed. Kenneth Hart Greene (Albany: State University of New York Press, 1997), 288. See also Thomas L. Pangle, "The Hebrew Bible's Challenge to Political Philosophy: Some Preliminary Reflections," in *Political Philosophy and the Human Soul: Essays in Memory of Allan Bloom*, ed. Michael Palmer and Thomas L. Pangle (Lanham, MD: Rowman and Littlefield, 1995), 67–92. The Egyptians under Pharaoh

and duchesses," had to be "enlightened." "The enlightenment was destined to become universal enlightenment." The spread of the new science and its democratizing "method," through formal education, *together with* the spread of an initial increase in prosperity, were the means to "weaning men away from concern with the bliss in the next world to work for happiness in this" (*LAM* 20, bottom). But the weaning, Strauss here indicates, was not, as it first seems, a mere means to the goal of having people receive the gifts of the new science. Rather, those gifts were part of the means to the *goal* of weaning, to a transformation of the people's consciousness, to its "enlightenment." "This *enlightenment* is the core of the new education. It is the *same* as the popularization or diffusion of the new science"; its "*results could be transmitted to all*" (20; emphasis added). The change from "bliss" to "happiness" is here especially telling: the goods produced by the new science were to reorient the people from a concern with "bliss" (*makariotes, beatiitudo*), an earned, superabundant happiness that humans cannot obtain on their own, to this-worldly happiness (*eudaimonia, felicitas*), which they could.[25] Unifying trade or commerce, "immensely facilitated by the new discoveries and inventions," took precedence over "religion, which divides the peoples." What might initially appear to be a merely tactical problem for the philosopher-scientists, in other words, is in truth its strategic objective: the "disenchantment" of the people, which entailed the homogenizing of "the peoples," was the very goal of the Enlightenment.

Two political consequences resulted from this growing shift to popular enlightenment. On one hand, with regard to liberal education, virtue, formerly understood as choiceworthy for its own sake, began to be understood instrumentally: the "*conversion* of men" from "the pre-moral if not immoral concern for worldly goods to goods of the soul" now gave way to "the calculating *transition* from unenlightened to enlightened self-inter-

---

"substitute, for religion or worship of deities, a very powerful human magic. Pharaonic despotism . . . embodies and exemplifies the power of human contrivance limited by no sense of a higher power limiting or humbling human arrogance" (73).

25. For a highly illuminating explication of this important shift, see Christopher Bruell, "Happiness in the Perspective of Philosophy," chapter 11 of *Recovering Political Philosophy: Essays in Honor of Thomas L. Pangle*, ed. Timothy W. Burns (Lanham, MD: Lexington, 2010), 147–59. In *Spinoza's Critique of Religion* (210), Strauss connects this shift (in Hobbes) with the foundation of technology: "Hobbes rejects the conception of *beatitudo* propounded by the ethical thinkers of antiquity, and replaces it by the prospect of endless progress from desire to desire, from power to ever greater power, and establishes, by reason of this conception of happiness, positive science as foundation of technology."

est."[26] (Enlightenment must therefore have meant the attempted erasure of concern for something beyond wordly goods, and hence of concern for immortality.) Even more: devising institutions that directed or channeled men to their long-range self-interest came to be seen as "more important than liberal education." On the other hand, the arguments that had been made, on the basis of scarcity, by aristocratic gentlemen in defense of their rule and their education gradually lost their force. The injustice of existing aristocracies became "clearer and more widely admitted" within modernity—not through the spread of Socratic dialectics, certainly, but rather—with the "increasing abundance of modernity." The removal of what had been the necessity of relative scarcity made it possible "to see and to admit the element of hypocrisy" in the rule of the gentlemanly aristocrats, or brought to light that they were actually "oligarchies."[27] That it also made *possible* an extensive public education of those hitherto condemned to poverty and lack of distinction did not at all mean, however, that liberal education was therefore to become more widely available and hence that democracy would become the "universal aristocracy" that scarcity had hitherto prevented. For the aim now was "enlightenment," something altogether different from conversion of the soul to virtue and public-spiritedness and in fact in tension with it. What came about, rather, was the argument for equality of "rights" understood as equality of opportunity to use unequal abilities in the "race" to this-worldly advancement, and thereby "the age of tolerance"—liberal, we may say, but not yet democratic—in which "humanity" became the crowning virtue and "goodness" became identical with compassion (toward those who did less well in the race). This development toward this-worldly advancement obviously moves in the opposite direction of return (*t'shuva*) to the right way given by divine law.[28] It is, as Strauss now explicitly calls it, a "progressive enterprise" (*LAM* 21, bottom).

That enterprise now reached a crucial period: since it was, as Strauss repeats, "originally" thought to be in the control of the "philosopher-scientist,"

---

26. *LAM* 21 (emphasis added).

27. *LAM* 15, 17, 21: It should be noted that while Strauss presents the "element of hypocrisy" in the aristocrats' claims of the justice of their rule in an economy of scarcity, he does not present the aristocrats' claims as simply hypocritical: with the overcoming of scarcity, and the arguments for equality that were made "increasingly easy" by it, "it became possible to abolish many injustices, or at least many things which had *become* injustices" (21; emphasis added).

28. See "Progress or Return?," 87.

his lack of power meant that he had originally to work through princes, enlightening them, with the people under his "tutelage." With the "progress of enlightenment," such tutelage was no longer needed—or almost so, since neither the princes nor the people always listened to the scientists. But need for the scientists grew with the change in the character of society brought about by their science, so that the people were "more and more compelled" to listen to the scientists merely "to survive." Yet a crucial "lag" between the "enlightenment coming from above" and "the way in which the people exercised its freedom" obtained. Strauss presents this lag time as engendering a "race": would the people come into their sovereignty before they became fully "enlightened?"[29] (The goal is not conceived, to repeat, a concern for the public-spiritedness of the sovereign people or their representatives, but their enlightenment.)

It is the "apparent solution" proposed at this point to this problem of enlightenment, Strauss argues, that brought about what we may call full democratization. It was part of an effort that appeared, Strauss argues,

---

29. *LAM* 22 (emphasis added). What Strauss has in mind, historically, may be gleaned from his glosses on three aspects of Rousseau's teaching: a) on the *First Discourse*'s teaching that "Bacon, Descartes, and Newton" are "teachers of the human race" and its demand "that scholars of the first rank should find honorable asylum at the courts of princes, in order from there to enlighten the peoples concerning their duties and thus contribute to the peoples' happiness" (*NRH* 259); b) on Rousseau's recognition that inhabitants of modern commercial republics like Geneva are "more concerned with private or domestic affairs than with the fatherland. They lack the greatness of soul of the ancients. They are bourgeois rather than citizens" (*NRH* 253); and c) on the fact that Rousseau "foresaw a revolution" (*NRH* 259). On the last, see especially the concluding section of Rousseau's *Second Discourse*, in which he makes clear that all forms of government have degenerated into hereditary despotisms and the "fatal right" to revolution is about to be exercised: "But the frightful dissensions, the infinite disorders that this dangerous power (right) would necessarily entail demonstrate more than anything else how much human governments needed a basis more solid than reason alone." Rousseau does not wish to rely on *revealed* religion for this basis, both on account of the wars and civil strife that result from it and because enlightenment and commerce are already causing revealed religion to atrophy. Jean-Jacques Rousseau, *The First and Second Discourses*, trans. and ed. Roger D. Masters and Judith Masters (New York: St. Martin's Press, 1964), 170–80. See also Leo Strauss, "Seminar in Political Philosophy: Rousseau A Course Offered in the Autumn Quarter, 1962," (Department of Political Science, University of Chicago; unpublished), 159: "The enlightened despotism became the ideal of these French *philosophes*, and they produced a big work called the *Encyclopédie*, which came out in 1751, I believe—for the first volume—and this preached enlightened despotism."

to be "a revolt *against* enlightenment," but was in truth directed against "enlightened *despotism*."[30] That is, it sought to retain or shore up a tottering enlightenment while attacking the despotisms that the enlightenment or partial enlightenment of princes had assisted or brought into being. Every man, it was now said, had a "right" to be part of the sovereign, by dint of his "dignity," as a moral being. This apparent solution entailed a redefinition of virtue, as something not difficult or rare but rather common or potentially universal. The new effort presented the "good intention" as "the only thing which can be held to be unqualifiedly good," and something possessed especially by the common man rather than the sophisticated. That is, the effort to guide the trajectory of the new science in its relation to the people further deprecated the claims to goodness of "contemplation of the eternal" or "cultivation of the mind" (to say nothing of Lockean "good breeding"), instead presenting each and every man's right to political freedom as resting on his "dignity" as a "moral being." The redefinition of virtue as "the good intention," or the activity of being guided by "the voice of nature" or a simple "conscience," was intended to call all citizens to a morality that would assist the enlightenment of self-interest, or would not

---

30. He has in mind (though he curiously does not name) Rousseau and his followers, especially Kant. This brief if enlightening historical presentation of Rousseauean activity should be supplemented with "On the Intention of Rousseau," *Social Research* 14, no. 4 (1947), 455–87; the section subtitled "Rousseau" in chapter 6 of *NRH* 252–94; and the section on Rousseau in "The Three Waves of Modernity," in *Political Philosophy: Six Essays by Leo Strauss*, ed. Hilail Gildin (Indianapolis: Bobbs-Merrill, 1975), 89–94. See also *The City and Man*, 43; and *What Is Political Philosophy?*, 47 (on Rousseau and the replacement of education to virtue with reliance on the conscience, resting on the [non-Christian] claim that "man is by nature good"). Its most conspicuous omissions are any mentions of "the general will," the "legislator" (or that Rousseau is in a sense the legislator), and the need for a rational, "civil religion" (like that of the Savoyard Vicar)—though Strauss does refer obliquely to the latter with the parallel he draws between treating all with equal dignity regardless of how they use their freedom, to the reasoning criticized by Locke, according to which one can "indeed behead a tyrannical king, but only with reverence for that king." See Locke, *Second Treatise*, secs. 232–39. The reasoning Locke amusingly opposes is that of William Barclay, "that great assertor of the power and sacredness of kings"; Barclay's injunction to "reverence" rests on the claim that "*Honour the king*, and *he that resists the power, resists the ordinance of God*" are "divine oracles." On Rousseau's recovery of the difference between civil society as essentially religious, and the philosophic life, and hence Rousseau's recovery of esoteric philosophical teaching, see especially *NRH* 258n15.

rely on or assist the former, revealed-religious orientation of the people;[31] it would invite them to obey a rational "moral law" that makes no reference to other-worldly ends but rather makes exclusive reference to the individual dignity and autonomy of each and all humans.[32] And this alteration in the

---

31. See Leo Strauss, "Seminar in Political Philosophy: Rousseau, A Course Offered in the Autumn Quarter, 1962," 13–14:

> The main point, what strikes us at first now in Rousseau I believe is the assertion of the supremacy of morality—not understanding, but acting morally is the only thing which ultimately counts. To show the peculiarity of this assertion (I do not say it is peculiar to Rousseau, but it is characteristic of part of his age): morality and not science, morality and not religion (that is the other side). Not religion. Religion means [positive] religion, Christianity, Judaism, or whatever it may be. Morality is the only thing which counts; morality is the only proper bond of society.

32. Compare *The City and Man*, 39–40: Whereas the argument for equality which the ancients addressed, equality of responsibility for becoming a good or bad man, led, against the conditions that as it were compel him to act badly, which would limit such responsibility, to the postulate that the world is the work of an omnipotent, sovereign God who has created the world *ex nihilo*, the Rousseauean equality rests on human autonomy and the conquest of nature:

> According to Rousseau, through the foundation of society, natural inequality is replaced by conventional equality; the social contract which creates society is the basis of morality, of moral freedom or autonomy; but the practice of moral virtue, the fulfillment of our duties to our fellow men is the one thing needful. A closer analysis shows that the core of morality is the good will as distinguished from the fulfillment of all duties; the former is equally within the reach of all men, whereas as regards the latter natural inequality necessarily asserts itself. But it cannot be a duty to respect that natural inequality, for morality means autonomy, i.e. not to bow to any law which a man has not imposed upon himself. Accordingly, man's duty may be said to consist in *subjugating the natural within him* and outside of him to that in him to which alone he owes his dignity, to the moral law. (emphases added)

The next step, by Fichte and Marx, depends on the further conquest of nature:

> The moral law demands from each virtuous activity, i.e. the full and uniform development of all his faculties and their exercise jointly with others. Such a development is not possible as long as everyone is crip-

conception of virtue helps to make intelligible "the assertion that was made at that moment: the assertion that virtue is the principle of democracy and only of democracy" (*LAM* 22). Far from emerging out of Christianity, the elevation of democracy to the status of the one best or only legitimate regime, because it recognizes the dignity of each man, emerges, in Strauss's account, as a tactical political corrective of the people made as part of the scientific, technological project of enlightenment.[33]

> pled as a consequence of the division of labor or of social inequality. It is therefore a moral duty to contribute to the establishment of a society which is radically egalitarian and at the same time on the highest level of the development of man. In such a society, which is rational precisely because it is not natural, i.e. *because it has won the decisive battle against nature*, everyone is of necessity happy if happiness is indeed unobstructed virtuous activity; it is a society which therefore does no longer have any need for coercion. (emphasis added)

That Strauss saw the new moral teaching as tied to the enlightening, technological intention of Baconian science appears also from "A Giving of Accounts," in *Jewish Philosophy and The Crisis of Modernity*, 463:

> Modern philosophy has a radically different character. In modern times the gulf between philosophy and the city was bridged, or believed to have been bridged, by two innovations: (1) the ends of the philosopher and the non-philosopher are identical, because philosophy is in the service of the relief of man's estate, or science for the sake of power; (2) philosophy can fulfill its salutary function only if its results are diffused among the non-philosophers, if popular enlightenment is possible. The high point was reached in Kant's teaching on the primacy of practical, i.e., moral reason, a teaching prepared, to some extent by Rousseau: the one thing needful is a good will, and of a good will all men are equally capable.

33. If the advance of enlightenment through technology required this doctrine of democratic rights, the converse also is true, that is, the doctrine relies on the advance of technology's conquest of nature, of our natural situation, and thereby affects the recent Thomistic claim of the "natural" character of democratic government. See Strauss's review of Yves R. Simon's *Philosophy of Democratic Government* (1951) in *What Is Political Philosophy?*, 310:

> This amounts to saying that the conditions required for democracy are the normal conditions, the conditions required by human nature. To judge of the validity of that contention, we must look at an example which Simon

But Strauss does not present this (Rousseauean-Kantian) attempt to guide the trajectory of the new science in its relation to the people as one that actually solved the problem of the "lag" or "race" that he has mentioned. He instead presents it as having had two different results: Jacobin terror, a new kind of secular and secularizing despotism[34]—owing to the punishment

---

discusses when speaking of democratic equality, *viz.*, the "equal right to protection against the risk of dying prematurely." "It is human nature which demands that human life be protected by the efforts of human society; this demand holds equally for all the bearers of human nature." But, as Simon notes, this demand of human nature approximates the status of a genuine right of all only by virtue of the modern technological development (205). One is forced to wonder whether what is true of this particular right, is not likewise true, *mutatis mutandis*, the abolition of "widespread ignorance" in a number of countries in the recent past (*cf.* 206–207). To express this generally, Simon does not show whether what he regards as the normal condition is not a condition which presupposes modern technology. He does not show, that is, whether what he regards as an improvement of our conscience is not the inevitable consequence of the application of an unchanged conscience to a situation, or an opportunity, created by modern technology. The condition created by modern technology would be the normal condition if modern technology itself were normal.

34. On the leader of that new, secular despotism or the leader of that terror, Robespierre, and the new secular "religion" he attempted to bring into being (the "Cult of the Supreme Being," authorized by the National Convention on May 7, 1794, as the civic religion of France), see Strauss's letter to Karl Löwith of August 20, 1946 (quoted above in chapter 1, note 13, p. 27) and Strauss's "Exoteric Teaching." In "Exoteric Teaching," *Reorientation: Leo Strauss in the 1930s*, ed. Martin D. Yaffe and Richard S. Ruderman (New York: Palgrave Macmillan, 2014), 285, Strauss argues that Lessing, having recovered the fundamental difference between the understanding peculiar to political society and to the philosophic life, and hence having seen the religious foundations of the former, found *unenlightened* despotism (insofar as it did not rely on force) preferable to emerging enlightened despotisms, and anticipated the terror of Robespierre:

Could Lessing have held the view that ecclesiastical despotism is two or three times better than secular despotism? Jacobi elsewhere says in his own name but certainly in the spirit of Lessing, that that despotism which is based "exclusively" on superstition, is less bad than secular despotism. Now secular despotism could easily be allied with the philosophy of enlightenment, and therewith with the rejection of exotericism strictly speaking, as is shown above all by the teaching of the classic of enlightened despotism: the teaching of Hobbes. But "despotism based exclusively on superstition,"

not only of crimes but also of intentions—and the (more abiding or universally made) claim that each man has equal rights and must be respected *regardless* of how he uses his "will or his freedom," or a newly moralistic insistence on official respect for the old democratic desire to live as one likes.[35] "It remains then at the race between the political freedom below and the enlightenment coming from above."[36] The people may come to use their new freedom in support of unenlightened despotism.[37]

---

i.e. not at all on force, cannot be maintained if the non-superstitious minority does not voluntarily refrain from 'openly' exposing and refuting the "superstitious" beliefs. Lessing had then not to wait for the experience of Robespierre's despotism to realize the relative truth of what the romantics asserted against the principles of J.-J. Rousseau, who seems to have believed in a political solution of the problem of civilization: Lessing realized that "relative" truth one generation earlier, and he rejected it in favor of the way leading to absolute truth, or of philosophy.

35. In *The City and Man* (89) Strauss suggests that this lowly fate of the stern Kantian "good will" is foreshadowed in Plato's *Republic* by the fate of Glaucon's definition of justice: "As for the view which Glaucon implicitly opposes to Thrasymachus' view, it cannot but remind us of Kant's view—of Kant's moving description of the simple man who has no quality other than the good will, the only thing of absolute worth. The opening statement of his *Foundations of the Metaphysics of Morals* makes it clear that morality as he understands it is more akin to justice than to any other virtue. Morality as Kant understands it is as much divorced from art and nature as justice is according to Glaucon: the moral laws are not natural laws nor technical rules. The fate of Glaucon's view in the *Republic* foreshadows the fate of Kant's moral philosophy." He later (on 137) gives an account of that fate, when describing the reaction of the "modern 'Idealists'" to the "Philistine" prescription of earthly rewards (divine and human) for the just.

36. *LAM* 22. In *Natural Right and History* Strauss argues that the Rousseauean state of nature which establishes the dreams of the rare and genuinely "free" solitary walker as approximating, on the level of developed humanity, the sentiment of existence available to natural man, "was the ideal basis for an appeal from society to something indefinite and undefinable, to *an ultimate sanctity of the individual as individual, unredeemed and unjustified*. This was precisely what freedom came to mean for a considerable number of men," that is, a freedom from rather than freedom for. But Rousseau, he argues, as opposed to his followers, "still saw clearly the disproportion between this undefined and undefinable freedom and the requirements of civil society" (*NRH* 294; emphasis added).

37. See "Leo Strauss on Thomas Hobbes and Plato," 16: "That is the meaning of sovereignty: no strings whatever attached, and you must not forget that the doctrine of the sovereignty of the people ascribes the same rights to the sovereign people, which Hobbes ascribes to the sovereign king. For example, if the sovereign American people

Yet as this shift to democracy, to complete equality of dignity, to the absolute right to do as one pleased, was taking place, Strauss notes, the hitherto understood or professed "enlightenment" from above ceased to be available: "science" and "philosophy" became divorced from one another, such that science no longer had any "essential connection with wisdom," with the determination of the right way of life. Thus liberal education ceased to be, as Strauss now calls it, a "fruitful tension between religious and liberal education" (*LAM* 22)—thereby indicating what he had only suggested to be the case in the prior sections concerning the former content of liberal education. The new science, which had in fact been from the start construc-tivist, eventually (in the late nineteenth century) shed its sometime pretense that its investigations, like those of the old science or philosophy, aimed at truth; it proclaimed that it can prescribe no "ought" on the basis of the "is" that it constructively discovers; it is "value-free."[38] Despite its authority

---

were to turn to Islam, there is no constitutional way to prevent it. . . . One can easily see in which direction it went: a prosperous society, a turning away from religious passion to property."

38. That the new science (both in its physical and political sides) was *always* to some (perhaps confused) degree constructivist Strauss makes clear in *Philosophy and Law*: "But precisely this new science could not long uphold the claim to have brought to light the truth about the world 'in itself'; its 'idealistic' explication already informs its beginnings." *Philosophy and Law: Essays Toward the Understanding of Maimonides and His Predecessors*, trans. Fred Baumann (New York: Jewish Publication Society, 1987), 14, 15. Originally published in German by Schocken Verlag, 1935. See also "Preface to Spinoza's Critique of Religion" in *Jewish Philosophy and the Crisis of Modernity*, 154: "The modern project as understood by Bacon, Descartes, and Hobbes demands that man should become the master and owner of nature, or that philosophy or science should cease to be essentially theoretical." And see Strauss's account of the Cartesian nature of Hobbes's political science in *Hobbes' Critique of Religion* and *NRH*, ch. 5. The political part of the new science was at first (in its Hobbesian variety) confusedly constructivist in that it relied initially on a notion of a natural end (comfortable self-preservation), but was already bent on a rational construction over and against nature, as Strauss argues in *The City and Man*, 42–45, a section that concludes (on 45) with the statement that "the rights of man are the moral equivalent of the *Ego cogitans*. The *Ego cogitans* has emancipated itself entirely from 'the tutelage of nature' and eventually refuses to obey any law which it has not originated in its entirety or to dedicate itself to any 'value' of which it does not know that it is its own creation." This result begins with the Baconian "resolve" to conquer nature (described on 42), for the sake of what was initially thought of as a natural end: "If one ponders over the facts which Aristotle summarizes by saying that our nature is enslaved in many ways, one easily arrives at the conclusion that nature is

in the modern world, it frankly claims now that "objectively" it cannot say that either the life according to reason (science) or the material prosperity, health, and extension of life it offers are "good or evil ends."[39] This final

not a kind mother but a harsh stepmother to man, i.e. that the true mother of man is not nature. What is peculiar to modern thought is not this conclusion by itself but the consequent resolve to liberate man from that enslavement by his own sustained effort. This resolve finds its telling expression in the demand for the 'conquest' of nature: nature is understood and treated as an enemy who must be subjugated. Accordingly, science ceases to be proud contemplation and becomes the humble and charitable handmaid devoted to the relief of man's estate. Science is for the sake of power, i.e. for putting at our disposal the means for achieving our natural ends. Those ends can no longer include knowledge for its own sake; they are reduced to comfortable self-preservation. Man as the potential conqueror of nature stands outside of nature." But from the very start the *social* end that is part of this project (that is, *making* man social) is not conceived of as "natural" but as "invented": "The end is not something towards which man is by nature inclined as something towards which he is by nature compelled; more precisely, the end does not beckon man but it must be *invented* by man so that he can escape from his natural misery" (43; emphasis added). The Hobbesian lowering of the goals of political life with the new, modern "natural laws" based on "natural rights," accordingly partakes of this constructivist character: the new physical, Cartesian science posits "natural laws as laws which *no one can* transgress because everyone is compelled to act according to them. Laws of the latter kind, it was hoped, would be the solid basis of a new kind of 'normative' laws which as such *can* indeed be transgressed but are much *less likely* to be transgressed than the normative laws preached up by the tradition. The new kind of normative laws did no longer claim to be natural laws proper; they were *rational laws* in contradistinction to natural laws; they eventually become 'ideals.' The ideal 'exists' only by virtue of human reasoning or 'figuring out'; it exists only 'in speech'" (44). For this reason the "rights of man," the moral equivalent of the *Ego cogitans*, eventually replaced the normative "natural laws" (45).

39. Precisely when the fact-value distinction comes into clear focus at this time Strauss does not here say, though it is obviously related to the previously sketched attempt to wean the people from their revealed-religious orientation, which (to Rousseau) appeared to require a remaking of human nature, whose possibility was established by the historical development of man, a historical development that became the basis of the new "ought," but that eventually led to the "depreciation of reason." See *City and Man*, 7:

> The modern project was originated as required by nature (natural right), i.e. it was originated by philosophers; the project was meant to satisfy in the most perfect manner the most powerful natural needs of men: nature was to be conquered for the sake of man who himself was supposed to possess a nature, an unchangeable nature; the originators of the project took it for granted that philosophy and science are identical. After some time

situation does not solve the underlying problem, but brings about a new tension, between "the ethos of technocracy" and "the ethos of democracy" (22). That is, the moral habits of each group are now understood in the terms of positivist social science; each is merely an "ethos," with no claim to offer rule or guidance to the other. Scientists, to be sure, continue to be guided toward what serves health, longevity, and extension of life, but they do so only through survival of "utilitarian habits," and their researches come to be guided by, or "respond to," their "customers," the people.[40] And

---

it appeared that the conquest of nature requires the conquest of human nature and hence in the first place the questioning of the unchangeability of human nature: an unchangeable human nature might set absolute limits to progress. Accordingly, the natural needs of men could no longer direct the conquest of nature; the direction had to come from reason as distinguished from nature, from the rational Ought as distinguished from the neutral Is. Thus philosophy (logic, ethics, esthetics) as the study of the Ought or the norms became separated from science as the study of the Is. The ensuing depreciation of reason brought it about that while the study of the Is or science succeeded ever more in increasing men's power, one could no longer distinguish between the wise or right and the foolish or wrong use of power. Science cannot teach wisdom.

40. That such "value-free" satisfaction was intended from the start by the new enlightening Baconian science, as the means to making philosophy respectable, or as a new, material kind of "rhetoric," Strauss suggests in his 1957 course on Plato's *Gorgias*, Leo Strauss Center, University of Chicago, 82–83 (see also 94), https://leostrausscenter.uchicago.edu/gorgias-winter-1957/:

If the end of philosophy will be not simply to know the truth, but by knowing the truth to contribute to the relief of man's estate, as Bacon said, to the increase of man's power over non-human things, as Hobbes thought, or to contribute to comfortable self-preservation, as Locke meant it—in other words, if the end of philosophy will be to be in agreement with the desire to have more, philosophy will become immensely popular. The demos will not merely be the recipient of scientific information, more or less superficial or unsubstantial, the demos will be, as it were, the customers of the merchandise supplied by philosophy or science; from which merchandise they would derive substantial enjoyment. In a word: The modern substitute for that public rhetoric which Plato seeks is technology based on science. That bridges the gulf between philosophy and the non-philosophers, a kind of speechless conviction of all people that philosophy or science is salutary. We can say that technology is public rhetoric

while certain "older traditions, fortunately, still retain their power" (23), the people (with the accelerated loosening of biblical restrictions, and hence of the distinction between liberty and license), come thereby to inhabit "mass society." What most characterizes our age can therefore be said to be "hardly more than the interplay of mass taste with high-grade but strictly speaking unprincipled efficiency" (23). Finally, as the sciences became more special-ized, all that is offered as an antidote to that specialization through liberal education is a "cinema" of "general civilization courses" that are "exciting and entertaining," or what Strauss elsewhere calls "sham universality," one that offers "conditioning" toward acceptance of the reigning opinions rather than a genuine "broadening and deepening" of human beings. Democracy has indeed emerged, but it cannot be said to be virtuous or to be guided by reason, nor, on the basis of the new science, to be the right, the best, a good, or even a decent regime. It could be so judged only on the basis of an older, political-moral understanding, which the new science actually attempted from the start to destroy.

With a brief mention of human "eros" that has as its goal "the per-fection of human nature," Strauss indicates, as he moves to his conclusion (at *LAM* 23), the classical understanding of the soul that had been denied or abandoned by the thinkers who began the modern scientific project, an understanding that, as we have seen, is intimately tied to awareness of mortality.[41] The alternative for liberal education within liberal democracy that he presents, on the basis of that understanding of eros, is one that takes advantage of the freedom that liberal democracy provides for all and hence *also* "to those who care for human excellence." With a genuine liberal education, such human beings may "set up outposts" within mass democracy, "which may come to be regarded by many citizens as salutary to the republic and as deserving of giving it its tone." In this way the liberally educated

---

of modern times. Even without advertising. . . . The problem which we have here to consider is not merely the A-bomb or the population bomb, as the enormous increase in the birthrate was called, but this new kind of philosophy or science which was made for the relief of man's estate leads to a new kind of political philosophy or social science in which relativism, as it is called, reigns supreme. The highest authority becomes science in this modern world, and science empowers every choice of ends by its inability to pronounce any ends.

41. *LAM* 23, bottom.

might "become again a power in democracy," assisting both democracy and the cause of excellence—though he indicates that this is attempted against very steep odds, "hoping against hope." This, then, is the "aristocracy within democracy" of which Strauss had spoken in his original talk on liberal education. That he here concludes by speaking of the "grandiose failures" of Karl Marx as "father of communism" and Friedrich Nietzsche as "stepgrandfather of fascism," as contemporary reminders of "the old saying that wisdom cannot be divorced from moderation," and that "hence," in our situation, "wisdom requires unhesitating loyalty to a decent constitution and even to the cause of constitutionalism," should make abundantly clear that Strauss, while by no means among the "flatterers of democracy," stands manifestly among "friends and allies of democracy."[42]

As we have seen, what is for much of this essay fairly unobtrusive bursts forth as a series of questions and then answers concerning the decay of *religious* and moral education within democracy. It declined owing to the very success of the scientific-technological enlightenment project and the material prosperity of the people, the overcoming of scarcity, and the Enlightenment's needed revolution in morality that are part and parcel of that project. In fact, if those who initiated that project were indeed motivated by biblical charity, then they were colossal bunglers in their exercise of that virtue, since they wiped out the very source of the virtue they found it so important to exercise. If on the other hand their claim to be motivated by biblical charity is disingenuous, as we have seen Strauss suggesting, then the result is much closer to what they in fact wished to achieve, or accords with their true motive.

A glance at the introductory chapter of Strauss's *Philosophy and Law* confirms that this is indeed how Strauss understands the matter. He there presents the "moderate Enlightenment," which presented itself as compatible with religion, as naively harboring the "radical Enlightenment," as part of a political dynamic inherent in the spread of the new constructivist natural science and its attempt to transform human consciousness away from religious orthodoxy, that is to say, away from belief in divine law, in revelation, in miracles, and above all in creation. This moderate enlightenment is characterized, first, by a belief that the " 'natural world image' " of the science of Aristotle and of the Bible had simply been replaced by the new Cartesian science as offering another account of the world as it truly is; and, second, by attempted "reconciliations" between the "modern world

---

42. *LAM* 24.

image" and the Bible, which "shot up like weeds in the seventeenth and eighteenth centuries and are attempted often enough even today." Calling the moderate enlightenment "the best first harvest of the radical Enlightenment," he indicates the use that was being made of it by its radical version; the moderate Enlightenment merely allowed "the new natural science" to enter "upon its successful campaign as the ally and pioneer of the radical Enlightenment." It depended on the continued, temporary rule over the "dispositions of men" of "the old concept of truth, which the Enlightenment had [in truth] already destroyed." Because of this continued rule of the defeated old disposition, for a short time "the ideal of civilization by means of modern natural science" was possible. Eventually, however, with the advance of modern natural science, "one was forced to ascertain that the 'goal- and value-free' nature of modern natural science could tell man nothing about 'ends and values,' that is, the 'Is' understood in the sense of modern natural science contains no reference whatsoever to the 'Ought,' and thus that the traditional view that the right life is a life according to nature becomes meaningless on the basis of modern presuppositions."[43] The new ideal of civilization proclaimed by the adherents of modern natural science was "Freedom," understood as "the autonomy of man and his culture." But "this view can be maintained," Strauss argues, "only if one confuses 'freedom,' understood as autonomy, with the [older notions of] 'freedom' of conscience, the 'freedom' of philosophizing, political "freedom" or the ideal of autarky of the philosophical tradition." And this "ideal was viable only during "an interval of calm, when the fight against Orthodoxy seemed to have been fought out and, correspondingly, the revolt of the forces unchained by the Enlightenment had still not broken out against their liberator." This was an interval "when, living in a habitable house, one could no longer see the foundation on which that house had been erected."[44]

While this description would have to be somewhat modified to accord with the differences between Europe and America at the time of which Strauss speaks, it nonetheless tells us a good deal about the very period during which the American Founding and its early life took place. The older "disposition" toward truth was toward discovery of nature and of a life led according to nature, which included the freedom to philosophize or the freedom of science, as the freedom that was necessary for the best way of life. The newer notion, of a nature that supplied *no* guidance as to

---

43. *Philosophy and Law*, 14, 15.

44. *Philosophy and Law*, 14–16.

the relation of the Is and the Ought (or was "value-free"), and hence also of a radical individual autonomy and the "mass society" that it produces, had not yet made itself fully apparent.[45]

The current situation of "mass society," in America and the West generally, may well be sufficiently attractive to those who sense that there is good reason to distinguish a decent constitutional democracy from its viable alternatives and one in which greatness can still burst forth. Other citizens of liberal democracy may wonder why, if the Enlightenment has indeed achieved its goal, one should stand opposed to that goal, rather than embracing it, if indeed democracy and its engine, modern science, achieves a decent society that, moreover, promises material well-being to those who had in the past suffered terribly and unjustly in its absence. But Strauss's "German Nihilism," a talk that analyzes the profound disgust at liberal democracy and the political movement to which it gave rise—one that required a world war to suppress—will help us to see better the deep precariousness of our situation.

---

45. That is to say, social science positivism or value-free social science is not simply a "German import" to America. It is the direct result of Cartesian constructivism. That American founders like Jefferson associated "enlightenment" with the new morality of natural rights is an example of the delusion that Strauss describes as predominating during this brief "period of calm." (See, e.g., Jefferson's Letter to Roger Weightman, July 4, 1826.) That period came to an end between 1860 and 1890. See Strauss, "Existentialism," in "Two Lectures by Leo Strauss," 308: "Modern science has not kept the promise which it held out from its beginning up to the end of the nineteenth century: that it would reveal to us the true character of the universe and the truth about man. You have in the *Education of Henry Adams* a memorable document of the change in the character and in the claim of science which made itself felt in the general public towards the end of the last century and which has increased since, in momentum and sweep. You all know the assertion that value-judgments are impermissible to the scientist in general and to the social scientist in particular." See also "Natural Right," Autumn 1962, lecture 2, October 10, 1962, pages 7 and 11–12 of the original unpublished transcript.

CHAPTER THREE

"German Nihilism"

The (admittedly weak) aristocracy that Strauss hopes to found within democracy is to be guided by contemporary examples of "greatness," and, as we have seen, he himself offered, within one of his own classes, the example of Churchill's greatness. We learn through "German Nihilism,"[1] a talk delivered twenty-three years before his classroom tribute to Churchill, that he thought this very same example could even have turned the German youth who were morally repulsed by the "mass society" of modern democracy, and intent therefore on the wholescale destruction of it, to instead support it, over and against the Call to action on behalf of its destruction—and learn what was behind that thought. Examining this talk will allow us better to understand the kind of nonhistoricist political reasoning that once characterized political life and that Strauss seems to think can, with adjustments to modernity, become vibrant again—if it can successfully gather those elements of its moral traditions that can sustain greatness. But examining this talk will also illuminate, through the light that it shines on three interrelated phenomena—"postmodernism" and its understanding of science; the German nihilists' "probity" and the atheism to which it led; and the

---

1. "German Nihilism," a talk delivered in the general seminar "Experiences of the Second World War" at the New School for Social Research, Graduate Faculty of Political and Social Science, February 26, 1941. My references will be to the version of the talk carefully edited and annotated by David Janssens and Daniel Tanguay, "German Nihilism," *Interpretation* 26, no. 3 (Spring 1999), 354–78. Strauss did not publish this talk, though he did publish a portion of it in his review of Dewey's *German Philosophy and Politics*, a review republished in *What Is Political Philosophy?*, at 280ff.

human longing for what is *good* rather than for the ancestral—a very great difficulty for modern democracy, a difficulty caused by the "partial victory of the Enlightenment," for any education or political reasoning that would seek a return to traditions. It therewith indicates the serious fragility of our current situation within liberal democracy. For better or worse, ours is a postmodern situation, even if we are successful in overcoming the so-called "historical sense" that Strauss considers the greatest obstacle both to sound politics and to genuine philosophizing.

Readers of "German Nihilism" will be struck by the similarity between what we have thus far seen and the claim Strauss makes in this talk that a reminder of human greatness, in the person of Churchill, is what was most needed—not by American youth, but—by the "very intelligent, and very decent, if very young, Germans" of Weimar, if they were not to succumb, as they did, to the thought of Nietzsche, Spengler, Moeller van den Bruck, Carl Schmitt, Ernst Jünger, and above all, Heidegger:

> Those young men who refused to believe that the period fol-
> lowing the jump into liberty, following the communist world
> revolution, would be the finest hour of mankind in general and
> of Germany in particular, would have been impressed as much
> as we were, by what Winston Churchill said after the defeat in
> Flanders about Britain's finest hour.[2]

The claim is part of Strauss's penetrating diagnosis, against the claims of Hermann Rauschning,[3] of what was informing German nihilism and hence of the appeal of National Socialism to these youth. Understanding what

---

2. "German Nihilism," 363.

3. The occasion of Strauss's talk was the recent US publication of an English translation of Hermann Rauschning's *Die Revolution des Nihilismus, Kulisse und Wirklichkeit im dritten Reich*, fünfte Auflage (Zurich: Europa Verlag, 1938); translated as *The Revolution of Nihilism: Warning to The West*, trans. E. W. Dickes (New York: Longmans, Green, 1939). It is worth noting that ten years after Strauss wrote this devastating critique of him, Rauschning was exposed as a fraud for his 1940 work, *The Voice of Destruction*, or *Hitler Speaks* (originally published as *Gespräche mit Hitler* [Conversations with Hitler]). In this later work Rauschning seems to have taken whole pages from Nietzsche and simply attributed them to Hitler, leading prominent historians such as Ian Kershaw to denounce his work.

Strauss saw as the "non-nihilistic root" of German nihilism, and the modern and postmodern understanding of reason that led that root to bear awful fruit in the miseducated souls of German adolescents, allows us to see the contours of admiration for greatness and its important place in a civilization whose two poles are, according to Strauss, morality, on one hand, and science or philosophy, on the other.[4]

In a series of increasingly precise definitions of nihilism, Strauss argues that nihilism is not fin de siècle ennui, nor a self-destructiveness explicable along the lines of contemporary psychology, but rather "a desire for the destruction of something specific: of modern civilization, . . . not guided by any clear positive conception" (357), a desire for its destruction as "far as modern civilization has a *moral* meaning" (358). That moral meaning is found in modern science's conquest of nature [Bacon], the doctrine of individual rights [Hobbes, Locke], and the greatest good of the greatest number [Bentham and Mill, the utilitarians]. It is found, in other words, not only in Marxists' vision of the end of history but in modern liberal democracy and its accompaniment, modern natural science. These forces

---

4. This is not to say that the longings of the German youth of whom he speaks in "German Nihilism" were in every important respect identical to those of thoughtful youth in America's democracy. In his attempt to explain the error of Rauschning's simple equation of nihilism with German bellicosity, Strauss notes both the peculiar communitarianism of the Germans and the peculiar Rousseauean form in which the Enlightenment arrived in much of Germany—that is, in the form of a *critique* of its bourgeois character and hence of the way in which the virtue of courage, and hence the call of war, became primary for the German youth: "German Nihilism," 370–71. (See also the autobiographical preface to *Spinoza's Critique of Religion*, 2: "Rousseau prepared not only the French Revolution and classical German philosophy, but also that extreme reaction to the French Revolution which is German romanticism. To speak politically and crudely, 'the romantic school in Germany . . . was nothing other than the resurrection of medieval poetry as it had manifested itself in art and in life.' The longing for the middle ages began in Germany at the very moment when the actual middle age—the Holy Roman Empire ruled by a German—ended, in what was then thought to be the moment of Germany's deepest humiliation. In Germany, and only there, did the end of the middle ages coincide with the beginning of the longing for the middle ages.") However, in his exchange with Alexander Kojève, Strauss predicts that a future manly rebellion against the universal and homogeneous state advocated by Kojève could well take the form of another nihilistic rebellion. See above, chapter 1, note 25. It may be necessary to add that, as all of his writings on Plato make clear, Strauss does not consider manliness to be a Socratic or philosophic virtue.

come together to produce modern society, and the German nihilists were protesting against it, as the "perfectly open society . . . which is as it were the goal of modern civilization"; they viewed it as "irreconcilable with the basic demands of moral life." For that society, as they saw it, was "the meeting ground of seekers of pleasure, of gain, of irresponsible power, indeed of any kind of irresponsibility and lack of seriousness."[5]

But how or why was the (morally) open society seen as necessarily the enemy of morality, of moral seriousness? Strauss explains:

> Moral life, it is asserted, means serious life. Seriousness, and the ceremonial of seriousness—the flag, and the oath to the flag—, are the distinctive features of the *closed* society, of the society which by its very nature, is constantly confronted with, and basically oriented toward, the *Ernstfall*, the serious moment, M-day, *war*. Only life in such a tense atmosphere, only a life which is based on constant awareness of the *sacrifices* to which it owes its existence, of the necessity, the *duty* of sacrifice of life and all wordly goods, is truly human: the sublime is unknown to the open society. The societies of the West which claim to aspire toward the open society, actually are closed societies in a state of disintegration: their moral value, their respectability, depends *entirely* on their still being closed societies.[6]

The root of nihilism was, then, *love of morality* seen as threatened by the principles of modern society, and the lack of moral seriousness, including the lack of a certain confrontation with mortality, that that society engendered. The open society—toward which, we must note, liberal societies tend even more today with the movement from liberal toleration to "diversity and inclusion"—precludes sacrifices and steadfast devotion to a distinctive, common way of life held to be good and worthy of devotion. The open society declares all former common ways of life mistaken, accepting only truncated or boutique versions of what were once parts of a vibrant, particular way of life held to be worthy of sacrifice; it accepts only "cultural" echoes of those ways manifested in textiles, gastronomy, and music, as its markets call for them, but carefully vetted for evidence of hatred of the

---

5. "German Nihilism," 358.

6. "German Nihilism," 358.

other, or "phobias." The open society, the liberal society outlined for the first time by Hobbes, says, "to get along, go along," or "better to switch than fight." It is cosmopolitan, eschewing oaths, sacred principles and customs, a serious way of life, things to which we bow, stand in awe or revere, to which we subordinate our own interests, and which one stands ready to defend with one's life.

Our own experience within contemporary liberal democracy might move us to associate the nihilists' defense of embattled morality, of the very possibility of sacrifice, with conservatism. But as Strauss makes clear, far from being conservative or "reactionary," the nihilists shared with Marxism a progressive understanding of reason or rationalism (and, we may add, the Marxists' glorification of struggle and sacrifice).[7] Theirs was an avante-garde movement that looked with contempt on Marxism (or "cultural Bolshevism") as historically backward, unable to see clearly, as the nihilists' allegedly more advanced (and equally atheistic) consciousness could, the destruction of the possibility of sacrifice, and hence of morality, that the Marxist warriors were, confusedly, aiming to bring into being. Strauss brings this home by presenting Marxists as almost a distant memory, not to say old-hat fuddy-duddies—not that he thought Marxism was dead, but in order to help capture the thinking of the German youth:

> The older ones in our midst still remember the time when certain people asserted that the conflicts inherent in the present situation would necessarily lead to a revolution, accompanying or following another World War—a rising of the proletariat and of the proletarianized strata of society which would usher in the withering away of the State, the classless society, the abolition of all exploitation and injustice, the era of final peace. It was this prospect, at least as much as the desperate present, which led to nihilism. The prospect of a pacified planet, without rulers and ruled, of a planetary society devoted to production and consumption only, to the production and consumption of spiritual as well as material merchandise, was positively horrifying

---

7. It is worth noting in this regard both the inspiration that the (nondeterminist) Marxist Georges Sorel gave to the fascist movement in Italy and his very high praise of *both* Lenin and Mussolini. See Georges Sorel, "For Lenin," *Soviet Russia* 2 (April 10, 1920), 356, and Sorel's March 1921 conversations with Jean Variot, published in Variot's *Propos de Georges Sorel* (Paris: Gallimard, 1935), 53–57, 66–86.

to quite a few very intelligent and very decent, if very young, Germans. They did not object to that project because they were worrying about their own economic and social position; for certainly in that respect they had no longer anything to lose. Nor did they object to it for religious reasons; for, as one of their spokesmen (E. Jünger) said, they knew that they were the sons and grandsons and great-grandsons of godless men. What they hated, was the very prospect of a world in which everyone would be happy and satisfied, in which everyone would have his little pleasure by day and his little pleasure by night, a world in which no great heart could beat and no great soul could breathe, a world without real, un-metaphoric, sacrifice, i.e., a world without blood, sweat, and tears.[8]

With this allusion to Churchill in "German Nihilism,"[9] Strauss links the example of Churchillian statesmanship to the youth's longing to preserve human greatness and sacrifice, and—tied to these—dissatisfaction with the emphatically materialist happiness promised by Marxism. Their rebellion was caused by the relative success of liberal regimes in wiping out the need for and call to sacrifice, and the prospect of the complete success of its "rational" successor, Marxist communism, in doing so. Even and precisely to those who were self-consciously the heirs of generations of atheists, of "disenchanted" men, this concern was their central concern. Modernity had not caused it to wither. Far from it.

Yet the example of Churchill came, Strauss makes clear, too late for the German youth to take it as their polestar. Their longing was, as their disgusted reference to one's "little pleasure by day and little pleasure by night"

---

8. "German Nihilism," 360.

9. In his first speech as prime minister to the House of Commons (May 13, 1940), Churchill had said, "I would say to the House, as I said to those who have joined this government: 'I have nothing to offer but blood, toil, tears and sweat.'" And a bit later: "We have before us many, many long months of struggle and of suffering. You ask, what is our policy? I can say: It is to wage war, by sea, land and air, with all our might and with all the strength that God can give us; to wage war against a monstrous tyranny, never surpassed in the dark, lamentable catalogue of human crime. That is our policy. You ask, what is our aim? I can answer in one word: It is victory, victory at all costs, victory in spite of all terror, victory, however long and hard the road may be."

suggest, still shaped by Nietzsche and especially by his Zarathustra's haunting account of the last man, and was otherwise—unshaped, or strictly negative:

> What to the communists appeared to be the fulfilment of the dream of mankind, appeared to those young Germans as the greatest abasement of humanity, as the coming of the end of humanity, as the arrival of the latest [last] man. They did not really know, and thus they were unable to express in a tolerably clear language, what they desired to put in the place of the present world and its allegedly necessary future or sequel: the only thing of which they were absolutely certain was that the present world and all the potentialities of the present world as such, must be destroyed in order to prevent the otherwise necessary coming of the communist final order: literally anything, the nothing, the chaos, the jungle, the Wild West, the Hobbian state of nature, seemed to them infinitely better than the communist anarchist-pacifist future.[10]

That Strauss is at pains here to bring out the youth's inchoate opposition to the *Marxist* goal should not hide from us the fact that the youth's stance, like that of the Marxists, grew out of a prior experience of deep dissatisfaction with (the even more backward consciousness of) liberal democracy;[11] the full and rational actualization of liberal democracy's potentialities lay, so far as the youth were concerned, necessarily in the direction of the more advanced consciousness of the communists.[12] And the generations-long, disillusioning work of modern science and of liberalism, we may say, had

---

10. "German Nihilism," 358–59.

11. See "German Nihilism," 359, bottom: "German liberal democracy of all descriptions seemed to many people to be absolutely unable to cope with the difficulties with which Germany was confronted. This created a profound prejudice, or confirmed a profound prejudice already in existence, against liberal democracy as such."

12. Consider also in this regard the following statement on Nietzsche from "Existentialism" (314): "As all continental European conservatives he saw in communism only the consistent completion of democratic egalitarianism and of that liberalistic demand for freedom which was not a freedom for, but only a freedom from. But in contradistinction to the European conservatives he saw that conservatism as such is doomed. For all merely defensive positions are doomed. All merely backward-looking positions are doomed."

stripped them of any hope that the object of their longing could possibly be found in conservative appeals to throne and altar. Yet if they were in this way prepared for the "creation" of new values, it was owing to an abiding love of morality and its sacrifices.

It is to these youth, Strauss argues, that the appeal to Churchillian greatness could have had a dramatic, reorienting effect. A Marxist might call such an appeal an attempt at co-optation of the consciousness of those German youth, such that their love of morality would no longer move them to oppose liberal democracy. And while Strauss does indeed wish that an appeal to Churchillian greatness could have been made, to this very end, this effect could not have taken place in a way that co-optation of consciousness can explain. It would, rather, have begun a liberation from the whole inherited, taken-for-granted notion of historical reasoning, from belief in a social progression of human consciousness, a "wheel of history"—a sense of belonging, to use a current phrase, to the "right side of History"—that would have begun to make possible the recovery of an older, truer understanding of reason. The example of Churchill's greatness could have reawakened this slumbering reason in them, by showing them the abiding possibility of moral life, of answering the call of duty and sacrifice, that still obtained in modern democracy, and indeed obtains "at any time."[13]

As things stood, the German youth remained in the thrall of historical reasoning, and thus found themselves in opposition to reason:

> It is hardly necessary to point out the fallacy committed by the young men in question. They simply took over the communist thesis that the proletarian revolution and proletarian dictatorship is necessary, if civilization is not to perish. But they insisted rather more than the communists on the conditional character of the communist prediction (*if* civilization is not to perish). That condition left room for choice: they chose what according to the communists was the only alternative to communism [the perishing of civilization]. In other words: they admitted that all rational argument was in favour of communism; but they opposed to that apparently invincible argument what they called "irrational decision."[14]

---

13. Consider also Strauss's letter to Karl Löwith of August 20, 1946: "A man like Churchill proves that the possibility of *megalopsychia* exists today *exactly* as it did in the fifth century b.c." *Independent Journal of Philosophy* 4 (1983), 105–19.

14. "German Nihilism," 360, bottom.

Told that their opposition to communism was necessarily against reason, the youth rejected reason and the modern civilization it was busy bringing into being, in a committed, and—one is tempted to say, "authentic"—life affirming "decision." Strauss thereby ties Schmittean/Heideggerian decisionism to the neglectful, taken-for-granted disposition toward historical reasoning of the Marxists and, more generally, toward Hegel and those who reacted to him—a disposition from which Strauss had freed himself. Taking advantage of his rediscovery of classical rationalism, he now presents the heart of his critique of both the Marxists and the nihilistic decisionists: there is, he argues, another kind of reasoning, which attempts to understand the world as it is rather than to transform it or engage it in accord with an alleged progressive consciousness. A case for the rulership of this kind of reasoning is a case for the rulership of what is "one and unchangeable," or what is always—precisely what "progressives" had abandoned. Against the nihilists' sense that a strong rain was needed to wash away civilization, the progressivists' teaching was in any case hopeless; to oppose the nihilists, one would have to have turned from modern reason to this older kind of reason.

As Marxists or half-Marxists, the teachers of the German youth were incapable of teaching them this older reasoning. They instead engaged in the paternalism peculiar to progressives, dismissing the nihilists' concerns as the result of a typical youthful enthusiasm. Strauss is harsher in his judgment of these teachers than he is of the youth, noting that the teachers have unleashed the movement by preaching emancipation of youth. It would not do, moreover, to think, as these teachers did, that one has refuted these youth by pointing to the inconsistencies in their positive vision, a vision given to them by Spengler, Carl Schmitt, Ernst Jünger (author of *Storm of Steel*, *The Worker*, and *Fire and Blood*), and Heidegger.[15] Their paternalistic

---

15. "German Nihilism," 362. See also "The Living Issues of Postwar German Philosophy" [1940], box 8, folder 9, Leo Strauss Papers; published in "Appendix: Two Previously Unpublished Lectures," in Heinrich Meier, *Leo Strauss and the Theologico-Political Problem* (New York: Cambridge University Press, 2006), 128: "A more radical expression of this [Carl Schmitt's] view is to be found in an essay by Ernst Jünger 'On pain' (in: *Blatter und Steine*). Jünger asserts that in our period all faiths and ideals of earlier times have lost their force and evidence. Consequently, all standards with reference to which we can judge ourselves and others are no longer valid. But there is one standard left: the ability or inability to stand pain, physical pain. Fortitude or courage is the only virtue which is still evident, the only virtue left—and this not without reason: ἀνδρεία is the original virtue." See also Heidegger's letter to Jünger, originally titled "Concerning the Line," changed to "On the Question of Being" [1955], *Pathmarks*, 295. " 'The Question concerning Technology,' " says Heidegger, "owes a lasting debt to the descriptions in

teachers "did not even try to understand the *ardent passion* underlying the negation of the present world and its potentialities. . . . These young men had come to doubt *seriously*, and not merely methodologically, the principles of modern civilization." The nihilists perceived the threat to morality as a threat to the possibility of leading lives that were at all significant or meaningful. Taking them seriously would have meant—still means—understanding both their deep longing for and sense of responsibility for threatened morality, and (therefore) their deep, unrelieved, even desperate revulsion at what the modern world, modern "civilization," has produced.

The foregoing allows us to appreciate Strauss's own, strikingly sympathetic attention to the youths' love of endangered morality, and prepares us for his claim that that love is neither new nor itself nihilistic. The youth's nihilism has a "non-nihilistic root," he argues, and that root—the concern for "embattled morality"—exists in both premodern and modern times. Quietly drawing again from his recovery of classical political philosophy and its modern alternatives, he espies and invites the reader to see that concern in the Glaucon of Plato's *Republic*, who had been talked deaf by Thrasymachus and wished Socrates to defend justice as the one thing most desirable; to see it in Rousseau's critique, in his *First Discourse*, of the modern bourgeois, who has forgotten the name fatherland and speaks only of money; and to see it, finally, in Nietzsche and his critique of the last man that had so moved the German youth.[16] The timeless example of Churchillian greatness within a

---

The Worker." He adds, a bit further, addressing Jünger, "For you no longer partake in that action of active nihilism that, already in *The Worker*, is conceived in a Nietzschean sense as oriented toward an overcoming" (296). In "The Rectorate: Facts and Thoughts" ("The Self-Assertion of the German University and The Rectorate 1933/34: Facts and Thoughts," 467), Heidegger relates the following:

> Ernst Jünger's essay on "Total Mobilization" [*Die totale Mobilmachung*] was published in 1930: in this essay the basic features of his book *The Worker* [*Der Arbeiter*], which was published in 1932, announced themselves. With my assistant Brock, I discussed these writings in a small circle and attempted to show how they express an essential understanding of Nietzsche's metaphysics, insofar as the history and present of the Western world are seen and foreseen within the horizon of this metaphysics. Using these writings and, still more essentially, their foundations, as a base for our thoughts we were able to think what was coming, that is to say, we attempted to face it in our confrontation with it.

16. The references to Rousseau and Nietzsche are to thinkers whom Strauss will later (in "The Three Waves of Modernity") present as emblematic of the second and third "waves"

liberal regime, we conclude, would have awakened, Strauss is claiming, the older moral reasoning because the passionate desire to defend morality, which is at the root of nihilism, is, importantly, long-standing or transhistorical (as are, as this also implies, attacks on morality).

The Place of the Old Moral Reasoning

The effect that Strauss suspects the example of Churchillian greatness would have had on Germany's nihilistic youth would certainly have accomplished a more difficult task, or been a greater achievement, than the effect he expected it to have on his American students within liberal democracy. Politically and most obviously, far from something that could be suspected of being an incipient *threat* to liberal democracy, that reminder could, Strauss argues, have changed the German youth's disposition toward "modern society and all of its potentialities." For by disclosing to them a moral potentiality within liberal democracy—which they, in their historical reasoning, had considered out of the question—it could have disposed them in the direction of liberal democracy. More importantly, by exposing the falsity of the claim concerning the alleged rational "necessity" of the communist potentialities, it could have begun a complete transformation in their moral thinking, from an historicist one to one that aimed at what their hearts desired: a transhistorical one. It would thereby have permitted them to begin a recovery of what was still available in England: "the prudence to conceive of the modern ideals as a reasonable adaptation of the old and eternal ideal of decency, of rule of law, and of that liberty which is not license, to changed circumstances."[17] In fact, Strauss indicates as much with his in-class statement twenty-three years later, when declaring that Churchill's *Marlborough*[18] is "not a whit less important" than Churchill's leadership in the defeat of the Nazi tyranny, as a work that offers an education in political wisdom and understanding. In Strauss's estimation Churchill, who himself wrestled with grave doubts about

---

of modernity, suggesting that the first wave, that of Machiavelli and Hobbes, bears some resemblance to the thought of the rhetoricians and sophists by whom Glaucon had been "talked deaf" and against whom he begged Socrates to "help out," in a defense of justice.

17. "German Nihilism," 372.

18. That is, the four-volume biography of Winston Churchill's celebrated ancestor, John Churchill, the late seventeenth- and early eighteenth-century English statesman and general, published between 1933 and 1938.

the direction of modern politics and modern technological science,[19] provided in *Malborough* a gift so great as to merit this extraordinary praise. Churchill presents Malborough not as someone engaged in antiquated politics, but as successfully confronting and accommodating himself, and England, to the post–Glorious Revolution politics of modernity.[20] Strauss's reminder of Churchillian greatness is healthy for democracy because it moves its listeners away from historicist reasoning and toward the older political reasoning.[21] There is, then, a very deep agreement, behind the apparent disagreement that we noted in chapter 1, between reminders of Churchillian greatness and liberal democracy.

But this agreement must be properly understood. As we have suggested, students of Strauss are mistaken to think that liberal democracy as conceived and put into place by the American founders is immune to the kind of *non*-nihilistic moral critique that lay at the bottom of the German youth's nihilistic rejection of modern civilization—to think, that is, that America was as it were the best regime until the import into it, during the Progressive Era, of foreign, "German" thought. As Strauss stresses, the historical thinking that eventually (in its most radical form) became historicist decisionism arose not as a reaction to anything peculiarly German, but as a moral reaction to the lived results of the spread of Enlightenment, including its doctrine of inalienable natural rights—a reaction, that is, to the problem posed by the new, secular societies of modernity brought into being by modern scientist-philosophers and their Enlightenment. While in Germany that reaction began with the historical school of jurisprudence, that school had equivalents in England (in Henry Sumner Maine),[22] in France,

---

19. See especially Winston Churchill, "Mass Effects in Modern Life," in *Thoughts and Adventures*, ed. James W. Muller (Wilmington, DE: ISI Books, 2009), and *The Aftermath* (New York: Scribner's, 1929), the added fourth volume of *The World Crisis*, whose first three volumes appeared in 1923, 1923, and 1927 (in two parts), respectively. The fifth volume, titled *The Eastern Front*, was published in 1931. And see Marjorie Jeffrey, *The Wars of Peoples: Science, Democracy, and International Politics in the Thought of Winston Churchill* (PhD diss., Baylor University, 2018).

20. See Charles Sullivan, "Churchill's Marlborough: The Character of a Trimmer," in *Interpretation* 46, no. 3 (June 2020), 513–32.

21. Tocqueville's counsel appears, by contrast, to have emerged out of an early version of the historical rationalism that bore full fruit in German nihilism, one that received its radical, atheist elaboration in the Nietzschean critique of progressive egalitarianism.

22. Henry Sumner Maine, *Ancient Law: Its Connection with the Early History of Society, and Its Relation to Modern Ideas* (London, 1861). A more recent edition is edited by C.

and in Italy, and Strauss even viewed Burke's notion of "prescriptive" to be the equivalent of the German notion of "historical."[23] "Today, we all are historicists to begin with. Where are the liberals who dare appeal to the natural rights of man? They prefer to appeal to the tradition of liberalism. Historicism is the basic assumption common to present-day democracy, communism, fascism."[24]

In addition, in his description of what was most needed by the German nihilists, Strauss never mentions "natural rights," no more than he does in his counsel to remind American students of Churchillian greatness. Moreover, as Strauss makes clear, "one cannot call the most radical critic of modern civilisation as such, a nihilist."[25] Finally, when explaining later in the talk the origins of the German militarism, of the German elevation of the virtue of courage, of which German nihilism was a radicalization, Strauss not only sketches his own understanding of modern civilization and its moral basis in "claiming one's rights" as a "debasement of morality," but offers very high praise of what he describes as the period (1760–1830) when Germany "reached the hey-day of her letters and her thought," in a deep criticism of modern, rights-based civilization:

> The ideal of modern civilisation is of English and French origin; it is not of German origin. What the meaning of that ideal

K. Allen (London: Oxford University Press, 1931).

23. See *NRH*, 83 with 319–20, together with Strauss's 1963 course on Vico, 10–12 of the original unpublished typed manuscript. See also "The Living Issues of Postwar German Philosophy," [1940] box 8, folder 14, Leo Strauss Papers; published in "Appendix: Two Previously Unpublished Lectures," in Meier, *Leo Strauss and the Theologico-Political Problem*, 123: "The fact that man does need tradition is shown by this, that the very same modern man who undermined all traditions was compelled to take refuge in history: history is the modern surrogate for tradition."

24. "Historicism," lecture to be delivered in the fall of 1941 in the general seminar of the New School for Research, typescript [no box or folder number supplied] (Patard, 206–31, at 210).

25. "German Nihilism," 366. Consider in this light Strauss's own statement on Carl Schmitt: "In order to launch the radical critique of liberalism that he has in mind, Schmitt must first eliminate the conception of human evil as animal evil, and therefore as 'innocent evil,' and find his way back to the conception of human evil as moral depravity. Only by so doing can Schmitt remain in agreement with himself, if indeed 'the core of the political idea is the *morally* exacting decision' " (*Politische Theologie* [1932], p. 56)." Strauss, "Comments on *Der Begriff des Politschen*, by Carl Schmitt," in *Spinoza's Critique of Religion*, 345 (emphasis in the original).

is, is, of course, a highly controversial question. If I am not greatly mistaken, one can define the tendency of the intellectual development which as it were exploded in the French Revolution, in the following terms: to lower the moral standards, the moral claims, which previously had been made by all responsible teachers, but to take better care than those earlier teachers had done, for the putting into practice, into political and legal practice, of the rules of human conduct. The way in which this was most effectually achieved, was the identification of morality with an attitude of claiming one's rights, or with enlightened self-interest, or the reduction of honesty to the best policy; or the solution of the conflict between common interest and private interest by means of industry and trade. (The two most famous philosophers: Descartes, his *generosité*, and no justice, no duties; Locke: where there is no property, there is no justice.) Against that debasement of morality, and against the concomitant decline of a truly philosophic spirit, the thought of Germany stood up, to the lasting honour of Germany.[26]

---

26. "German Nihilism," 370–71. That Strauss does not here explicitly mention technological science does not at all mean that he does not consider it an essential part of the utilitarian "lowering" of the goals of modern civilization. Not only does he mention here "industry and trade" as part of the modern effort, but he considered that very lowering to be part of the social engineering begun by Machiavelli. See Strauss, "What Can We Learn from Political Theory?" [lecture to be delivered in the general seminar of the summer course, July 1942), *Review of Politics* 69, no. 4 (2007), 515–52 (at 523): "The traditional utopianism of the philosophers and, we may add, of the theologians, was gradually replaced by the modern utopianism of the social engineer." Second, in addition to Strauss's explicit inclusion, in "German Nihilism," of Baconian "relief of man's estate" (358) in the thinking that has brought forth the situation to which the nihilists object, and their Nietzschean understanding of that situation, we have in Strauss's eulogy of Kurt Riezler ("Kurt Riezler, 1882–1955," *Social Research* 23, no. 1 [Spring 1956], 3–34) a specific inclusion of the "technological-scientific development" as part of the "politically relevant cosmopolitanism" that confronted Germany. Riezler, says Strauss, "distinguished genuine cosmopolitanism from spurious and superficial cosmopolitanism, and he discerned the root of the former in the depth of the individual. The individual is part of his nation, but he is not merely part of his Nation" (10–11) But Riezler "believed that nationalism stands for something more noble than cosmopolitanism, or at least that cosmopolitanism which is politically relevant. The politically relevant cosmopolitanism was supported by the modern economic-technological-scientific development. But this development did not strengthen, it rather weakened, the human in man. It increased man's power but not his wisdom. One could see with special clarity in Germany that this development was

The older moral reasoning to which the German youth were to be reawakened is not, then, bound to the modern doctrine of inalienable rights that

---

accompanied by a decay of spirit, of taste, of the mind. It compelled men to become ever more specialistic, and at the same time it tempted them with a sham universality by exciting all kinds of curiosities and stimulating all kinds of interests. It thus made ever more difficult concentration on the few things on which man's wholeness entirely depends" (6). That Strauss agreed with this (Riezler's) assessment is clear from Strauss's own description, in "Existentialism" (307), of the problems besetting liberal democracy, in which he speaks of "industrial mass democracy" and of Nietzsche's lament that "the morning newspaper has replaced the morning prayer":

> Are there no dangers threatening democracy not only from without but from within as well? Is there no problem of democracy, of industrial mass democracy? The official high priests of democracy with their amiable reasonableness were not reasonable enough to prepare us for our situation: the decline of Europe, the danger to the west, to the whole western heritage which is at least as great and even greater than that which threatened Mediterranean civilization around 300 of the Christian era. It is childish to believe that the U.N. organization is an answer even to the political problem. And within democracy: it suffices to mention the name of France and the commercials and logical positivism with their indescribable vulgarity. They have indeed the merit of not sending men into concentration camps and gas chambers, but is the absence of these unspeakable evils sufficient? Nietzsche once described the change which had been effected in the second half of the nineteenth century in continental Europe as follows. The reading of the morning prayer had been replaced by the reading of the morning paper: not every day the same thing, the same reminder of men's absolute duty and exalted destiny, but every day something new with no reminder of duty and exalted destiny. Specialization, knowing more and more about less and less, practical impossibility of concentration upon the very few essential things upon which man's wholeness entirely depends— this specialization compensated by sham universality, by the stimulation of all kinds of interests and curiosities without true passion, the danger of universal philistinism and creeping conformism.

Third, it is helpful to consider Strauss's presentation of Nietzsche's disposition toward the modern project, in "The Origins of Political Science" (Oct. 27, 1958), *Interpretation* 23 no. 2 (Winter 1996), 137: "The modern project stands or falls by science, by the belief that science can in principle solve all riddles and loosen all fetters. Science being the activity of reason par excellence, the modern project appears as the final form of rationalism, of the belief in the unlimited power of reason and in the essentially beneficent character of reason." For the full understanding of this statement, consider "The Problem of Socrates" (1970) in "Two Lectures by Leo Strauss," 223 (emphases added): To Nietzsche,

lies at the heart of the American order; in important respects, and certainly in that doctrine's widespread effects, it is at odds with it. Those who might be led by Strauss's stress on Churchillian greatness to find Strauss advancing a rationalism that perceives what is just by nature will find the matter to be far more complicated than this easy jump would suggest. It was after all the attempt to produce a "rational society" that led to the present crisis.

And yet neither is the appeal to Churchill simply conservative. To say nothing of Strauss's silence on the stance taken by Crown Prince Rupprecht of Bavaria against "the wheel of history,"[27] Strauss identifies the "barbarian"—"the non-Greek barbarian as well as the Greek barbarian"—as one who "believes that all his questions are solved by, or on the basis of, his

> [Socrates] is the prototype of the rationalist and therefore of the optimist, for optimism is not merely the belief that the world is the best possible world, but also the belief that the world can be *made into* the best of all imaginable worlds, or that the evils which belong to the best possible world can be rendered harmless by knowledge: thinking can not only fully *understand* being but can even *correct* it; *life* can be *guided* by science; the living gods of myth can be replaced by a *deus ex machina*, i.e. the forces of nature as known and used in the service of 'higher egoism.' Rationalism is optimism, since it is the belief that reason's power is unlimited and essentially beneficent or that science can solve all riddles and loosen all chains. Rationalism is optimism, since the belief in causes depends on the belief in ends or since rationalism presupposes the belief in the initial or final supremacy of the good. The full and ultimate consequences of the change effected or represented by Socrates appear only in the contemporary West: in the belief in universal enlightenment and therewith in the earthly happiness of all within a universal society, in utilitarianism, liberalism, democracy, pacifism, and socialism.

As we have seen, Strauss disagrees with Nietzsche's (and Heidegger's) understanding of *ancient* theoretical or scientific reasoning as having this character; he distinguishes it much more radically than does Heidegger from the modern understanding on this basis. One may say that Heidegger mistakenly ascribes to the investigations that belong to the theoretical life, which is the investigation both of beings and being, the understanding of being as a "being," as if those investigations grew out of and were meant to inform and "correct" their practical, political-moral lives. He does not see dialectics as the path to the justification of the (quite different) theoretical investigation of both being and beings. See Martin Heidegger, "The Self-Assertion of the German University and The Rectorate 1933/34: Facts and Thoughts," 467–502, at 472–73, and see below, chapter 4.

27. "In about these words: 'Some people say that the wheel of history cannot be turned back. This is an error.' " "German Nihilism," 359.

ancestral tradition."[28] Above all, he objects to Rauschning's identification of nihilism with the "destruction of all traditional spiritual standards" on the ground that "not all traditional spiritual standards are, by their nature, beyond criticism and even rejection," and justifies this with reference to Aristotle: "We seek what is good, and not what we have inherited. . . . In other words, I believe it is dangerous, if the opponents of National Socialism withdraw to a mere conservatism which defines its ultimate goal by a specific tradition. The temptation to fall back from an unimpressive present on an impressive past—and every past is as such impressive—is very great indeed. We ought not, however, cede to that temptation."[29] The education Strauss hopes to awaken within liberal democracy is not hagiographic or even one that aims simply at an increased devotion to a *specific* ancestral tradition.[30] But if Strauss is pointing us neither to the modern doctrine of individual rights nor to guidance by a specific tradition, to what—within liberal democracy—is he pointing?

He is pointing to a moral reasoning that he understands to be universally available—though by no means universally practiced—one that has been distorted by modern civilization and the philosophers who initiated it but that remains present and recoverable in that civilization, in liberal democracy. To understand what Strauss has in mind, it will be helpful to say a word or two about the modern doctrine of rights and its incoherence and its potentialities.

It is not difficult to see the confused or self-contradictory character of the Marxists' moral struggle to bring about a world in which there is no longer any possibility of moral struggle. It may be more difficult for us citizens of liberal democracy to see that that confusion, or incoherence, has a counterpart in the morality of liberal democracy,· one that is visible in the original argument for the doctrine of inalienable natural rights.[31] That

---

28. "German Nihilism," 366.

29. "German Nihilism," 367.

30. In fact, the decisionism of the nihilists entailed a "reflective" embrace of the present that the past has thrown us into, an existentialist embrace of a re-made past.

31. See above, chapter 1, pp. 10–11. And see Timothy W. Burns, "Modernity's Irrationalism," in *After History? Francis Fukuyama and His Critics* (Lanham, MD: Rowman and Littlefield, 1998), ch. 9, espescially 146–48; "John Courtney Murray, Religious Liberty, and Modernity: Part I: Inalienable Natural Rights," *Logos* 17, no. 2 (Spring 2014), 13–38, especially 24–28. Also David Bolotin, "Is There a Right to Do as We Please? (So Long as We Respect the Right of Others to Do the Same)," unpublished

argument wishes to secure the primacy of inalienable, self-regarding claims and thereby reduce all duties, or natural laws, to subsequent, prudential rules of reason that show the best means of securing those claims. The argument rests on the assertion that whatever steps are deemed *necessary* by individuals, in dangerous circumstances, for their preservation, are not only "generally allowed," but "ought to be allowed." But this "ought" can have no meaning without an appeal to justice, to a perceived, preexisting moral law, one that obliges us to serve a common good, a law that in normal circumstances forbids many voluntary acts, such as murder and theft, that would (in Hobbes's words) "augment" our "dominion." The argument thus states, on one hand, that we are compelled to seek our own interest, by a permanent necessity—so permanent that it justifies "inalienable" selfish claims—even as it makes, on the other, a quiet or surreptitious appeal to an obligatory law that presumes our freedom from such necessity, a freedom and a duty to act for the common good, limiting and sacrificing our own good in accord with it.[32] And in his extended reflection on Isaiah Berlin's case for the "negative freedom" secured by this doctrine, or the (permissive) "freedom to live as one prefers" that is at the heart of the morality of modern Western democracies, Strauss notes a version of this contradiction: the doctrine of "freedom from" simultaneously declares the nonexistence of *any and all moral absolutes* that would guide one to a "freedom for," *and* claims that there is a *morally absolute right* to be left alone.[33]

As an aspect of its very incoherence, however, the liberal democratic doctrine of rights preserves within it, and must preserve, the older moral reasoning. Strauss points out that Isaiah Berlin knows, concerning the mere "negative freedom," that "even in the modern Western world it is cherished

---

talk given at St. John's College, Santa Fe, New Mexico, January 25, 2002. Strauss calls attention to this incoherence in *NRH*, 168 with 196n39.

32. See Hobbes, *Leviathan* 13.4 with 18.3, and *De cive* 1.8–1.9. The moral character of this right is not established or claimed by (the more consistent) Spinoza, who makes right coextensive with power. See Spinoza, *Theologico-Political Treatise*, ch. 16, and *Political Treatise* 2.4, and see his correspondence with Jarig Jelles, December 14, 1673 (ep. 50): "With regard to political theory, the difference between Hobbes and myself, which is the subject of your inquiry, consists in this, that I always preserve the natural right in its entirety, and I hold that the sovereign power in a State has right over a subject only in proportion to the excess of its power over that of a subject. This is always the case in a state of nature." Spinoza, *Complete Works*, Michael Morgan, ed. Samuel Shirley, trans. (Indianapolis: Hackett, 2002), 891–92.

33. " 'Relativism,' " chapter 7 of *Relativism and the Study of Man*, ed. Helmet Schoeck and James W. Wiggins (Princeton, NJ: D. Van Nostrand, 1961), 135–57.

by some individuals rather than by large masses; there is no necessary connection between negative freedom and democracy."[34] That is, the majority of its citizens continue to be moved by a positive notion of freedom and hence of excellence. They continue to respond to appeals to greatness and sacred duty and all that those appeals imply. (And, of course, neither premodern democracies nor nonliberal modern democracies had or have constitutions based on the concept of negative freedom.) Even those among our own youth who might wonder what is at all unattractive about a society in which there is, in the words of one of their favorite poets, "nothing to kill or die for," may at some point wonder what the ground is for their insistence on the moral limitation of their and others' selfish actions, and may even be driven by their wonder to see the incoherence of the doctrine of individual rights that underlies their thinking and to which they adhere.

But as the existence of such youth suggests, the long-range tendency of liberal democracy is away from moral seriousness and toward permissiveness. And this tendency, together with Strauss's ability to discern within liberal democracy the abiding character of an older, premodern moral reasoning, and even its full flowering in the speeches and writings of Churchill, moved him to see the need to promote the founding, within the cultural, subpolitical, or private sphere, of an "aristocracy within democracy." The moral reasoning of its members would endeavor to keep liberal democracy "closed" not only to tyranny but also to the depravations brought on when license displaces liberty.

Moral Reasoning and Ancestral Traditions

What, then, according to Strauss, does the older moral reasoning look like—the moral reasoning that guides liberal democracy, at its best, and

---

34. "'Relativism,'" 136. Incidentally, the recent claim that Strauss's thought is best understood as a distortion of Western thought made for the sake of Cold War anti-communism overlooks the fact that Strauss's critique of Isaiah Berlin indicates that this is far from his own theoretical intention: "It would be short-sighted to deny that Berlin's comprehensive formula [that is, that any old subjective basis for an "absolute stand" in favor of negative freedom will do] is very helpful for a political purpose—for the purpose of an anti-Communist manifesto designed to rally all anti-Communists. But we are here concerned with a theoretical problem, and in this respect we are forced to say that Berlin contradicts himself" (138). Similarly, Strauss goes so far as to sternly warn readers of *Natural Right and History* (6) who are looking to find a basis for natural right, not to be led by the spirit of fanatical obscurantism that characterized their nihilistic foes.

is to guide the "aristocracy within democracy" that Strauss wishes liberal education to found? And what is its relation to science or philosophy?

First, and most obviously, it is a kind of reasoning, and aims at *knowledge*. As Strauss says of the German nihilists, instead of expecting "the answer to the first and the last question from "History," from the future as such, the German nihilists might have begun to be "guided by a *known* and *stable* standard": by a standard that is stable and is "known and not merely believed."[35] Second, the knowledge at which it aims has more to do with *means* than with ends: "Decent and noble conduct has to do, not so much with the natural aim of man, as with the means toward that aim: the view that the end sanctifies the means, is a tolerably complete expression of immoralism";[36] the ends of the moral life within which its reasoning takes place are for the most part *given*, rather than an object of "reasoning." And third, relatedly and crucially, this reasoning and the "knowledge" it yields is *not* "scientific." In fact, Strauss draws a sharp distinction between morals and science—between practical and theoretical reasoning, in his definition of "civilization," that which the nihilists wished to destroy:

> By civilisation, we understand the conscious culture of humanity, i.e. of that which makes a human being a human being, i.e. the conscious culture of reason. Human reason is active, above all, in two ways: as regulating human conduct, and as attempting to understand whatever can be understood by man; as practical reason, and as theoretical reason. The pillars of civilisation are morals and science, and both united. For science without morals degenerates into cynicism, and thus destroys the basis of the scientific effort itself; and morals without science degenerates into superstition and thus is apt to become fanatic cruelty.[37]

---

35. "German Nihilism," 364.

36. "German Nihilism," 365.

37. "German Nihilism," 365. The turn away from this distinction, which begins with Bacon and Hobbes, shows itself also in contemporary "political theory": see Strauss's attribution, to contemporary "political theory," of the end of Baconian science, in "What Can We Learn from Political Theory?," 515–52 (at 515): "The term 'political theory' implies that there is such a thing as theoretical knowledge of things political. This implication is by no means self-evident. Formerly, all political knowledge was considered practical knowledge, and not theoretical knowledge. According to that division, political philosophy, or political science, together with ethics and economics, belongs to the

The distinction Strauss here draws between science and morality is, we note, not between *modern* natural science and morality; it is between morality and science as originally conceived, science as philosophy, or "theory."[38] And while morality shares with science or philosophy a wish to know what is unchangeable, its concern is with living and acting. While the world of theory is a world "of mere objects at which we detachedly look," that of morality is one "of 'things' or 'affairs' which we handle."[39] Morality's practical orientation is, to be sure, ever informed by a "view of the whole," but its view is one that is in line with its concern for "regulating human conduct" and with "stability." The "unchanging" nature of scientific or theoretical knowledge,[40] by contrast, is knowledge of necessities by which motion or *change* comes about, the necessities that underlie all change.

---

practical sciences, just as mathematics and the natural sciences belong to the theoretical sciences. Whoever uses the term 'political theory' tacitly denies that traditional distinction. That denial means one of these two things or both of them: (1) the denial of the distinction between theoretical and practical sciences: all science is ultimately practical (*scientia propter potentiam*); (2) the basis of all reasonable practice is pure theory. A purely theoretical, detached knowledge of things political is the safest guide for political action, just as a purely theoretical, detached knowledge of things physical is the safest guide toward conquest of nature: this is the view underlying the very term political theory."

38. "Science is the attempt to understand the universe and man; it is therefore identical with philosophy; it is not necessarily identical with *modern* science." "German Nihilism," 365.

39. See "History of Philosophy: Its Nature and Its Function," lecture to be delivered on November 12, 1947, general seminar, the New School (Patard, 288), with *NRH* 79. The distinction Strauss draws here is, notably, closely parallel to that drawn by Heidegger, in *Being and Time*, between our primordial experience of being "in the world" and its association with inner-wordly beings, on one hand, and the modification of this experience in theoretical investigation of or disinterested looking at "objective" beings.

40. "German Nihilism," 364: "I frankly confess, I do not see how those can resist the voice of that siren who expect the answer to the first and the last question from 'History,' from the future as such; who mistake analysis of the present or past or future for philosophy; who believe in a progress toward a goal which is itself progressive and therefore undefinable; who are not guided by a known and stable standard: by a standard which is stable and not changeable, and which is known and not merely believed. In other words, the lack of resistance to nihilism seems to be due ultimately to the depreciation and the contempt of reason, which is one and unchangeable or it is not, and of science. For if reason is changeable, it is dependent on those forces which cause its changes; it is a servant or slave of the emotions; and it will be hard to make a distinction which is not arbitrary, between noble and base emotions, once one has denied the rulership of reason."

If we consider more closely the dangers faced by "science without morals," we can better understand this distinction that Strauss draws between the two ways of reasoning. The danger to science is "cynicism," which "destroys the basis of the scientific effort itself." What Strauss means by this cryptic statement might best be grasped by other statements he makes concerning the scientific or philosophic effort and disposition. Among the most revealing was made in a class in the 1940s that considered, among other thinkers, John Dewey, who in his effort to elaborate a standard or ideal of conduct, a "social theory," for the "moral engineering" that he deemed necessary in modern democracy, had dismissed as "an idle luxury" the attempt to elucidate the best or "ideal" life, and in particular, had dismissed "the classic view," as one in which "the idea belongs ready-made in a noumenal world . . . while to the modern, an idea is a suggestion of something to be done or of a way of doing." In response, Strauss spells out the goal of Socratic *political* philosophy, its turn to the serious questions of moral and political life—the Socratic turn uncovered and recovered by the contemporary shattering of the "old beliefs":

> I have said that we are in need of a reflection more radical than that of epistemology, a reflection devoted to the question: <u>why</u> science?, a reflection which would elucidate why science, quest for truth, is not just one hobby among many hobbies, but something <u>serious</u>. Now, we assume that something which concerns the whole community is more serious than what concerns an individual only: for what is most serious for me (my death e.g.) is not serious at all for almost all other people; it is then only relatively serious; but what concerns the whole community, is "absolutely" serious. Or, the other way around: the serious things of an individual—the job, health, family, reputation . . .—<u>depend</u> largely on the serious things of general, of public concern—economic stability, peace, victory . . .—. The question of the whole policy of the country can be said to be the most serious question. It is a <u>question</u>, as is shown by the fact that there are different <u>parties</u>, different <u>trends</u>. If that question is clarified, it is the question of what is the right aim of living together? what is the <u>standard</u> with reference to which all actions and institutions are to be judged? This <u>most</u> <u>serious</u> question is the <u>primary</u> justification of "quest for truth." It is from <u>this</u> question that the philosophic tradition, the tradition founded

by Socrates, starts. We can see from here how unjust Dewey's view of that tradition is: "They have transformed knowing into a morally irresponsible estheticism." One only has to remember Plato's indictment of poetry and Dewey's praise of "art" in order to see that Dewey's position implies a complete misinterpretation of the original meaning of philosophy. In which sense the basic question is "<u>historical</u>": it turns up after the old beliefs have been shattered—but this does not make that question "relative," since it is <u>evidently</u> necessary.[41]

As noted above in chapter 2, political philosophy allows the philosopher "to give an account of his doings by answering the question, 'why philosophy?' . . . [which] is only a special form of the general question 'what is the right way of life?' "[42]

What Strauss means by the scientific or philosophic life itself, and its need for the justification in question, becomes clearer in the rest of his critique of Dewey, in which he sketches the radical difference, in a crucial respect, of classical philosophy or science from modern science—a critique that explains why Strauss draws so clear a distinction between philosophy or science, on one hand, and morals, on the other. Dewey's "pragmatic" standard for social life was sought, Strauss argues, without an attempt to discover "knowledge of human nature," something that "in its turn requires knowledge of the place of man in the universe." Dewey simply took for

---

41. " 'Sociology of Knowledge' in Pragmatism," lecture 3 [on Dewey] of "Philosophy and Sociology of Knowledge," lectures delivered in the summer of 1941 at the New School for Social Research, box 6 folder 9, Leo Strauss Papers (series of sheets written with a pen, with the general titles "Philosophy and Sociology of Knowledge I" and "Philosophy and Sociology of Knowledge II," without clear division between these two) (Patard, 457–539; quotation is from 492).

42. Strauss, "Farabi's *Plato*," *Louis Ginzberg: Jubilee Volume* (New York: American Academy for Jewish Research, 1945), 366. See also "How to Begin to Study Medieval Philosophy," *Interpretation* 23, no. 3 (Spring 1996), 329: "We are again confronted with the question, Why philosophy? or, Why science? This question was in the center of discussion in the beginnings of philosophy. One may say that the Platonic dialogues serve no more obvious purpose than precisely this one: to answer the question, Why philosophy? or, Why science? by justifying philosophy or science before the tribunal of the city, the political community . . . [or] before the tribunal of the law." Consider also Strauss's statement that philosophy proper is the actual investigation of each of all the beings, but "a way of life is a 'thing,' not a 'being.' " "Farabi's Plato," 389.

granted the (deeply flawed) modern understanding of science and man's place in the universe: according to Dewey, " 'knowledge is power to transform the world.' " Strauss asserts against this modern or "pragmatic" understanding of science that "no earlier philosopher had indulged in such fantastic notions about the power of man. An active attitude toward the universe is absurd: the only possible attitude toward the universe is theoretical attitude, i.e. the attitude guided by the interest in knowing only." And he adds that purely *theoretical* knowledge of the whole is the "only possible foundation for 'scientifically' guided action within that limited sphere, within which action is possible at all." He then lays out the great difficulty with—the "delusion" behind—the active, conquering disposition of modern science, and its deep opposition to the "philosophic attitude" required for genuine science or theorizing:

> Science teaches us that the existence of man on this planet will come to an end sometime in the future: in a distant future, to be sure, but certainly at some time: all achievements of the human race will sink into oblivion, into nothingness. It is not morose preachers advising us to prepare ourselves for the last day who uphold that teaching, but the this-worldly scientists of the modern time. Maybe they are wrong—the fact or the possibility that all human achievements are destined to perish completely without leaving the slightest trace, is at the basis of the philosophic attitude. For it is of the essence of the philosophic attitude: to strive to live without delusions. As regards that fact, most people deceive themselves about it by simply not thinking about it: they forget "themselves" by engaging in all sorts of business, ambitions, desires, fun. . . . Those alone who see clearly the corruptibility of all human achievements, who are penetrated by that insight, and who have no hope for any miracle, and who bear this fact with serenity—they alone are philosophers; they alone look at all things *sub specie aeternitatis.*[43]

---

43. " 'Sociology of Knowledge' in Pragmatism" (Patard, 457–539; quotations from 493–94). See also "Restatement on Xenophon's *Hiero*," 197–98, and compare Plato, *Laws* 967a. Compare also *Philosophy and Law*, 18: "The last and purest basis of justification for the revolt against the tradition of revelation in the end turns out to be a new form of bravery. It forbids every flight from the horror of life into consoling illusion. It rather takes the eloquent depictions of the misery of man without God as a proof of the goodness

Nor does Strauss consider this turning away from the crucial philosophic awareness of the perishing of all human things to be peculiar to current practitioners of social or natural science. As noted in the previous chapter, he considers it to belong to even the greatest of modern thinkers, from Hobbes and his "illustrious contemporaries" to Hegel, and, finally, to Heidegger, as he argues in *Natural Right and History*.[44]

Strauss's description of the loss of the decisive philosophic or theoretical disposition, not only by modern scientists but modern political philosophers,

---

of its case. This new bravery, understood as the readiness to hold firm while gazing on the abandonment of man, as the courage to endure fearful truth, as hardness against the inclination of man to deceive himself about his situation, is probity." One may say that Nietzschean "probity," which grew out of the "idealist" tradition of modernity, was linked by Nietzsche to the biblical doctrine of examination of conscience and its demand for truthfulness. Probity is understood by Strauss instead to have always been a vital part of the philosophic nature (as hatred of the "lie in the soul"—Plato, *Republic* 382a4-c1; see also 485c3-d5, and *The City and Man*, 135), to belong properly to that nature and that nature alone, and hence to go together with a certain serenity rather than misery or anguish. It does not share with the Nietzschean version the sense of having been "abandoned" by God, which appears instead to be related to the early moderns' disappointed hope in providence and their sense of a "right to rebel." See above, chapter 1, pp. 33–35, note 24. The "esotericism" of the ancients is tied to this original philosophic probity; see *Reorientation: Leo Strauss in the 1930s*, appendix F, supplement 1: Early Plan of "Exoteric Teaching," 289: "Esoteric philosophy sees man in his insignificance."

44. See above, chapter 2, p. 51, note 17. It may be helpful to point out here that the moderns' hope for "enlightenment" is based on their opinion that it is the ancients who did not permit themselves to accept how awful our situation is. So Bacon, in articulating "the idols of the tribe" (*The New Organon*, aphorism 48), argues that ancient philosophers were resistant to knowledge of general principles of the sort Bacon proposes ("laws of nature") because, like people at large, they longed to find instead principles that can be referred to "final causes," disclosing purpose and purposefulness in all that exists. Bacon associates this with a desire for a beneficent, divine ruling power. The new "laws of nature" will by contrast enable scientists to bring to a haphazardly ordered nature an imposed order that is conducive to the satisfaction of human desires and purposes. In other words, Bacon and the moderns who followed him (Descartes, Hobbes) sought to make this haphazard order—our harsh beginning—universally accepted on the premise of an anticipated, universally manifest progress in the defeat of that harsh beginning, by "art" or technology. The initial, promising, technological overcoming—through manifestly successful *human* providence—dissipates the great obstacle that has always existed to that awareness. Strauss is exposing both the absence of genuine resignation in that stance, and the moderns' overlooking of the genuine resignation to the ultimate destruction of all things that had in fact characterized the ancients.

reminds us that to Strauss, the activity of the classical political philosopher, in his engagement with the (prescientific, or commonsense) opinions of his political community, does not lead to a rational ethics, the spelling out of a scientific morality, but instead to the justification of a way of life that, for the citizen who acts in a morally serious way, with a sense of his or her moral significance as a member of a morally significant community, has little part in the philosophic way of life. The significant difference between the moral life (and hence moral reasoning) and the philosophic life (of theoretical reasoning) is not that the latter is "open" to various ways of life while the former is "closed" or particular; it is not fundamentally about openness to different ways of life over and against an attachment to one's own. It is, rather, that the moral life as such affirms a deeper significance to one's life and that of one's community than does the philosophic. That affirmation is founded on hope for immortality, a hope that the philosopher does not, in the face of the destruction of all human things, allow himself. Yet in the face of this gulf Strauss nonetheless sees or calls for a "union" of the two ways of life as the vital components of "civilization." How can this be? In what way are the two "united" within civilization?

Serious moral reasoning is reasoning about the *means* to given ends, as Strauss, following Aristotle, has said. This means that for it, the ends are *given*. But by what are they usually given? We could say: by one's upbringing in the ways or traditions of one's ancestors. While there is a great deal of truth in this—and we will return to it—it is not simply the case: traditions manifestly accrue and change. Moreover, the question is simply pushed back by this answer: by what were these ancestors' notion of the ends given to *them*? A clue is provided, in the first part of his refutation of Dewey cited above, by Strauss's allusion to awareness of one's own individual death, to "what," by contrast to that individual concern, "concerns the whole community" and so "is 'absolutely' serious." In this statement, as we've seen, Strauss goes on to describe the manner in which most human beings flee awareness of death: "by engaging in all sorts of business, ambitions, desires, fun." This response—fully known to the ancients, who attempted to correct for it—was actually encouraged by the moderns' liberation of the individual,[45] and became, as we have seen, characteristic of life in modern

---

45. Consider Aristotle, *Politics* 1257b–1258a and context, as well as *Politics* 3.9, and *Nicomachean Ethics* 1180a24–29 with 1103b4–5, 1103b22–23 and 1137b16–18. Contrast Locke, *Second Treatise*, sections 32–35, 37, 41, 48, and Montesquieu, *The Spirit of the Laws* 20.1 with 15.3, 10.3, 25.13, 22.13, 23.4, 24.11, 28.23, 28.38. Heidegger's

societies. The "serious" and deeper response of the political community, by contrast, takes up and preserves this awareness even and precisely in the hope of overcoming it, in noble and just actions, in heeding of the call of conscience, in redemptive labors, and above all by dutiful attention to divine law.[46] The morally serious life carries within it awareness of mortality.

In a speech given at Harvard University in 1978, Aleksandr Solzhenitsyn arrived at a similar conclusion concerning the opposition between awareness of mortality and opposition to the life found in the commercial, technologically driven West. He, too, traced the origin of that West back to sixteenth-century humanism. And he concluded:

> If humanism were right in declaring that man is born to be happy, he would not be born to die. Since his body is doomed to die, his task on earth evidently must be of a more spiritual nature. It cannot be unrestrained enjoyment of everyday life. It cannot be the search for the best ways to obtain material goods and then cheerfully get the most out of them. It has to be the fulfillment of a permanent, earnest duty so that one's life journey may become an experience of moral growth: to leave life a better human being than one started it.[47]

As the reader will by now have seen, that which tends to emerge from and guide the moral life, in its premodern political reasoning, is ends supplied by *religious* experience, and the rich, thoughtful traditions to which such experiences give rise. It is for this reason that Strauss can say of "morals without science" that they "degenerate into superstition." Our own

---

frequently illuminating presentation of inauthentic being of Da-sein, in its falling prey to "the They" (*das Man*), also often appears to capture what Strauss here has in mind.

46. Hence Strauss can say, in "The Three Waves of Modernity" (86) that "in the crucial respect there is agreement between classical philosophy and the Bible, between Athens and Jerusalem, despite the profound difference and even antagonism between Athens and Jerusalem. According to the Bible man is created in the image of God; he is given the rule over all terrestrial creatures: he is not given the rule over the whole; he has been put into a garden to work it and to guard it; he has been assigned a place; righteousness is obedience to the divinely established order, just as in classical thought justice is compliance with the natural order; to the recognition of elusive chance corresponds the recognition of inscrutable providence."

47. Aleksandr Solzhenitsyn, *A World Split Apart* (New York: HarperCollins, 1978), 57–59.

inclination as inhabitants of late modernity is likely to be the equation of religion and superstition. But Strauss, like Weber, distinguished a "genuinely religious impulse of a very high order" from mere "superstition."[48] Mere "superstition" represents a severe decline from such a "religious impulse."

We suggest, then, that what Strauss has in mind by the "union" of science or philosophy and the moral life, as the pillars of civilization, is the following. Both religious experience and philosophy are responses, albeit radically different ones, to the unplanned human encounter with mortality. That encounter awakens in all serious human beings a yearning for the noble, for a dignified life, one devoted to, and prepared to sacrifice for, what is elevated or noble, a devotion that permits us to hope to overcome the limits of our mortal existence, through miraculous interventions of providential gods or God, accounts of which, in the permanent absence of genuine scientific knowledge of that out of which the whole is constituted, cannot be lightly dismissed. It is through the painful, dialectical purification of this yearning and of the thoughts to which it gives rise, a yearning which in the classical political philosophers is called "erotic," that philosophers secure the serene if sad resignation to necessity that, according to Strauss, marks the philosophic-scientific disposition or attitude. Without it, the philosophic disposition does not emerge and cannot be secured.[49] The Socratic dialectical examination of the moral-political opinions that one sees, as Strauss states, in the Platonic dialogues are the means through which the philosopher achieves the confirmation he needs that his is the right way of life.[50] In the "German Nihilism" talk, Strauss alludes—but only alludes—to the central confusion carefully uncovered in such dialectic: in the stress put during the

---

48. NRH 51–52. See also 111n44, and see What Is Political Philosophy?, 21: "A man who cannot distinguish between a profound religious thought and a languishing superstition may be a good statistician; he cannot say anything relevant about the sociology of religion."

49. Thomas L. Pangle, in his extraordinarily illuminating account of this erotic response, also spells out Montesquieu's inadequate grasp of it, and his corresponding attribution of the desire for immortality to accidental/historical indoctrination, his hostility to "theory," his desire to encourage evasion of awareness of mortality, his neglect of the conscience and its call, and his failure to anticipate the horrific twentieth- and twenty-first century despotisms emerging from communistic and nihilistic revolts against comfortable self-interest and commercialism that he promoted. Thomas L. Pangle, The Theological Basis of Liberal Modernity in Montesquieu's "Spirit of the Laws" (Chicago: University of Chicago Press, 2010), 133–136.

50. See NRH, 146–152.

heyday of thinking, in Germany, "to its lasting honor," on "self-sacrifice and self-denial," in their battle with the Enlightenment's denigration of the noble and elevation of self-interest: the German thinkers "insisted on it so much, that they were apt to forget the natural aim of man which is happiness."[51]

But what we have seen of the role that awareness of mortality plays in the development of moral and religious traditions should also make us aware of the true philosopher's admiration for, and desire to help sustain in nonphilosophers, the serious moral and religious life that thus takes up this awareness, even as that life hopes to overcome the necessities announced by that awareness.

To sum up: By proposing the nihilists' transformation, through the Churchillian example of abiding greatness within modern civilization, Strauss is by no means simply endorsing the Enlightenment morality that has brought about the characteristics of modern civilization that were so repulsive to the nihilists. To the contrary, he is claiming that *even* within *that* civilization is still visible an older notion of, calling to, and achievement of greatness, or that the modern political philosophers who attempted to refound civilization on a new, allegedly "rational," morality had failed—and failed in a rather big way—to so refound it. It is owing not to the modern philosophers' success, but to their failure, that the young nihilists might have been won over by the example of Churchill. The moderns made a crucial mistake in thinking that they could through enlightenment transform humanity in such a way as to make morality a matter of mere useful rules (eventually, "values") erected or chosen by a society or individuals in the pursuit of individuals' earthly goods. And now the longing for morality, unhappy with the modern world, was striking back. The older, true rationalism—premodern philosophy—did *not* make this mistake, and it was not for reasons of any backward consciousness. It was instead by dint of a superior wisdom about the human soul, which led them to distinguish sharply between theoretical reasoning, in resigned contemplation of necessities or causes, and practical or political reasoning, guided by ancestral, religious traditions and the exigencies of practical life as they were understood within those traditions. Philosophers offered their limited guidance to the latter only when looking at things as the statesman does. Strauss points, in other words, to the supremacy of the "prudence" of the statesman and *away* from the characteristically modern ruling guidance of statesmen by philosophers.

---

51. "German Nihilism," 371.

Tradition and the Health of Liberal Democracy

While the older moral reasoning still obtains, as we have seen, in the modern world, and hence in a world transformed by philosophy-science, that older moral reasoning is not in its essence a philosophic, but rather a prephilosophic, prescientific reasoning. It is in fact abiding evidence of the "natural" consciousness or "natural understanding" or "natural horizon of human thought" that Strauss, following Husserl, had attempted to recover, in his effort to recover the understanding of which philosophy, as the attempt to understand the whole, could claim to be the natural perfection.[52] Far from being based on an understanding of nature, that understanding or

---

52. Strauss, "Political Philosophy and History," in *What Is Political Philosophy? and Other Essays*, 5–6, 24–25. See also the earlier formulation in "History of Philosophy: Its Nature and Its Function," lecture delivered on November 12, 1947, general seminar at the New School for Social Research, 13 sheets, written on both sides with a pen, box 6, folder 14, Leo Strauss Papers, pp. 4 recto–4 verso (Patard, 273–307, at 283–85). Consider also Strauss, "Existentialism," 305: "Science, Husserl taught, is derivative from our primary knowledge of the world of things; science is not the perfection of man's understanding of the world, but a specific modification of that pre-scientific understanding. The meaningful genesis of science out of pre-scientific understanding is a problem; the primary theme is the philosophical understanding of the pre-scientific world." This pre-scientific understanding, or world image, was to be replaced by the Enlightenment, but the replacement required for its success, as we have seen in chapter 2, the temporary retention of key aspects of the older world image that was eventually to be replaced. Finally, Strauss considered the recovery of the "natural horizon of human thought," available in the Platonic dialogues, to be something that historicism had put into "oblivion" (and his use of this word, which Heidegger uses to describe Being's situation in the modern world, indicates the seriousness of the need for a recovery of this "natural horizon"): "Historicism sanctions the loss, or the oblivion, of the natural horizon of human thought by denying the permanence of the fundamental problems." Strauss, "On Collingwood's Philosophy of History," *Review of Metaphysics* 5, no. 4 (June 1952), 586. See also Strauss's comment on *Sein und Zeit* sect. 21 (pp. 98–99) in "Philosophy as a Rigorous Science and Political Philosophy," in *Studies in Platonic Political Philosophy*, 31:

> Heidegger went much further than Husserl in the same direction: the primary theme is not the object of perception but the full thing as experienced as part of the individual human context, the individual world to which it belongs. The full thing is what it is not only in virtue of the primary and secondary qualities as well as the value qualities in the ordinary meaning of that term but also of qualities like sacred or profane: the

awareness precedes and (in some cases) gives rise to awareness or discovery of nature. What characterizes it is a reasoning within the horizon of one's moral and religious, which is to say ancestral, tradition.

This claim may surprise those who have noted Strauss's warning against ceding to the "temptation to fall back from an unimpressive present on an impressive past." But if human beings seek the good and not the ancestral—that is, their own good, happiness—their longing for the ancestral nonetheless obviously exists, and so must somehow be understood in light of, as a particular form of, the (more primary) longing for the good. Strauss has, moreover, identified the form that this version of the longing for one's good takes as longing for the "noble." And this disposition is clearly tied to the ancestral, to what is old and is one's own way. Besides, Strauss is abundantly aware, and even stresses on other occasions, that the very passage of Aristotle that he quotes concerning the human desire for the good over the ancestral warns about the limit to (though certainly not about the possibility of) philosophically/scientifically based "progress" in laws, in political life, rather than in philosophic reasoning about the whole, where it is not problematic.[53] As we will see in the next chapter, in Strauss's extensive review of Eric Havelock's *The Liberal Temper in Greek Politics*, he spells out

---

full phenomenon of a cow is for a Hindu constituted much more by the sacredness of the cow than by any other quality or aspect. This implies that one can no longer speak of our "natural" understanding of the world; every understanding of the world is "historical."

53. See for example *The City and Man*, 17–23, especially 22, and see below, chapter 4, pp. 127–28 and pp. 139–41. See also "Progress or Return?," in *The Rebirth of Classical Political Rationalism*, ch. 10, p. 236: "The idea that . . . [intellectual and social progress] are necessarily parallel or that intellectual progress is accompanied in principle by social progress was known to the classics. We find there the idea that the art of legislation, which is the overarching social art, progresses like any other art. Yet Aristotle, who reports this doctrine, questions this solution, and he notes the radical difference between laws and arts or intellectual pursuits. More generally stated, or more simply stated, he notes the radical difference between the requirements of social life and the requirements of intellectual life." On the great significance of the Hippodamus section of the *Politics*, see Thomas L. Pangle, *Aristotle's Teaching in the* Politics (Chicago: University of Chicago Press, 2013), 8–24 and 83–84. We note that both in *The City and Man* and in his 1958 "Six Lectures on Socrates" (*Interpretation* 23, no. 2 [Winter 1996], 130) Strauss uses a sentence that equates progress in the arts with "technological change" or "technological

the ancients' awareness of the ground of this warning,[54] and goes so far on this occasion as to insist, on the basis of this Platonic knowledge, that the *"first duty of civilized man is to respect the past,"* a duty that leads one to elevate the "Founding Fathers" and the aged, and hence leads logically to the "belief in perfect beginnings or in the age of Kronos."[55] Precisely the most radical thinkers have dutifully employed the "Muses" to sustain accounts of the past that sustain civilization, in a manner that accords with the needs of most human beings—that is, with their political-moral lives, and hence, ultimately, with the needs also of the philosophic life.

But why, or in what way, exactly, is the elevation of the ancestral so crucial to the moral life? As Strauss indicates in many places,[56] it is at least in part so crucial because by and through accounts of beings or a

---

progress": "When examining this proposal, Aristotle brings out the fact that Hippodamus hadn't given thought to the tension between political stability and technological change. On the basis of some observations we have made closer to home, we suspect the existence of a connection between Hippodamus's unbridled concern with clarity and simplicity and his unbridled concern with technological progress."

54. "The Liberalism of Classical Political Philosophy," *LAM*, 26–64. The long review essay, originally published in the *Review of Metaphysics* 12, no. 3 (March 1959), 390–439, is devoted to demolishing Havelock's claims that modern liberal democracy and technological progressivism were embraced by ancient Greeks. The positivist Havelock, Strauss has frequent occasion to note, is fiercely anti-religious, and condemns the intolerance of "even the most humane" religions. Compare *NRH* 84: "Pre-philosophic life is characterized by the primeval identification of the good with the ancestral. Therefore, the right way necessarily implies thoughts about the ancestors and hence about the first things simply." See also "A Giving of Accounts," in *Jewish Philosophy and the Crisis of Modernity*, 463–64: "Philosophy is as such transpolitical, transreligious, and transmoral, but the city is and ought to be moral and religious."

55. "The Liberalism of Classical Political Philosophy," *LAM* 41. See also Strauss's characterization of his friend Kurt Riezler's early opposition, in Germany, to the "modern ideal," in "Kurt Riezler, 1882–1955," *Social Research* 23, no. 1 (Spring 1956), 3–34 (at 6–7): "Riezler's thought may be expressed as follows: the modern ideal does not leave room for reverence, the matrix of human nobility; reverence is primarily—that is, for most men at all times, and for all men most of the time—reverence for one's heritage, for tradition; but traditions are essentially particularistic, and therefore they are akin to nationalism rather than to cosmopolitanism."

56. See *The City and Man*, especially 38–39 and 129; *NRH*, especially 83–84, 95–97, 150n24; "Jerusalem and Athens: Some Preliminary Reflections," in *Jewish Philosophy and*

being who can guarantee the conditions that might otherwise be thought to impede our ability to be or become just or unjust, noble or base. The manifest harshness, sufferings, and imperfections that accompany the lives of most human beings, particularly those who must, as most did prior to modernity, till the soil, would make it unreasonable to expect justice from men if the original condition of man as man, prior to his own artful efforts, was even worse—if that condition was one of such habitual and extreme penury that men would have been *compelled* to violence.[57] Only an original life of ease and bounty enables one to say that there is no genuinely compelling inducement to harshness, violence, or injustice—that life as we know it would in fact be as free of troubles as our sense of justice tells us it would be were it not for the ways of wicked, lawless men. The expectation that humans be just thus not only accords with but presupposes the view that the early conditions of human life were good. The moral life, in its insistence on our freedom to choose what is right or noble—and on which all sense of gratitude, anger, remorse, and guilt depend—is informed by the belief, conscious or unconscious, in a golden age or a perfect beginning. By guaranteeing that evil or suffering or harshness is due to human fault—that evil is not compelled but *voluntary*—this belief guarantees that man is morally free, or "responsible."[58] But only the providence of certain kinds of gods or God, of an immortal being or beings who can from the beginning act upon the world with an artisan's purposefulness, forethought, and concern for human activity, could provide for this original perfection, by creating it or bringing it into being. By guaranteeing a good beginning, such gods, or God, guarantee the sense of responsibility, or moral freedom, upon which the moral life depends. If the just or noble life is to be choiceworthy, as something good in itself and not as a mere means (which can be dispensed with when other means prove more effective), then our original condition must be good, and so the first things simply

---

the Crisis of Modernity, 385; "Progress or Return?," in The Rebirth of Classical Political Rationalism; "Notes On Lucretius," in LAM, especially 84, 86, 97,100,116–17,122, 131; "The Law of Reason in the Kuzari," in Persecution and the Art of Writing (Glencoe, IL: Free Press, 1952), especially 114, 139–41. In Natural Right and History, Strauss explicitly ties "the question of the status of man within the whole" to the question of "man's origin." NRH 275–76.

57. See e.g., Thucydides 3.82.2, and cf. 3.45.4–5.

58. Cf. Aristotle, Nichomachean Ethics 1114a15–20, 1114a31–b16.

must be immortal, powerful, creative gods.[59] A divine being or beings are needed by the social being, man, to secure the moral life.[60] This is what lies behind Strauss's statement, in "German Nihilism," that "every past is as such impressive."

In "Progress or Return?" by way of explaining the importance of a perfect beginning to the moral life, Strauss states the following: "Repentance is return, meaning the return from the wrong way to the right one. This implies that we were once on the right way before we turned to the wrong way. Originally we were on the right way; deviation or sin or imperfection is not original. Man is originally at home in his father's house. He becomes a stranger through estrangement, through sinful estrangement. Repentance, return, is homecoming." And this in turn helps us to understand why, in the praise of the English with which he concludes "German Nihilism," Strauss praises the English preservation of "traditions," or, more specifically, a tradition: "the classical tradition":

---

59. This means the absence of causality, the assumption that the world is the product of divine will and not of necessities. In his essay on Isaac Abravanel, Strauss argues that "the beliefs peculiar to the law are founded upon and, as it were, derived from one fundamental conviction: the belief in creation *ex nihilo*." "On Abravanel's Philosophic Tendency and Political Teaching," in *Isaac Abravanel*, ed. J. B. Trend and H. Loewe (Cambridge University Press: Cambridge, 1937), 201. The note accompanying Strauss's sentence (201n10) reads: "Cp. Abravanel, *Rash 'Amana*, h. 22, with: Maimonides' *Guide*, Pt. II, ch. 25, in the beginning, and Pt. III, ch. 25 in the end." In the same essay (at 119n1) Strauss calls to our attention the anti-rationalist direction of this tendency as it manifests itself in Abravanel's work: "Restating the genuine teaching of the Bible against Maimonides' rationalist and therefore political teaching, Abravanel goes sometimes farther in the opposite direction than does the Bible itself. The most striking example of this which occurs to me is his interpretation of Judges 1, 19: Judah 'could not drive out the inhabitants of the valley, because they had chariots of iron.' Abravanel explains this passage in the following way: 'Judah could not drive out the inhabitants of the valley, not because they had chariots of iron.'"

60. As for the characteristically modern, "progressive" understanding of justice, or "natural rights," its acceptance and eventual rejection manifests the same belief. It required for its initial success, after all, a Christian appearance that Strauss brings out (in his effort to show what lies behind it) in his essay on Locke in *Natural Right and History* (ch. 5, 165–66, 202–51; on the "state of nature" and original "penury" versus the biblical Garden of Eden and the Fall, see especially 215–216, 221, 234–246). And Rousseau's subsequent "corrective" of the politics of modernity entailed a new state of nature doctrine in which men were

This taking things easy, this muddling through, this crossing the
bridge when one comes to it, may have done some harm to the
radicalism of English thought; but it proved to be a blessing to
English life; the English never indulged in those radical breaks
with traditions which played such a role on the continent.
Whatever may be wrong with the peculiarly modern ideal: the
very Englishmen who originated it, were at the same time versed

---

innocent, free, and happy, and a rhetorical appeal to man in civil society as offending
"the author of one's being" if he failed to defend his (moral) "freedom": "I shall not stop
to inquire whether, freedom being the most noble of man's faculties, it is not degrading
one's nature, putting oneself on the level of beasts enslaved by instinct, even offending the
author of one's being, to renounce without reservation the most precious of all his gifts and
subject ourselves to committing all the crimes he forbids us in order to please a ferocious
or insane master; nor whether this sublime workman must be more irritated to see his
finest work destroyed than to see it dishonored." Rousseau, "Discourse on the Origin and
Foundations of Inequality among Men," in *The First and Second Discourses*, trans. Roger
D. Masters and Judith R. Masters, 167. Consider also Strauss's interpretation of Burke in
Natural Right and History: for Burke, who held that the best constitution is not the work
of reason but is instead the result of "growth," the age of the French Revolution is the
worst of ages. "One is tempted to say that it is the age of perfect sinfulness. Not admiration, but contempt of the present; not contempt, but admiration of the ancient order
and eventually of the age of chivalry, is the sound attitude—everything good is inherited.
What is needed is not 'metaphysical jurisprudence' but 'historical jurisprudence' " (316). The
subsequent displacement of "Nature" by "History" by the Historical School in Germany,
for which Burke "paves the way," according to Strauss (*NRH* 316), entails an attempt to
recover, finally, the particular standards of a people in its past (when it was, that is, in
fact directed by an understanding informed by a notion of a divinely established golden
age or good beginning). But "what came to be called 'historical' was, for Burke, still 'the
local and accidental.' What came to be called 'historical process' was for him," Strauss
initially argues, "still accidental causation or accidental causation modified by the prudential
handling of situations as they arose. Accordingly, the sound political order for him, in the
last analysis, is the unintended outcome of accidental causation" (*NRH* 314–15). Yet, as
Strauss puts it a bit later, "it almost goes without saying that Burke regards the connection
between 'the love of lucre' and prosperity, on the one hand, and 'a great variety of accidents'
and a healthy political order, on the other, as part of the *providential* order; it is because
the processes which are not guided by human reflection are part of the *providential* order
that their products are infinitely superior in wisdom to the products of reflection. From
a similar point of view, Kant has interpreted the teaching of Rousseau's *Second Discourse*
as a vindication of Providence." (*NRH* 316; emphasis added). (See also the reference to
"sacred powers behind that [historical] process," stated at *NRH* 18.) Yet seeing that divine

> in the classical tradition, and the English always kept in store a
> substantial amount of the necessary counter-poison.[61]

Using here the same term that he would later use in "What Is Liberal Education?" Strauss presents the preservation of traditions or of a tradition as
a "counter-poison" to modernity's inevitable production of "mass culture."
While Strauss joins Heidegger in speaking of the need for a *destruktion* of
the *philosophic* tradition, to unearth its foundations, and even in his "German Nihilism" talk speaks of the great difficulty of referring to the "Western
tradition," owing to its heterogeneity (Voltaire and Bellarmine would both
have opposed Nazism, but otherwise have so to speak nothing in common),
he is here, when speaking of *political* or moral reasoning, perfectly willing
to speak of and to praise traditions or a tradition.

But before we can examine that tradition and what it may offer to
the "aristocracy within democracy" that Strauss hopes liberal education may
found, we must say a brief word about Strauss's statements on the radi-
calizing effect of "the romantic judgment" on German militarism. For that
judgment, whose deleterious effect on German thought and action Strauss
singles out for blame, might well appear to some readers to be identical with
traditionalism's elevation of the remote past. Strass defines this "romantic
judgment," after all, as "a judgment which is guided by the opinion that
an absolutely superior order of human things existed during some period
of the recorded past."[62] Yet as we've seen, the older moral thinking that
produces or relies on an opinion of the remote past as good, understands
that past as a peaceful state, without harsh necessities, one created by God

---

providence as "scrutable" (*NRH* 317) inclines one to view the outcome of the historical
process as *good*, and to view "what it has defeated as evil." It is only a short step from
this thought of Burke to the supersession of the distinction between good and bad by
the distinction between the progressive and the retrograde, or between what is and what
is not in harmony with the historical process" (*NRH* 318). "Transcendent standards can
be dispensed with if the standard is inherent in the process; 'the actual and the present
is the rational.' What could appear as a return to the primeval equation of the good
with the ancestral is, in fact, a preparation for Hegel" (*NRH* 319). The eventual revolt,
prepared by Kierkegaard and Nietzsche, of "existentialism" against Hegel in support of "a
human life which has a significant and undetermined future" (*NRH* 320–21), includes
an attempt to return, in the face of the "death of God," to a radical "rootedness" and
culminates in the view that "only a god can save us."

61. "German Nihilism," 372. *LAM* 40–41 (emphasis added). The reference to "muddling
through" is perhaps the third and final (and quietest) to Churchill.

62. "German Nihilism," 370.

or gods, and lost by free acts of disobedience to an original divine law; return to it by an individual or community is done in repentance, return (*t'shuva*) for having lost the right way, the way indicated by that divine law. German romanticism was, by contrast, a reflective judgment on the course of "the whole modern development," or was close to what we would today call postmodern; it relied on reflective judgment of that development.[63] It accordingly sought not a perfect beginning, a Garden of Eden or golden age, but a past in which "an absolutely superior order of *human* things" to that of modernity existed, and found it in a (typically modern) "state of nature," in which the virtue of courage could be the predominant virtue. The German nihilists, "sons and grandsons and great-grandsons of godless men," sought nothing that bespoke a "very good" world created by a providential God, who provided it along with his binding law, to which one found oneself in need of return. They blamed not themselves but modern civilization, and retained that civilization's emphasis on autonomy. They therefore sought a return to an uncivilized past in order to "begin again," from a fertile, pristine situation, over and against the path that modernity or Western civilization had taken, one in which, unlike the situation in which they found themselves, the completely self-sacrificial virtue of *cour-*

---

63. See "On Collingwood's Philosophy of History," 576–77: "True Romanticism regards the highest possibility of the nineteenth or twentieth century, 'futile' longing, as the highest possibility of man, in so far as it assumes that the noble fulfillments of the past were based on delusions which are now irrevocably dispelled. True Romanticism believes that while the past was superior to the present as regards 'life' or 'culture' or 'art' or 'religion' or the nearness of God or gods, the present is superior to the past as regards the understanding of 'life' or 'culture:' etc. It believes therefore that the present is superior to the past in regard to knowledge of the decisive truth, i.e., in the decisive respect."

64. "German Nihilism," 370. See also Strauss's "Comments on Carl Schmitt's *Concept of the Political*" [1932], trans. Harvey Lomax, in *Carl Schmitt and Leo Strauss: The Hidden Dialogue*, by Heinrich Meier (Chicago: University of Chicago Press, 1995), 115 [paragraph 29 of the German original]: "The affirmation of the political is the affirmation of the state of nature. Schmitt opposes the affirmation of the state of nature to the Hobbesian negation of the state of nature. The state of nature is the *status belli*, pure and simple. Thus it appears that the affirmation of the state of nature can only be bellicose. That appearance fades away as soon as one has grasped what the return to the state of nature means for Schmitt. The affirmation of the state of nature does not mean the affirmation of war but 'relinquishment of the security of the status quo' (93). Security is relinquished not because war would be something 'ideal,' but because it is necessary to return from 'splendid vicarage,' from the 'comfort and ease of the existing status quo to the 'cultural or social nothing,' to the 'secret, humble beginning,' 'to undamaged, noncorrupt nature' (93) so that 'out of the power of a pure and whole knowledge . . . the order of the human things can arise again' (95)."

age would find a fertile home.[64] Tellingly, their teachers included Georges Sorel and Paul LaGarde, whose disposition toward the past was toward a self-consciously created myth.[65] The romantic judgment was, in short, self-consciously "creative" or constructivist, rather than a vision that emerges out of the natural human consciousness.

Moreover, the nihilists had learned from Nietzsche to attribute to secularized Christianity the desire to abolish all suffering. They had thereby been brought to stifle in themselves any attraction to the virtues that demanded attention to the weak and the vanquished. The artificially, historicist-indoctrinated, "disinterested" pleasure that Strauss attributes to them, pleasure in "the business of destroying, and killing, and torturing," and pleasure from "the aspect of the strong and ruthless who subjugate, exploit, and torture the weak and helpless," together with "their anti-Jewish policy," clearly have no place in the virtues of those who rely on a perfect beginning that is the work of a providential God or gods.[66]

Still, the path taken by the German nihilists is not one that can be ignored or simply forgotten by those who, in our present situation, might find Strauss's appeal to "Return" to the ancestral inviting. The nihilists would, Strauss argues, have been moved by—they sought—educators who might guide them by "a known and stable standard: by a standard which is stable and not changeable, and which is known and not merely believed." That is, precisely to the extent that they were moved by the older moral reasoning, they sought *knowledge*, and not mere belief. Within modern "secular" political regimes, of course, such knowledge they deemed unavailable to human beings. One of Strauss's indications of the effect of this secularization is his elaboration on Nietzsche's late echo of Hegel: "The morning newspaper had

---

65. Georges Sorel, *Reflections on Violence* (New York: Macmillan, 1961), and the anti-Jewish, anti-Christian Lagarde's *Über das Verhältnis des deutschen Staates zu Theologie, Kirche und Religion. Ein Versuch Nicht-Theologen zu orientieren* (On the Relationship of the German State to Theology, Church and Religion: An Attempted Orientation for Nontheologians) and *Über die gegenwärtige Lage des deutschen Reichs: Ein Bericht* (On the Current Situation of the German Reich: A Report; 1875).

66. "German Nihilism," 368–69.

67. Strauss, " 'Existentialism,' " in "Two Lectures by Leo Strauss," 307. For Nietzsche's remark, see *The Will to Power*, aphorisms 44 and 71; cf. 132. The echo is of Hegel: "Aphorismen aus Hegels Wastebook" (1803–6), in *Werke*, ed. Eva Moldenhauer and Karl Markus (Frankfurt: Surhkamp, 1969–71), 2:547. An English translation of the passage from Hegel is available in *Miscellaneous Writings*, ed. Jon Stewart (Evanston, IL: Northwestern University Press, 2002), 247.

replaced the morning prayer."[67] This effect is not unintended and it will remain with us: for one thing, liberal democracy goes hand-in-hand with the secular state, that is, the separation of church and state. It must treat what had been considered divine law as a matter of private opinion. It aims thereby to replace biblical divine commandments and all other duties by enlightenment concerning natural rights.[68] For another, as Strauss's statements about the German nihilists' atheism indicate, this secularization, along with modern science and its technological transformations of our everyday life, has not been without effect on religious opinion.[69] That effect is something Strauss was quite precise about, in its bearing on the matter of the older moral reasoning. Where Handel's *Messiah* (1741) could include an aria titled "I *know* that my redeemer liveth," much of our contemporary religious opinion confines itself to speaking instead of "belief." As Strauss put it in *Philosophy and Law*:

> Yet even though the Enlightenment's attack on Orthodoxy failed, the battle of the two hostile powers still had a highly consequential and positive result for the Enlightenment. Let us take an example that is more than an example. Even if it could not prove the impossibility or the unreality of miracles, the Enlightenment could demonstrate the unknowability of miracles, and thus protect itself against orthodoxy's claims. What holds for the Enlightenment's aggressive critique does not hold its defensive critique. The quarrel between the Enlightenment and Orthodoxy made clearer and better known than before that the presuppositions of Orthodoxy (the reality of creation, miracles, and revelation) are not known (philosophically or historically) but

---

68. As Strauss put it in a lecture in 1946, "The principle of modern natural right cannot be understood if one does not take into account its theological implications. The primacy of right over duty presupposes the denial of any superhuman order or will. On the other hand, the complete absence or at least relative weakness of the doctrine of rights of man prior to the 17th century is doubtless due to the overwhelming influence of the Biblical teaching." Lecture to be delivered on January 19, 1946 in the general seminar and in February 1946 in Annapolis (Patard, 398).

69. Consider *NRH* 79: "The world in which we live is already a product of science, or at any rate it is profoundly affected by the existence of science. To say nothing of technology, the world in which we live is free from ghosts, witches, and so on, with which, but for the existence of science, it would abound."

are only believed, and thus lack the peculiarly binding character of the known. . . . The formation of the new science thus led to the result that fundamental teachings of the tradition, which had also been counted as knowable by the presuppositions of the older science, came more and more to be viewed as merely believed.[70]

On account of the transformation of the given world that had been carried out by the Enlightenment, including its technology, simple probity made belief difficult to sustain for a number of "very intelligent if very young" Germans. While Strauss did not find such probity sufficient for philosophy to overcome the challenge of revelation and, moreover, after his recovery of classical political philosophy, found the late, Nietzschean *account* of probity as dubious as all other secularization-of-Christianity theses, he does not deny probity's manifest influence on the German nihilists, nor its likely, abiding influence on the older political reasoning that is to be found within modernity—the very reasoning that he is recommending. Equally clear, however, is that Strauss saw the exercise of such probity as necessary and proper to the philosophic life, and saw its emergence with such force in modern political life, with its mistaken attempt at Enlightenment, as manifestly problematic. Its result was atheist nihilists who wished to preserve morality and who were prepared to jettison the other half of civilization—science, reason, philosophy—that appeared to threaten it. The classical political philosophers, more politically sober because more radically disposed toward the truth of the crackings of the walls of the world—did not create a political movement of atheists who actively rebelled against science or philosophy in the name of morality; they saw clearly the great divide between the philosophic and the political life. The situation of both philosophy and of moral reasoning, which relies on tradition, is more perilous in the modern world.

The divide between the philosophic and political life, between the life of theory or contemplation and the life of practice, was overlooked above all by Heidegger. His existentialism followed from the attempts of Kierkegaard and Nietzsche "to recover the possibility of practice, i.e., of a human life which has a significant and undetermined future," but whose attempts "destroyed, as far as in them lay, the very possibility of theory."[71]

---

70. *Philosophy and Law*, Baumann trans., 11–12. See also 13–14.

71. *NRH* 320–21.

Heidegger led the effort to direct German youth away from what he considered the catastrophic understanding of truth first enunciated by Plato, sharpened by Thomas Aquinas, further sharpened by Descartes, and reaching its culmination in Nietzsche and his effort to wrest himself free of it in the name of "life."[72] Heidegger also undertook, in a series of classes on Aristotle throughout the 1920s and 1930s, serious, very careful, and sometimes illuminating studies of Plato's and Aristotle's writings, in an effort to recover in Aristotle the remains of an inquiry into Being and truth that had been buried or forgotten by Plato. Impressive as they are, these studies are made in complete oblivion of the esotericism practiced by the ancients and recovered by Strauss. A similar if infinitely less impressive effort to recover in ancient thought the very opposite—remnants of an ancient liberalism, democratic "values," positivism, "technological society and an international commercial system," guiltlessness, humanism, progressivism, and relativism—appeared in 1957 in Eric Havelock's *The Liberal Temper in Greek Politics*.[73] A study of Strauss's essay review of that work will provide us with a better understanding of Strauss's own careful approach to ancient texts and his agreements and disagreements with Heidegger concerning technology, political or practical science, democracy, and theory or contemplation.

---

72. The clearest statement of this of which I am aware is Heidegger's "Plato's Doctrine of Truth" (1931; published in 1940), trans. Thomas Sheehan, in *Pathmarks*, ed. Thomas McNeil (Cambridge: Cambridge University Press, 1998). See below, chapter 4, pp. 143–45.

73. Eric Havelock, *The Liberal Temper in Greek Politics* (New Haven, CT: Yale University Press, 1957).

CHAPTER FOUR

"The Liberalism of Classical Political Philosophy"

Eric Havelock's *The Liberal Temper in Greek Politics* appeared in 1957. Strauss's review essay of it, "The Liberalism of Classical Political Philosophy," was published in March 1959 and incorporated as chapter 3 of *Liberalism Ancient and Modern* in 1968.[1] In the essay Strauss lays out the multiple errors of a work that, conforming as it did to contemporary prejudices, was likely to become influential.[2] And examining the extraordinarily careful arguments by which Strauss refutes Havelock's thesis is instructive: he manifests a relentless demand for caution, clarity, coherence, probity, and finesse. I will however focus my examination on an unobtrusive but important argument that is woven into this thumping. Strauss himself suggests the need to do so. For Havelock's book is of such poor scholarship that Strauss is moved in his conclusion to explain why he even bothered reviewing it. Such works, he explains, are no longer unusual, and so scholarship, which is supposed to

---

1. Havelock, *The Liberal Temper in Greek Politics*; Strauss, "The Liberalism of Classical Political Philosophy," *Review of Metaphysics* 12, no. 3 (March 1959), 390–439; republished as "The Liberalism of Classical Political Philosophy" in *LAM* 26–64. Page references appearing in parentheses in the text are to the latter.

2. In fact it was Havelock's next book, *Preface to Plato* (1963), that became influential. It relied on Milman Perry's thesis concerning oral traditions to argue that the difference between fifth and fourth century BC works reflected a cultural shift from oral to written culture, from "Homeric" associative and temporal thinking about particular things to a "Platonic" insistence on general static ideas. Just after its publication, Havelock moved from Harvard to Yale.

be a "bulwark of civilization against barbarism," is becoming, even among classicists, "an instrument of re-barbarization." In particular, the work shows how the modern liberal demand for tolerance can turn into a "ferocious hatred of those who have stated most clearly and most forcefully that there are unchangeable standards founded in the nature of man and the nature of things" (*LAM* 63). Strauss certainly brings out Havelock's hatred; he is even moved to attribute to Havelock the fanatical motto *Fiat liberalismus pereat Plato*.[3] But the unchangeable standards to which he here refers are less clear, and are in fact indicated only incidentally in the course of the review.

Moreover, during the review's composition Strauss wrote the following to Seth Benardete:

> I am reading Havelock's book on Greek liberalism. It is utterly contemptible on all possible grounds: religious, political, moral and scholarly; I say nothing of philosophic. I plan to write a 30-page article since this will give me an opportunity to elaborate some footnotes of *Natural Right and History*. Compared with this kind of "liberalism," Jaeger is a giant.[4]

The review thus has as its indirect purpose the elaboration of some points made in the footnotes to *Natural Right and History*, which Strauss had published four years earlier.

Since that book represented Strauss's most sustained address to date of the work of Heidegger,[5] it is not surprising that the review of Havelock

---

3. "Let liberalism be done, let Plato perish" (*LAM* 61). The famous phrase Strauss echoes, *Fiat justitia et pereat mundus* ("Let justice be done and let the world perish") appears in Johannes Manlius's *Loci communes* (1563). The phrase was used by Kant, without the "et," in *Perpetual Peace*.

4. Strauss to Benardete, September 22, 1958. Quoted in Patard, 843n120. Strauss's reference in the letter to Benardete is to Werner Jaeger, author of *Paideia: The Ideals of Greek Culture*, the first volume of which was published originally in German as *Paideia: Die Formung des griechischen Menschen* (Berlin: Walter de Gruyter, 1934), and in English as *Paideia: The Ideals of Greek Culture* (New York: Oxford University Press, 1939–44). Strauss had attended Jaeger's courses in 1924–25, and as his correspondence with Klein makes clear (October 10, 1939), he did not have a high opinion of his work.

5. Heidegger appears in the first chapter of *Natural Right and History* as "radical historicism," or "existentialist" historicism (32), in the final chapter as "existentialism" (321), and toward the middle of the book (176) as the unnamed thinker who understands the "highest principle" as "the mysterious ground of 'History,'" a ground that, "being

proper is preceded and prepared by two paragraphs on positivism and existentialism, the two predominant schools of thought in our age which had according to Strauss rejected classical political philosophy as "obsolete" (*LAM* 27). The opening is an abbreviated sketch of the movement that a thoughtful adherent to positivism will necessarily make *to* existentialism, a movement that Strauss describes at somewhat greater length in his "Existentialism" talk on Heidegger.[6] Strauss here notes that proponents of positivism oppose classical political philosophy on two grounds: that it is nonscientific in mode and that it is nondemocratic in substance. Since positivists claim that value judgments cannot be validated by science, however, positivism's opposition to what is "nondemocratic" is by its own lights a nonscientific opposition, as is the sympathy for a "certain kind of democracy" that one finds among positivism's practitioners. Strauss points in this way to the "dogmatism," or hidden premises, of positivism, a dogmatism it hides by loudly proclaiming its "skepticism."

But Strauss predicts that positivism will be "the last form in which modern rationalism appears," because it is "that form in which the crisis of modern rationalism becomes almost obvious to everyone" (*LAM* 26). He does not here elaborate on that crisis, but he has already suggested one aspect of it: the alleged need to abstain from value judgments must, of course, be applied to modern science itself, which therefore cannot consistently claim (as it once claimed) to provide, through its rational results, guidance to human beings on the right way to act—that is, cannot claim that acting rationally or in accord with the findings of modern science is right or good. Positivism as value-free science has abandoned "the notion that man is a rational being who perverts his being if he does not act rationally."[7] He to whom the crisis becomes obvious therefore abandons positivism and "if he adheres to the modern premises, he has no choice but to turn to existentialism," that is, to a school of thought at whose core, as Strauss says in his talk on existentialism,[8] is Heidegger. And as he does in that talk, Strauss here presents existentialism as superior to positivism in its manifest willingness

---

wedded to man and to man alone, is so far from being eternal that it is coeval with human history."

6. "Existentialism," in "Two Lectures by Leo Strauss," 303–20, at 308–11. See also *What Is Political Philosophy? and Other Studies*, 17–27, especially 25–27.

7. "Existentialism," 308–9.

8. "Existentialism," 304. See also Strauss's "Philosophy as Rigorous Science and Political Philosophy," in *Studies in Platonic Political Philosophy*, 29–37, at 30.

to face "the situation with which positivism is confronted but which it does not grasp: the fact that reason has become radically problematic"—that is, the inability of positivistic science to say that its practice and adherence to its findings are good or right for man, or its new, astonishing claim that the choice to act rationally is an unguided "free" choice, or is what existentialism calls a "decision" made over the abyss of freedom.

But if existentialism is, as this indicates, superior to positivism, any attempted return to classical political philosophy faces in existentialism a more serious opponent than it faces in positivism.[9] For existentialism, too, finds classical political philosophy "obsolete," on three grounds. In elaborating these grounds Strauss stresses the religion-friendly and even mystical nature of existentialism. Its first ground against classical political philosophy is that the premises upon which it rests are "not evident." In fact, says the existentialist, "all thinking rests on unevident but non arbitrary premises," for "man is in the grip of powers which he cannot master or comprehend, and these powers reveal themselves differently in different historical epochs." Second, classical political philosophy is "rationalist"; it claims indeed to be universal but it is unconsciously indebted to the historical community of Greeks that was not made but "grew." (Here Strauss silently alludes to the indebtedness of Heideggerian existentialism to the German historical school of jurisprudence, which sought to ground justice in a notion of a nation's sacred, organically grown tradition.) Third, "by denying the dependence of man's thought on powers which he cannot comprehend, classical political philosophy was irreligious." It recognized indeed the need for religion in political communities but it unjustifiably subordinated the religious to the political, making the priesthood "fifth and first," for example, in Aristotle's elaboration of offices (*LAM* 26–27).

Having in this way shown the greater willingness of existentialism to face the current situation of reason, and shown the movement from positivism to existentialism to be a movement toward an elevation of the religious disposition or what was once a religious disposition, Strauss turns to Havelock, whom he introduces as a "positivist" (and hence as representing a logical and "historical" step backward from existentialism) and even as an adherent of an "obsolete version" of positivism. For while Havelock wishes to be nonjudgmental, he still speaks of "savages" rather than (as a more current positivist would) of "pre-literate" men, and of "progress" rather

---

9. On this point see also "What Is Political Philosophy?," 26.

than of (the morally neutral) "change." The inconsistent, dated positivism of Havelock moves him to declare himself (proudly) a "liberal," enabling Strauss to raise the question of what a liberal is and what it means to be a liberal today. But in the course of examining this question, and Havelock's search for his pre-Socratic liberal counterparts half hidden or buried in classical texts, Strauss will not simply leave behind the other, more formidable critic of classical political philosophy, existentialism, which he has so forcefully and conspicuously drawn to our attention. In fact, his most serious purpose may be to bring into doubt the threefold existentialist critique of classical political philosophy that he has presented, or to cause the premises of existentialism, "the modern premises," to which, he implies, existentialists adhere, to be called into question.

The work has four sections, marked simply by an extra space between the paragraphs.[10] The first and longest (*LAM* 26–41) lays out Havelock's procedure and examines his attempt to demonstrate ancient liberals' philosophy of history through his examination of Hesiod's *Works and Days* and Plato's *Laws*. A short second section (41–45) addresses how Havelock "begins to disinter Greek liberalism" by examining his account of Aeschelus's *Prometheus*, Sophocles's *Antigone*, and Diodorus Sicilus's histories. A third, long section (45–59) is devoted largely but not exclusively to Havelock's interpretation of Plato's *Protagoras*. The fourth section (59–64) addresses Havelock's culminating argument on the political theory of the ancient liberals as disclosed in the fragments of the writings of the sophist Antiphon. We will go through each in turn.

Havelock's Liberalism

Strauss first sketches his understanding of the true classical liberal—the possessor of the virtues of a free man rather than those of a slave—as the classical liberal appears in the thought of Aristotle. This liberal comes to associate liberalism especially with freedom from stinginess or greed. Following Aristotle, Strauss suggests that this is a result of the gentleman dimly perceiving that there is an activity that is good in itself rather than for whatever monetary profit might come out of it: the mind's activity (*LAM*

---

10. The section breaks in the original *Review of Metaphysics* article are present but less visible. Its four sections are these: 390–409, 409–15, 415–33, and 433–39.

28–29; cf. Aristotle, *Politics* 1334a–b). That activity represents man at his best and subject to no authority, and provides the basis for the authority to which all other human activities are, to the genuine liberal, indeed subject: that authority must "be a reflection through a dimming medium of what is highest," and so cannot be tyrannical or despotic. The genuine classic liberal is republican and a gentleman. Strauss contrasts him with today's liberal, brought into being by modern political philosophy and described by Havelock. Today's liberal is the opposite of the classical liberal. He puts greater stress on liberty than on authority, which he understands as derived solely from society (consent). He denies fixed norms, finding all norms to be responses to historical needs and so changing as the "historical process" changes. Today's liberalism is "optimistic and radical," democratic and egal-itarian, and considers human characteristics to have been acquired through an historical process, by the pressures of groups. It is "a genuine human-ism which is not guilt-ridden." It is "in full sympathy with technological society and an international commercial system." It is pragmatic, scientific, nontheological, and nonmetaphysical (*LAM* 29). It is, one could say, deeply indebted to Hegelianism or "implies a philosophy of history" (33). And the picture Strauss thus paints of it shows us at once that it stands in opposition not only to what Strauss has presented as authentic classic liberalism ("To quote Havelock . . . Plato is not a liberal thinker") but likewise—especially in its guiltless commercial and technological humanism—in opposition to Heideggerian existentialism.[11] We will thus be able to see in Strauss's

---

11. In *Being and Time* Heidegger had presented atheistic alternatives to the biblical understanding of the fall, of the call of conscience, and of guilt. The fall is "falling prey" to entanglement in the "They." The conscience is naked, thrown-into-nothingness, not-at-home Da-sein's silent summoning of itself back from its refuge of lostness in the They to its own authentic, uncanny, unique, innermost potentiality of being, revealed in *Angst*. Primordial (and inescapable) guilt is guilt in the uncanny ground of our being; it is the burden or weight borne by authentic Da-sein, as a consequence of *thrownness*, of our nullity, viz., "never to gain power over one's ownmost being from the ground up," and hence includes the burdensome fact of "nullity," of not being able to choose, or having to relinquish, many possibilities in one's existentelle project. "The summons calls back by calling forth: forth to the possibility of taking over in existence the thrown being that it is, back to thrownness in order to understand it as the null ground that it has to take up into existence. The calling back in which conscience calls forth give Da-sein to understand that Da-sein itself—as the null ground of its null project, standing in the possibility of its being—must bring itself back to itself from its lostness in the they, and this means that it is guilty. . . . Summoning to being-guilty means a calling forth

examination of Havelock's thesis both Strauss's agreement and disagreement with Heidegger.

For in at least one respect, Havelock appears to follow or parallel Heidegger. Unlike most contemporary liberals, Havelock looks for a "pure" liberalism in pre-Platonic or pre-Socratic thought, on the assumption that the modern thinkers who are thought to be responsible for the rise of liberalism (Locke and Jefferson) remain, in their appeal to "nature" or to a nonnegotiable "natural right," under the influence of Plato and his alleged metaphysical "absolutism." In his search for a pre-Socratic ancient liberal, Havelock makes a newer, cruder version of an old claim (made by Hegel): the German idealists stand to the French Revolution as Plato and Aristotle stand to the sophists. Unlike Hegel, however, Havelock takes the side of the sophists or pre-Socratics in the alleged fight between them and Plato and Aristotle. As we will see, Strauss quietly indicates that this fight is significantly overblown—that Plato and Aristotle are in some very important and overlooked respects in agreement with the pre-Socratics. Critiquing it will allow Strauss to articulate his understanding of the pre-Socratics also in implicit opposition to Heidegger's.

Everyone grants, Strauss argues, that there were pre-Socratic or pre-Platonic thinkers who were atheistic, materialist, and Epimethean, who recognized progress in the arts and inventions as having pulled humanity out of an originally "poor and brutish" beginning, and who held all morality to be of merely human origin. Strauss himself grants in addition that the pre-Platonic thinkers in question share this set of doctrines with modern liberals. What he denies is that this set of doctrines is "the sufficient condition of liberalism" (*LAM* 30–31). What, then, according to Strauss, is the needed addition?

Havelock himself does not say, or "never meets the issue" (*LAM* 32). Strauss finds the needed addition that produces liberalism in three related things. First, for the ancients, the specialty of the "special sort of animal,"

---

to the potentiality-of-being that I always already am as Da-sein. Da-sein need not first burden itself with 'guilt' through failures or omissions; it must only be authentically the 'guilt' that it is. . . . In the summons, the they-self is summoned to the ownmost being-guilty of the self. Understanding the call is choosing, but it is not a choosing of conscience, which as such cannot be chosen. What is chosen is having a conscience as being free for one's ownmost being-guilty." *Being and Time*, Stambaugh translation, secs. 34–38, 54–61; *Sein und Zeit* (Tübigen: Max Niemeyer Verlag, 1927), pp. 167–80, 254–301. Quotations are from pp. 262 and 264–65 of the Stambaugh's translation of pp. 284 and 287–88 of *Sein und Zeit*).

man, is his capacity to "look at the universe or look up to it," the recognition of which can "easily lead to the non-liberal conclusion that the distinctly human life is the life devoted to contemplation as distinguished from the life of action and production" (31). Second, the ancient thinkers did not lose sight of the fact that since the universe has come into being, it will perish, in an infinite repetition; "there were and there will be infinitely many universes." The pre-Socratics' "contemplation" of the whole, then, Strauss immediately makes clear, is not infused by any hope to overcome its inevitable decline, or to "conquer nature." That contemplation is instead infused, as we have seen, by a resignation to what Strauss in *Natural Right and History* had, following Lucretius, called the crackings of the walls of the world, a resignation accompanied by the recognition of the relative insignificance of human action and production. For this reason the ancients attached importance not so much to the progress of social institutions, which would inevitably decay, as to "understanding the permanent ground or character of the process or to the understanding of the whole within which the process takes place and which limits the progress" (32–33). What Havelock calls the "flamboyant optimism" of the modern liberals manages, by contrast, to be somehow unaffected by the inevitability of decline, which, as Strauss had emphasized in a note in *Natural Right and History*, should confront the moderns even in the findings of their own science.[12] Unlike the pre-Socratics, the modern liberal does not actually permit himself to see the inevitable decline and hence ultimate futility of all human deeds.

In the midst of articulating this second difference between modern liberals and their alleged ancient counterparts, Strauss raises a deeper question:

> Here the question arises as to whether there can be a universe without man: is man's being accidental to the universe? In other words, is the state of things prior to the emergence of man and the other animals one state of the universe equal in rank to the state after their emergence, or are the two states fundamentally different from one another as *chaos* and *kosmos*? (*LAM* 31)

---

12. See again *NRH* 175–76, including note 10 on 176, which contains quotations from Engels and Bachofen addressed to this question. See also "The Liberalism of Classical Political Philosophy," *LAM* 40.

The modern liberals, Strauss argues, who find man's being to be accidental to the universe, accordingly find no significant difference between the two states of the universe (prehuman and human), and Strauss wonders if "their ancient predecessors—the 'Greek anthropologists'—agree[d] with them." His formulation implies that they did not, and that this disagreement is significant. Human being was for them not accidental to but necessary to any ordered whole or cosmos, which is to say that they understood the human mind and its noetic and sense perceptions to play a decisive role in the formation or being of that ordered whole (which, incidentally, can be the case only if there is no divine mind). And as Strauss indicates in *Natural Right and History* (*NRH* 32 and 176), the finitude of man and hence this question of the being of the cosmos without man is central also to the thinking of Heidegger. Is Heidegger, then, correct to seek among the pre-Socratics a kind of thinking closer to his own?

The third distinction that Strauss draws between the ancients and contemporary liberals indicates otherwise:

> Finally, liberalism is empirical or pragmatic; it is therefore unable to assert that the principle of causality ("nothing can come into being out of nothing and through nothing") is evidently and necessarily true. On the other hand it would seem that the Greek anthropologists or rather "physiologists" did regard that principle as evidently true because they understood the relation of sense perception and *logos* differently than do the liberals. (*LAM* 32)

Here a major difficulty for positivist science, upon which modern liberalism depends, comes into focus: positivist science cannot defend the principle of causality; it can strictly speaking give us only observations. Strauss here traces this inability of the liberals' science to their doubt (starting with Descartes) of our sense perception of the given world—to the Cartesians' rejection of sense perception as providing a natural knowledge of the world as it is. The ancient "physiologists," by contrast, while breaking with the prephilosophic life and prephilosophic orientation—the orientation guided by law or custom—accepted the principle of causality (cf. *NRH* 89–90) because they did not reject prephilosophic *knowledge* available through sense perception, a knowledge which as knowledge relies on that principle. (Sense perception shows us trees and rivers, for example, while it does not show us spirits and witches, even if specific human groups may *believe* them to exist.)[13] This would mean, however, that the pre-Socratic physiologists in question, no less than Socratics, stand against Heidegger, according to whom all things come to be out of nothing and by nothing.[14] We may therefore say that contra Heidegger, awareness of mortality and recognition of the central role of the thinking being, man, in the being of the cosmos, which as Strauss has already shown, characterized the thinkers in question, does not dispel or bring into question the fundamental tenet of all philosophy—Socratic or pre-Socratic—that no being emerges without a cause.

That which does drive Heidegger to assert that all things come into being out of nothing and through nothing is, Strauss suggests in *Natural Right and History*, Heidegger's unquestioned *historicism*, that is, his belief in history as a "dimension of reality" that had allegedly "escaped classical thought."[15] Havelock's liberalism, too, assumes "history" as a " 'dimension of reality' " (*LAM* 33), and Havelock is eager to find belief in it or awareness of it among the ancient thinkers whom he wishes to call liberal. As Strauss brings out, Havelock can do so only at the expense of philological discipline: Havelock translates words for "becoming" or "all human things" as "History," distorting the text in his own image. But Havelock's broader case for the existence of ancient historicism is that his ancient "liberals" were conscious that moral beliefs changed over the course of a humane progress from imperfect beginnings, while their religiously orthodox and Platonic opponents held to belief in a perfect, Edenic or golden, first age that was lost through guilt. What for Nietzsche had been the catastrophic awareness of the historical relativity of all values is to Havelock a ground for optimism, held by both ancient and modern liberals, and so the basis of a progressive moral crusade against conservatives ancient and modern. By examining Havelock's argument concerning perfect versus imperfect beginnings—a subject to which, as we saw in the previous chapter, Strauss called his readers' attention on a number of other occasions, and one that

---

13. See Strauss's "Note on 'Some Critical Remarks on Man's Science of Man,' " December 26, 1945, typed manuscript with 9 numbered pages, box 14, folder 9, at 6, Leo Strauss Papers (Patard, 579). The "Note" is an unpublished manuscript review of Kurt Riezler's "Some Critical Remarks on Man's Science of Man," *Social Research* 12, no. 4 (1945), 481–505.

14. See "The Problem of Socrates," 321–38, at 327–29.

15. *NRH* 33.

will become a theme of this essay—Strauss addresses more fully the issue of historicism, and so the true ground of Heidegger's opposition to ancient science and its principle of causality.

Havelock begins his search for the ancient historicism with Hesiod. He reads Hesiod's account of the five races of men as a tale of successive failures and woe told by "an ageing conservative . . . who cannot come to terms with . . . changing conditions." Strauss certainly does not, as some of his critics would lead one to expect, defend Plato and Aristotle and an unchanging morality against this progressivist attack. He instead notes that Hesiod's account of the five ages is much more complex than Havelock's reading allows: only three of the five human races—the silver, bronze, and iron races—are failures, and they did not fail on account of human guilt but instead began to decline from the golden race (as Havelock himself notes elsewhere) when Zeus dethroned Kronos; Zeus, not man, is responsible for the failures. Moreover, the race of heroes, made by Zeus, coming as it does between the bronze and the iron ages, represents an ascent, not a decline, and the next race after our iron age will likely also be an ascent. The poet appears to teach not decline upon decline, but that better and worse races of men follow indefinitely one after another, until the end of the age of Zeus (*LAM* 35).

But Strauss does not leave it at refuting Havelock's claim that Hesiod regarded "History as Regress." As he will many times in this essay (see *LAM* 35, 36, 40, 47, 49, 52, 55, 58), he invites his reader to consider "the context," specific and general, of the passages under consideration, in order to develop a more adequate reading of the text under consideration. This too may surprise those who have been led by Strauss's critics to expect a disregard of contexts. In fact, however, Strauss (and his better students) consider context more carefully than almost any other readers. Where they differ from most contemporary interpreters is in their assumption that truly great thinkers are not determined in their thinking by the opinions that reign in their time, but are able to transcend those opinions (their "cave") in a manner that can be seen only when the context, and the permanent contextual need to pay lip service to those opinions, is recognized. In this case the immediate context is three Hesiodic tales, of which the tale of the five races of man is the second. The tale of the five races is sandwiched between the tale of Prometheus and Pandora, on one hand—in which work decline is presented as a curse—and the tale of the hawk and the nightingale, on the other. Calling the latter tale "very pertinent to the history of Greek liberalism," Strauss explains its teaching as follows: the hawk, that is, the king, tells the nightingale, that is, the singer, that he who resists the stronger is a fool, doomed to suffer pain and disgrace; yet the king is unaware that the nightingale has a power of its own.

As Strauss's subsequent account of the "broad context" of the poem brings out, the power of the singer—of Hesiod—rests in part on his capacity to hide his critique of the king—that is, of Zeus the king—from most of his listeners. The "works and days" of men chronicled by Hesiod are accordingly preceded by "exhortation to work as the only proper thing for just men and as a blessing, by answers to the question as to why the gods compel men to work, and by the praise of Zeus the king, the guardian of justice." This surface teaching, according to which there are two ways of life, that of unjust idlers and that of just workers, conceals a teaching that appears on "closer inspection." According to this more muted teaching there are three ways of life or kinds of men: those who understand by themselves, those who listen to and obey the former, and those who do neither. The singer is the highest example of the first way of life or kind of man. He does not work (and so does not belong to the righteous) nor is he idle (and so does not belong to the unjust), but has a kind of activity that "transcends" both and that "belongs to the night." His activity must transcend both because work is not in truth simply a blessing but is also "toil," the "brother of forgetting," while "the Muses are the daughters of Memory." The suggestion of Strauss is that Hesiod, the singer who understands, is philosophic, in search of the truly oldest or first things, aided in this search by what he poetically calls the Muses, who "are indispensable for knowledge of the things that shall be and of the things that were in the olden times as well as of the gods who are always." Hesiod's highest theme is "Zeus" as the (popular) alternative to the genuine first things.[16] (Contrary to Heidegger, the thinking of "the Greeks" did not, for the philosophic among them, take place in a historical

---

16. *LAM* 37. As for the "philosophic" character of Hesiod's understanding, consider what Strauss says concerning the Muses' possible instruction of "the men of the age of Kronos" and of the present (iron) age (37), together with the remark, in the next section, on Plato's *Statesman*: "the question of whether men led a blessed life under Kronos, when the gods took care of men, is left unanswered on the ground that we do not know whether men then used their freedom from care for philosophizing . . . Hesiod compelled us to raise a similar question regarding the golden age" (38). See also Strauss's letter to Jacob Klein, October 10, 1939, in *Leo Strauss Gesammelte Schriften*, ed. Heinrich Meier (Stuttgart: J. B. Metzler, 2001), 3:581–82; trans. in Patard, 21–23.

situation "guarded" by belief in gods; instead the Greek thinkers "guarded" their speech, or practiced moderation.[17])

Havelock misses all of this because he is "too certain of his answers to all questions," especially those provided by contemporary psychology and sociology (*LAM* 36, bottom), or as Strauss also suggests, because he is amusic and unable to perceive ambiguity. At any rate Strauss states that a wiser beginning than Havelock's attempt to interpret Hesiod would have been a consideration of the "nonmusic and unambiguous discussion of the problem of progress which we find in the second book of Aristotle's *Politics*" (37, bottom), that is, the final part of the discussion of Hippodamus of Miletus's

---

17. In his rectoral address, Heidegger presents the science or knowing of Germans (and through them, all humans) as taking place in a new, "unguarded" situation, one quite different from that of the Greeks: they must now engage in science in light of the finding of Nietzsche, "that passionate seeker of God," that "God is dead," and hence "face up to the forsakenness of modern man in the midst of what is." See above, chapter 1, p. 32, note 22, and see below, pp. 135–39. With his introduction here of the esotericism of the ancients (in this case, of Hesiod), Strauss indicates both the "unguarded" or radical character of ancient thought *and* the ancient thinkers' perceived need to convey such thoughts only to their most thoughtful readers. He does not thereby disparage political/ moral reasoning, but rather encourages it. Compare *What Is Political Philosophy?*, 26–27, on the rectoral address:

> The crucial issue concerns the status of those permanent characteristics of humanity, such as the distinction between the noble and the base, which are admitted by the thoughtful historicists: can these permanencies be used as criteria for distinguishing between good and bad dispensations of fate? The historicist answers this question in the negative. He looks down on the permanencies in question because of their objective, common, superficial and rudimentary character: to become relevant, they would have to be completed, and their completion is no longer common but historical. It was the contempt for these permanencies which permitted the most radical historicist in 1933 to submit to, or rather to welcome, as a dispensation of fate, the verdict of the least wise and least moderate part of his nation while it was in its least wise and least moderate mood, and at the same time to speak of wisdom and moderation. The biggest event of 1933, would rather seem to have proved, if such proof was necessary, that man cannot abandon the question of the good society, and that he cannot free himself from the responsibility for answering it by deferring to History or to any other power different from his own reason.

scheme of honoring citizens for innovations (*Politics* 1268b22–1269a27). Strauss's formulation of Aristotle's position brings out how well disposed is the alleged conservative Aristotle to progress in the arts and sciences: Aristotle assumes "as a fact that the change from the old manner in the arts and sciences to the new manner has been beneficial." He simply "wonders whether a corresponding change in the laws would be equally beneficial," or he questions "whether there is a necessary harmony between intellectual progress and social progress." There is certainly *some* such harmony for Aristotle—since all humans seek not the ancestral but the good—but "his answer is not unqualifiedly in the affirmative." The apparent tendency of such thinkers as Hesiod and Aristotle to "look backward" arises, it seems, not from any irrational conservative motives but from a limit that their reason perceives to "social progress," both "after and before the emergence of science" (*LAM* 37). But what, then, is that limit?

The subsequent few paragraphs, on Plato's *Statesman* and its myth of the ages of man (*LAM* 37–38), suggest an answer, or rather make clearer the answer that Strauss has already pointed to. The Eleatic Stranger, the "philosopher" who describes those ages, says "disconcertingly" of the only age of which we have knowledge by perception—that is, the present age—that "there is in it no divine providence, no care for men." The former ages are known only by "hearsay" or myth; of the first, the age of Kronos, it is said that gods took care of men, but it is hard to know if men were happy then, since it is unknown if they used their leisure to philosophize rather than to mythologize. The reader is "compelled" by this argument of the Eleatic Stranger, Strauss says, to raise the question of whether there could be philosophy when there was (under divine care) no need for arts, hence no arts, hence no genuine knowledge of what it means to know something, or of "what philosophy is" (38). Havelock is thus correct to say that Plato's Socrates considers the arts second in rank, but as all of this makes clear, that is a "high rank." Strauss adds that if Plato's Eleatic Stranger speaks of the arts as divine gifts, as Havelock complains, he does so only momentarily. "Plato," says Strauss, "admits in the myth of the *Statesman* the imperfect character of man's beginnings." As this indicates, "Socrates" has not been given this whole argument, but it is the argument of "Plato." The limit to social progress would seem then to be tied to the need of most human beings for belief in divine providence. Or (as Aristotle suggests in the *Politics*) social progress is limited by the law's lack of a *rational* hold on man—by the fact that law derives its strength from habituation, especially, we may add, from the as it were natural habituation of most human beings toward belief in divine providence.[18]

This is borne out in the sequel, in which Strauss turns with Havelock to a passage in Plato's *Laws*. Here the story of the age of abundance under Kronos is again told, as a way to show men of the present that "not men but a god, or the immortal mind within us, must rule over men if the city is to be happy." That is, Plato's Athenian Stranger suggests that one need not long for the age of Kronos, since it would be possible in principle (however remotely in practice) to achieve it now, with the rule of the human mind. And as Strauss notes, Plato's more thematic account of the first age presents it as the age of men who survived a cataclysm, not as an age of men ruled by Kronos, and of men who are moreover initially praised highly but are said to be lacking in wisdom or prudence and therefore inferior to the best of later men, that is, philosophers. Eventually these men of the first age are even said to have been savages and cannibals. The Athenian Stranger's account does indeed, as Havelock complains, include a limit to human inventions or "history," but that is a rational inference rather than evidence of prejudice; the "liberal's science" should tell Havelock the same thing (*LAM* 39–40).

Strauss concludes the first section by noting that Havelock is right to assert that the net effect "on the imagination" of reading the archeology of book 3 of the *Laws* is to see early human life as a "wholly admirably and happy thing," and that this effect is contradicted by Plato himself. Strauss argues that the reason is however not, as Havelock would have it, Plato's desire to avoid an open fight with the alleged ancient liberals. It is instead the following: "Plato knew that most men read more with their 'imagination' than with open-minded care and are therefore much more benefited by salutary myths than by the naked truth" (*LAM* 40). Havelock himself cites Protagoras's awareness that insights such as the human origin of morality are an invaluable acquisition, a heritage for later men that " 'must never be lost' or 'is too precious to be gambled with.' " Strauss implicitly agrees with Havelock that morality, if not indeed "historical," is of "human origin," and that this insight is a valuable part of the heritage of civilization. Where he disagrees is in his assessment of who constitutes the enemies of civilization. Strauss finds the greatest of them to be not the "narrow but loyal preservers" of civilization, but rather those who through contempt for the past

---

18. See Strauss's analysis in *The City and Man* (21–22) of Aristotle's account of Hippodamus, and see below, pp. 139–41.

"squander the heritage." Civilization, he argues, "is much less endangered by narrow but loyal preservers than by the shallow and glib futurists who, being themselves rootless, try to destroy all roots and thus do everything in their power in order to bring back the initial chaos and promiscuity" (41).[19] While this statement sounds (and is doubtless meant to sound) like that of an alarmist conservative, it has the less obvious but deeper purpose

---

19. On the need for "rootedness" for civilization, Strauss is in some agreement with Heidegger, who equates rootlessness or homeless wandering with contemporary nihilism. See Heidegger's letter to Jünger, titled "Concerning the Line" (1955), or (as it was later titled) "On the Question of Being," trans. Thomas Sheehan, in *Pathmarks*, 292: "as the unconditional will to will [nihilism], wills homelessness [*Heimatlosigkeit*] as such." And see Strauss, "Philosophy as Rigorous Science and Political Philosophy," 33:

> Both thinkers [Nietzsche and Heidegger] regard as decisive the nihilism which according to them began in Plato (or before)—Christianity being only Platonism for the people—and whose ultimate consequence is the present decay. Hitherto every great age of humanity grew out of *Bodenständigkeit* (rootedness in the soil). Yet the great age of classical Greece gave birth to a way of thinking which in principle endangered *Bodenständigkeit* from the beginning and in its ultimate contemporary consequences is about to destroy the last relics of that condition of human greatness. Heidegger's philosophy belongs to the infinitely dangerous moment when man is in a greater danger than ever before of losing his humanity and therefore—danger and salvation belonging together—philosophy can have the task of contributing toward the recovery or return of *Bodenständigkeit* or rather of preparing an entirely novel kind of *Bodenständigkeit*: a *Bodenständigkeit* beyond the most extreme *Bodenständigkeit*, a being at home beyond the most extreme homelessness.

Unlike Heidegger, Strauss neither holds out any such hopes for philosophy, which he calls "these fantastic hopes, more to be expected from visionaries than from philosophers" (34), nor does he see the original task of philosophy as prescribing a new moral or ethical education, for "the Greeks" or for humanity; nor does he see the healthy traditions in which healthy political life moves as guiding the philosopher in his philosophizing, but rather as the object of the dialectical examination through which the philosopher privately ascends out of the "cave" of his society; nor does he see Plato or his metaphysics as the source of the present nihilism or homelessness. That source is rather modern philosophy and its attempted enlightenment, its "politicization of philosophy" (*NRH* 34). The German historical school of jurisprudence and the historicism that grew out of it was an effort to combat this homelessness born of the Enlightenment:

of confirming not only Plato's but Strauss's agreement with Havelock on the important matter of the *chaotic* character of man's beginnings. He insists, on account of this very awareness, however, that the "first duty of civilized

> By denying the significance, if not the existence, of universal norms, the historical school destroyed the only solid basis of all efforts to transcend the actual. Historicism can therefore be described as a much more extreme form of modern this-worldliness than the French radicalism of the eighteenth century had been. It certainly acted as if it intended to make men absolutely at home in "this world." Since any universal principles make at least most men potentially homeless, it depreciated universal principles in favor of historical principles. (*NRH* 15–16)

Yet precisely this effort ended in nihilism/homelessness:

> Yet the unbiased historian had to confess his inability to derive any norms from history: no objective norms remained. . . . The only standards that remained were of a purely subjective character, standards that had no other support than the free choice of the individual. No objective criterion henceforth allowed the distinction between good and bad choices. Historicism culminated in nihilism. The attempt to make man absolutely at home in this world ended in man's becoming absolutely homeless. (*NRH* 17–18)

Taking for granted this experience of homelessness at which historicism had arrived as the historically disclosed truth, Heidegger made the attempt to explain the structure of *existenz* in such a way as to offer a home or dwelling to human beings that could emerge in a committed or resolute stand over and against that homelessness. In this way—and despite his sustained critique of Cartesianism—he continued the modern politicization of philosophy. *That* Heidegger's whole effort is directed toward the overcoming of nihilism is clear from these sentences in the open letter to Jünger, "On the Question of Being," 315: "'What is metaphysics?' At the peril of becoming long-winded and of repeating things that have been said on other occasions, I would like to take the opportunity of this letter to elucidate once more the meaning and import of that question. Why? Because *your* intention *too* is concerned with assisting in the overcoming of nihilism in your own way. Such overcoming, however, occurs in the realm of a recovery of metaphysics" (emphases added). Or, as he says even more clearly later, "the overcoming of nihilism, i.e., the recovery of the oblivion of being" (319). And again: "The essence of nihilism, which finds its ultimate consummation in the domination of the will to will, resides in the oblivion of being. . . . This higher ambiguity lets us experience to what extent the overcoming of nihilism demands a turning it into its essence, a turning it whereby the desire to overcome becomes untenable. The recovery of metaphysics calls thinking into a more originary calling" (319–20).

man is to respect the past," a duty that leads one to elevate the "Founding Fathers" and the aged, and hence logically to the "belief in perfect beginnings or in the age of Kronos."[20] Fully aware of the ramifications of their discoveries concerning early man, and therefore without hope in any saving power, be it gods or History, to preserve civilization, the most radical thinkers employ the "Muses," or appeal to the imagination of readers, to sustain the conservative myths that sustain civilization, in a manner that accords with the needs of most human beings.

What, then, has Strauss's initial argument disclosed concerning not only Havelock but Heideggerian existentialism? The latter was what one is led to from positivism, according to Strauss, if one "adheres to the modern premises." A key "modern premise," clearly assumed by Havelock but assumed no less by Heidegger, is that the findings of philosophers have always been, and ought to be, made apparent to everyone. This premise causes Havelock, and likewise Heidegger, to fault those thinkers who to him appear unable to live with the thoughts that there is no divine or eternal order to the whole, that our beginnings were imperfect, and that morality is of human origin. Heidegger's analysis of classical thought, in his early period, was of course infinitely more impressive than that of Havelock. Yet it was limited, no less than Havelock's, by his failure to see the accommodations that classical philosophers and poets, Socratic and pre-Socratic, were making on the surface of their works to the reigning religious orthodoxies of their times. This failure made it easier for Heidegger to be given over to the reigning modern orthodoxy according to which thinkers are determined by their historical situation, by "History," or by the disclosure of Being peculiar to their age. To him, the Platonic or Aristotelean philosophers were unable to accept "flux," or were engaged in a flight from their mortality, an intellectual flight from the decay and death that *time* entails.[21] Strauss has made as clear as circumstances permit how mistaken a view of Socratic or Platonic philosophy this is.

---

20. *LAM* 40–41. Compare *NRH* 83b–84t.

21. See, e.g., Martin Heidegger, "Letter on Humanism" (1946), in *Basic Writings of Heidegger*, rev. and exp. ed., ed. David Farrell Krell (New York: HarperCollins, 1993), 217–65. See also his 1924–25 Marburg winter semester course, *Plato's "Sophist,"* trans. Richard Rojcewicz and André Schuwer (Bloomington, IN: Indiana University Press, 1997). Originally published in German as *Platon: Sophistes* (Frankfurt: Vittorio Klostermann, 1992). Commenting therein on book 10, chapter 7 of Aristotle's *Ethics*, Heidegger says:

Disinterring Greek Liberalism: Aeschylus and Sophocles

The short second section of Strauss's essay (*LAM* 41–45) is devoted to Havelock's comments on three passages taken from the three major Greek tragedians who allegedly possessed a "progressivist view" and thus a "scientific anthropology."

According to Havelock, Aeschylus's *Prometheus* drastically "corrects" Hesiod's "scheme": Prometheus's philanthropic theft of fire saved man from the tyrant Zeus and allowed man to learn all of the arts and thus rescue himself by means of "understanding," or by his own achievement, from his prehuman and not divinely created condition; "technology" also allowed him to save himself and fellows, compassionately, from liquidation by the tyrant Zeus. Aeschylus is even a "progressive evolutionist," who, by presenting an eventual reconciliation of Zeus and Prometheus, shows future progress to be infinite (*LAM* 41). To make this case, Havelock resorts to what would today be called a Straussian reading: "on the surface of the drama" Prometheus is a god, but if the fire that he brings is, as the play suggests, the true teacher of the arts for man, then the arts are "to some extent man's own achievement" (41–42).

Strauss finds this argument "reasonable," but asks what, then, Prometheus's achievement is, or what he stands for. Havelock's answer is "Intelligence." To this conjecture Strauss objects that Prometheus claims to have put "blind hopes" in men "as a remedy for having made them stop to foresee their doom, their death." Prometheus further claims to have invented a medicine that would cause man to think that he has abolished man's mortality. "Is he a boaster?" Strauss asks. He points again, that is, to how crucial to classical judgment of intelligence versus foolishness is a full

---

For what always is, which is thematic in this comportment, is constantly predelineated in such a way that even the presence of Dasein to it is determined as constant and persevering. Herein resides the peculiar tendency of the accommodation of the temporality of human Dasein to the eternity of the world. The abiding with what is eternal, θεωρεῖν, is not supposed to be arbitrary and occasional but is to be maintained uninterruptedly throughout the duration of life. There resides for man a certain possibility of ἀθανατίζειν (1177b33), a mode of Being of man in which he has the highest possibility of not coming to an end. This is the extreme position to which the Greeks carried human *Dasein* (122; 177–78 of the German).

awareness of mortality, or how far from intelligence are the blind hopes that hide this awareness. Havelock, for his part, appears to have such hopes. For as Strauss goes on to argue, Aeschylus's Prometheus has in fact learned that art is "far weaker than necessity." And this means that (contrary to Havelock's hopes and reading) "there is . . . no infinite progress." Human death, and mortality more generally, limit progress. Since Prometheus comes to this knowledge only late in Aeschylus's play, Strauss is moved to say of him that "the well-meaning bringer of blind hopes was himself the victim of a blind hope." The punished Prometheus comes to regret having chosen to side with Zeus over Kronos. Aeschylus causes us to wonder, though, as had Hesiod, whether Zeus is not wilier than Prometheus, teaching man "to learn wisdom by suffering . . . and not through the arts."

But as he had done in the examination of Hesiod, so does Strauss in this examination of Aeschylus proffer not merely a rebuttal but his own alternative reading, on the basis of a consideration of the broader context of the play (*LAM* 42–43). It is the first play of a trilogy, he notes, and Zeus, the great Prometheus's antagonist, does not appear on stage in it, perhaps as a tribute to his greater wisdom: he *appears* as a tyrant before he can fully manifest himself or his plan. Even Zeus's desire to destroy the "witless" race of men created by Kronos contains a praise of Zeus. Only Prometheus's theft of fire gave man wits, after all, and it is possible that Zeus had intended to create a race of men "worthy of him and free of blind hopes." He instead now uses Prometheus's kind but non-Promethean, non-foreseeing deed in a "foreseeing, in a royal manner." He decides to use man's new power as a means to teach him wisdom through the suffering that comes from the arts.

Strauss concludes his alternative reading by stressing, over and against Havelock's esoteric reading, the need to dwell "on the surface of the play" rather than moving too quickly to find a concealed meaning in it. He thus may be said to provide a corrective for the type of investigation that he had recommended in the opening section on Hesiod. In any event, Aeschylus's change of Hesiod's story is due not, as Havelock would have it, to a "scientific source" of information concerning the human origin of the arts (for which, Strauss points out, one could much more easily credit the arch-Edenic Biblical account—he has in mind especially Genesis 4:17–24) but to a "somewhat different meditation on things divine-human."[22]

---

22. For Strauss's reflections on Aristophanes's account, in the *Frogs*, of Aeschylus's thoughtful conservatism in divine matters, see Strauss, *Socrates and Aristophanes* (New York: Basic Books, 1966), 251–253.

∾

In this interpretation of Aeschelus's words on art and necessity Strauss provides, quietly, an alternative to the interpretation that Heidegger provided in his rectoral address, an interpretation that Heidegger expected would assist his listeners in being up to the task of "the German fate in its most extreme distress." Heidegger asks those listeners to consider what science is as it discloses itself in its beginning, among the ancient Greeks. As part of this effort he quotes Aeschelus's Prometheus, who, he notes, was said to be the first philosopher: "τέχνη δ' ἀνάγκης ἀσθενεστέρα μακρῷ (*Prom.* 514)." In Heidegger's translation of the passage, *techne* is "knowledge," so that what might be translated as "art is by far weaker than necessity" becomes "knowing, however, is far weaker than necessity." And in his subsequent sentence, *anagke* becomes "fate": "This is to say, all knowing about things has always already been delivered up to overpowering fate and fails before it."

Heidegger then identifies this "knowing"—stemming from *techne*—as "contemplation" (θεωρία) and attacks the notion that it meant disinterested contemplation—unattached, as it were, to one's people:

> But what do the Greeks mean by θεωρία? One says: pure contemplation, which remains bound only to the thing in question and to all it is and demands. This contemplative behavior—and here one appeals to the Greeks—is said to be pursued for its own sake. But this appeal is mistaken. For one thing, "theory" is not pursued for its own sake, but only in the passion to remain close to and hard pressed by what is as such. But, for another, the Greeks struggled precisely to conceive and to enact this contemplative questioning as one, indeed as *the* highest, mode of human ἐνέργεια, of human "being-at-work." They were not concerned to assimilate practice to theory. Quite the reverse: theory was to be understood as the highest realization of genuine practice. For the Greeks, science is not a "cultural good" but the innermost determining center of all that binds human being to people [*volklich*] and state [*stoat/Wit*]. Science, for them, is also not merely a means of bringing the unconscious to consciousness, but the power that hones and embraces being-there (*Dasein*) in its entirety.[23]

---

23. "The Self-assertion of the German University and The Rectorate 1933/34," 472–73.

While this statement on the contemplative life of a philosopher appears to have important similarities to that life as Strauss speaks of it—as a life of desire to know the truth and as one that, while entailing a serene if sad resignation to necessity, is the fulfillment of his human nature and the highest realization of practice—Heidegger is actually saying something quite different from Strauss. For he subsequently presents knowing not as resignation but as "defiance" of the ultimate failure implied in Prometheus's statement, a defiance that opens one up to the "unfathomable inalterability" of what is. And he presents the possible activity of science or knowing to be undertaken by Germans in a similarly defiant posture, yet one that takes place in a *new* situation, a situation quite different from that of the Greeks: his listeners must now engage in science in light of the finding of Nietzsche, "that passionate seeker of God," that "God is dead," and hence "face up to the forsakenness of modern man in the midst of what is."[24] Hence, "what was in the beginning the *awed perseverance* of the Greeks in the face of what is" now "transforms itself into the *completely unguarded exposedness to the hidden and uncertain*, i.e., the questionable."[25] The questioning of the "Greek" philosophers, he implies, radical as it was, remained under the "guard" of their belief in the gods; it was for this reason but "a preliminary step" intended "to give way to the answer, and thus to knowledge," but that can no longer be the case. Now "*questioning* becomes the highest form of knowing."[26] Such questioning, Heidegger promises, "exposes science once again to the fertility and the blessing bestowed by all world-shaping powers of human-historical being (*Dasein*), such as nature, history, language; people, custom, state; poetry, thought, faith; disease, madness, death; law, economy, technology." "If," he continues, "we will the essence of science understood as *the questioning, unguarded holding of one's ground in the midst of the uncertainty of the totality of what-is, this* will to essence will create for our people its world, a world of innermost and most extreme danger, i.e. its truly spiritual world." While *Da-sein* is now faced with the difficult (because fully exposed) possibility of defiant free creation of a "world," *against* necessity/fate, or the *new* possibility of *existenz*, it has always been engaged, *through science*, in

---

24. "Self-assertion," 474.

25. "Self-assertion," 474 (emphasis added).

26. "Self-assertion," 474 (emphasis added). Compare his criticism of *eidos* and Platonic "procedure" that leads to science as "correspondence," rather than as "addressing and discussing," at *Being and Time* (Stambaugh translation) 58 and 374; *Zein und Seit*, 61–62 and 408.

"world-shaping activity"; not only is poetry one of its powers, but poetry, making (*poein*) is *essential* to its defiant activity as *techne*.[27]

---

27. See also *The Question Concerning Technology*, 34–35:

> There was a time when it was not technology alone that bore the name *techne*. Once that revealing that brings forth truth into the splendor of radiant appearing also was called *techne*.
>
> Once there was a time when the bringing-forth of the true into the beautiful was called *techne*. And the *poiesis* of the fine arts also was called *techne*.
>
> In Greece, at the outset of the destining of the West, the arts soared to the supreme height of the revealing granted them. They brought the presence [*Gegenwart*] of the gods, brought the dialogue of divine and human destinings, to radiance. And art was simply called *techne*. It was a single, manifold revealing. It was pious, *promos*, i.e., yielding to the holding-sway and the safekeeping of truth.
>
> The arts were not derived from the artistic. Art works were not enjoyed aesthetically. Art was not a sector of cultural activity.
>
> What, then, was art—perhaps only for that brief but magnificent time? Why did art bear the modest name *techne*? Because it was a revealing that brought forth and hither, and therefore belonged within *poiesis*. It was finally that revealing which holds complete sway in all the fine arts, in poetry, and in everything poetical that obtained *poiesis* as its proper name.
>
> The same poet from whom we heard the words
>
> > *But where danger is, grows*
> > *The saving power also.*
>
> says to us:
>
> > *. . . poetically dwells man upon this earth.*
>
> The poetical brings the true into the splendor of what Plato in the *Phaedrus* calls to *ekphanestaton*, that which shines forth most purely. The poetical thoroughly pervades every art, every revealing of coming to presence into the beautiful.
>
> Could it be that the fine arts are called to poetic revealing? Could it be that revealing lays claim to the arts most primally, so that they for their part may expressly foster the growth of the saving power, may awaken and found anew our look into that which grants and our trust in it?
>
> Whether art may be granted this highest possibility of its essence in the midst of the extreme danger, no one can tell. Yet we can be astounded.

Moreover, the new poetic "making" of science is to be on behalf of one's people or through them, the authentic *existenz* of all humanity. It is in the service of the spiritual needs of all. The practice of science thus understood "guarantees the people greatness," under the leadership of the university teachers, who will be "empowered by the deepest vocation and the broadest obligation" that, it appears, is entailed in this science, or rather that emerges from Heidegger's scientific analysis of *existenz*, his articulation of fundamental ontology that is to guide it, together with awareness of our new situation, and the "courage" bestowed by and manifest in such science. This will enable the teachers "to elevate" their already "awakened" students' "own purpose, so that it becomes a grounded, knowing truth." Heidegger can thus present this activity of questioning, which is to guide science, as in accord with the third of the three bonds of service given in the German law: the *Arbeitsdienst* (labor service), the *Wehrdienst* (armed service), and the *Wissensdienst* (knowledge service).[28] The new theorizing is to be in the service of the German people. It is true that Heidegger claimed, with some plausibility, in his 1949 "Facts and Thoughts" on the rectoral address, that "knowledge service" was stated last in this list "not because it is subordinated to the former [two], but because knowing is what is authentic and

---

Before what? Before this other possibility: that the frenziedness of technology may entrench itself everywhere, to such an extent that someday, throughout everything technological, the essence of technology may come to presence in the coming-to-pass of truth.

Compare Strauss, 1957 course on Plato's *Gorgias*, 15–16:

I often translate the Greek word "techne" as "art" but you must understand that has a very broad meaning in Greek. It embraces the art of the shoemaker as well as the art of Homer. It may even embrace, and indeed it does embrace in Plato, all science. Let us say tentatively, an art is a pursuit which can be transmitted from teacher to pupil because it consists of rules. That is a good beginning. So in other words, whether it is a shoemaker . . . you have to think of shoemaker and Homer at the same time if the word art occurs without any addition.

Despite their agreement, Strauss does not present the art of Plato as pious, as the bringing forth of the true into the beautiful, nor as a "dialogue of divine and human destinings," which, in Heidegger, means belief in the demiurge. Strauss sees the beautiful/noble, as well as artful gods, as subject to a radical if private *critique* in Plato's dialogues.

28. "Self-assertion," 476–77.

highest."[29] But it is no less in the service of the German people. Besides, he actually says quite clearly in the rectoral address itself something quite different. He there says that the "three bonds . . . are equally primordial to the German essence. . . . And the three services—Labor Service, Armed Service, and Knowledge Service—are equally necessary and of equal rank."[30]

It accords with this that for Heidegger, *techne* is considered a manner of knowing that does not differ in kind from contemplation, and hence the ancients' allegedly "disinterested" pursuit of the truth of Being and of beings through contemplation was in fact meant to yield a framework for a "correct" set of answers, one that would guide ordinary life, through correspondence with the "ideas," toward what is "rational." This "metaphysical" framework is, as he argues elsewhere, what eventually led to the modern technocratic science and the catastrophe of modern life, in its technological oblivion of Being and its self-disclosure or uncovering. Heidegger has made clear indeed that his *substitute* for ancient contemplation—namely, thinking informed by the analysis of *existenz*—was far from the "political science"—that is, politicized science—being demanded by the Nazis, who disapproved of his address. He even claims that he offered a quiet but radical critique of the Nazis' politicized science: his version of science was not "racial," as the Nazis wished science to be. Yet Heidegger's science was not without a deliberate attention to *care*, not only for Germany and the revival of German thinking within the West, over and against the coming global technological forgetting of being, but thereby for the whole world.

For Strauss, on the other hand, *techne* (art) is to be distinguished from (even if it stems from and hence will be related to) the knowing that is available as *dianoia* or as *episteme*; *techne*, as rules prescribing a transformation of what is given, already shows within it the conscious possibility of technology, and its possible autonomy from political control—an autonomy rejected by the ancients. Hence in his commentary on Aristotle's account of the political thought of Hippodamus of Miletus, Strauss can refer to Hippodamus's proposal for awards to be given for proposed improvements of the city as awards for "technological change" and "technological progress":

> Hippodamus had not given thought to the difference between innovation in the arts and innovation in law, or to the possible tension between the need for political stability and what one

---

29. "Self-assertion," 487.

30. "Self-assertion," 477.

might call technological change. On the basis of some observations made nearer home, one might suspect a connection between Hippodamus' unbridled concern with clarity and simplicity and his unbridled concern with technological progress.[31]

Technological progress, progress in the arts in conjunction with science, Strauss then explains, has a deeply problematic relation to progress in *law*:

> His scheme as a whole seems to lead, not only to confusion, but to permanent confusion or revolution. At any rate Aristotle cannot elucidate innovation without bringing out a most important difference between the arts and law. The arts are susceptible of infinite refinement and hence progress and they do not as such in any way suffer from progress. The case of law is different, for law owes its strength, i.e. its power of being obeyed, as Aristotle says here, entirely to custom and custom comes into being only through a long time. Law, in contradistinction to the arts, does not owe its efficacy to reason at all or only to a small degree. However evidently reasonable a law may be, its reasonableness becomes obscured through the passions which it restrains. Those passions support maxims or opinions incompatible with the law. Those passion-bred opinions in their turn must be counteracted by passion-bred and passion-breeding opposite opinions which are not necessarily identical with the reasons of the law. The law, the most important instrument for the moral education of "the many," must then be supported by ancestral opinions, by myths—for instance, by myths which speak of the gods as if they were human beings—or by a "civil theology." The gods as meant in these myths have no being in and by themselves but only "by law." Yet given the necessity of law one may say that the principle of the whole both wishes and does not wish to be called Zeus.[32]

Hippodamus, the first political scientist, had studied natural science and had wished to direct political life in accord with its principles. One may say with only some exaggeration that Hippodamus's activity, which Aristotle

---

31. *The City and Man*, 21–22.

32. *The City and Man*, 22.

presents as comically inept, does not differ in kind from what Heidegger thinks Aristotle and Plato were engaged in. Strauss, on the other hand, finds Aristotle pointing, as had Plato, to the deep gulf separating the moral/political life from the philosophic or contemplative life, and to arts/technology as destructive of that by which a healthy society (as opposed to the philosopher) must take its bearings. Philosophy *is* not technology, does not *lead* to technology, is *aware* of "technological" thinking, and *opposes* its liberation from political control.

In the present review of Havelock, as we have seen, when addressing the very passage from *Prometheus* that Heidegger quotes in the rectoral address, Strauss, too, presents Prometheus as having learned, late, and through his suffering, a limitation, but it is not a limitation on "knowing"; it entails "knowing." It is a limitation on *art*: "Art is by far weaker than necessity (vv. 514–518)."[33] Strauss draws the conclusion that "Prometheus' love of man

---

33. There is, of course, a "kinship," according to Strauss, between the "humble knowledge" of the artisan and philosophy. In "The Mutual Influence of Theology and Philosophy," 12, Strauss presents that kinship as residing in a common reliance on sense perception:

> This quest for the beginnings proceeds through sense perception, reasoning, and what they called *noesis*, which is literally translated by "understanding" or "intellect," and which we can perhaps translate a little bit more cautiously by "awareness," an awareness with the mind's eye as distinguished from sensible awareness. But while this awareness has certainly its biblical equivalent and even its mystical equivalent, this equivalent in the philosophic context is never divorced from sense perception and reasoning based on sense perception. In other words, philosophy never becomes oblivious of its kinship with the arts and crafts, with the knowledge used by the artisan and with this humble but solid kind of knowledge.

He goes on to distinguish this awareness, informed by sense perception, from the biblical alternative, which is also nonmythical but whose nonmythical character moves in the opposite direction of the nonmythical character of philosophy. Philosophy turns to examine the "impersonal forces" like *moira*, which, in mythology, struggle with the gods, *as necessities*. The bible *removes* necessities, attributing all things to one omnipotent, mysterious God who has revealed himself and established a free covenant with men, whose experiences of God are *not* based on sense perception:

> To give some meaning to the term mythology which I am here forced to use, I would say that mythology is characterized by the conflict between gods and impersonal powers behind the gods. What is in Greek sometimes called *moira*, for example. Now philosophy replaces this impersonal fate, as

cannot overcome the power of necessity. There is no "infinite progress," as Havelock had claimed that there is on the basis of "human achievement" or "technology."[34] Not only does Strauss translate *techne* as "art" rather than "knowledge"; he adds references to the four subsequent lines from Aeschylus's play (where a reference to one line, 514, might seem to have sufficed, as it did for Heidegger). The four additional lines (515–518) include the Chorus' (bewildered) inquiry "Who is the helmsman of Necessity?"; Prometheus's reply that it is the "three-shaped Fates and mindful Furies"; the Chorus' (astonished) response, "Can it be that Zeus is weaker than they?"; and Prometheus' confirmation, "Yes, in that even he cannot escape what is destined." And what is poetically understood as destiny or fate, Strauss goes on to say, is what philosophers understand as "necessary." Whereas for Heidegger the Germans (and through them, all humans) must now engage in thinking, science in light of the finding of Nietzsche, "that passionate seeker of God," that "God is dead," and hence "face up to the forsakenness of modern man in the midst of what is,"[35] for Strauss what is entailed in this facing up was already achieved in the "meditation on things divine-human" of Aeschylus (*LAM* 43). But Aeschylus, a poet with an awareness of his civic responsibility, did not broadcast it.

The second portion of a poetic work Havelock adduces to show the influence of science consists of lines, delivered by the chorus in Sophocles's *Antigone*, listing the most outstanding inventions of the awful or wondrous being, man. Havelock notes that the figure of Prometheus has here "disappeared," which Strauss agrees would demonstrate Havelock's thesis were it the case that unscientific man is unable to be aware "of the human origin of the

we might say, by nature and intelligible necessity. The Bible, on the other hand, conceives of God as the cause of everything else, impersonal necessities included. . . . The biblical God is known in a humanly relevant sense only by his actions, by his revelations. The book, the Bible, is the account of what God has done and what he has promised. It is not speculation about God. In the Bible, as we would say, men tell about God's actions and promises on the basis of their experience of God. This experience, and not reasoning based on sense perception, is the root of biblical wisdom.

34. *LAM* 42–43.

35. "Self-assertion," 474.

human arts"; he adduces a passage from Plato's *Laws* (677d4) to demonstrate that this is not so. So too Havelock presents a passage of Euripides's *Suppliants* as evidence of a pious, "skillful re-write" of a "scientific original," but Strauss again notes that there is no actual evidence of the alleged original. Havelock's only possible evidence is that Euripides contradicts himself by "theistically" praising the kindness of heaven but "nontheistically" blaming heaven's harshness. Against this Strauss cites the words of the play itself: not Euripides but one of his characters, Theseus, says that a god "taught man to protect himself against . . . another god." Yet Havelock "knows that Euripides speaks in the person of Theseus." For a second time, Strauss cites the surface—this time the obvious literary character of the work as a play, with *dramatis personae*, none of whom can be said to be the playwright's mouthpiece—over and against an alleged deeper but in fact purely conjectural teaching. And here again, an important critique by Strauss has a bearing on the works of Heidegger.

For while he often proceeds with remarkable, probing caution in analyzing ancient texts, and with an acute and illuminating awareness of the distortions that the texts have undergone in the scholastic tradition, there is a significant neglect of the *literary* character of the ancient texts that Heidegger examines. In "Plato's Doctrine of Truth," for example, he begins as follows: "In order to experience and to know for the future what a thinker left unsaid, whatever that might be, we have to consider what he said. To properly satisfy this demand would entail examining all of Plato's 'dialogues' in their interrelationship. Since this is impossible, we must let a different path guide us to the unsaid in Plato's thinking."[36] What remains "unsaid" in Plato's thinking is according to Heidegger "a change in what determines the essence of truth. The fact that this change does take place, what it consists in, and what gets grounded through this transformation of the essence of truth—all of that can be clarified by an interpretation of the 'allegory of the cave.' "[37]

That Heidegger puts the word "dialogue" in quotation marks is indicative of the fact, visible in the rest of the essay, that he considers Socrates to be in fact Plato's mouthpiece.[38] And what Heidegger means by what "Plato

---

36. "Plato's Doctrine of Truth," 155.

37. "Plato's Doctrine of Truth," 155.

38. See also "The Problem of the Ontological Difference" [1927], in *The Basic Problems of Phenomenology*, trans. Albert Hofstadter (Bloomington: Indiana University Press, 1982), pt.

left unsaid" is what Plato conveyed without being aware of it. "Plato's thinking subjects itself to a transformation in the essence of truth that becomes
the hidden law governing what the thinker says." This transformation is
not spoken of in the dialogue, but, Heidegger argues, can today become
visible to *us*; its doing so is "made necessary from out of a future need."[39]
The transformation consists of moving from an understanding of truth as
"unhiddenness," ἀλήθεια (with stress on the privative) to what has "for a
long time now in Western thinking," been assumed, truth as "the agreement
of the representation in thought with the thing itself: *adaequatio intellectus
et rei*." The transformation is visible in the allegory of the cave, where "the
'idea' is the visible form that offers a view of what is present. The ἰδέα is
pure shining in the sense of the phrase 'the sun shines.' . . . The essence of
the idea consists in its ability to shine and be seen [*Schein-und Sichtsamkeit*].
This is what brings about presencing, specifically the coming to presence of
what a being is in any given instance. A being becomes present in each case
in its whatness. . . . What the idea, in its shining forth, brings into view
and thereby lets us see is—for the gaze focused on that idea—the unhidden
of that as which the idea appears. . . . Only in this Platonic revolution do
νοεῖν and νοῦς (apprehending) first get referred essentially to the 'idea.' The
adoption of this orientation to the ideas henceforth determines the essence
of apprehension [*Vernehmung*] and subsequently the essence of 'reason'
['*Vernunft*']. . . . 'Unhiddenness' now means: the unhidden always as what
is accessible thanks to the idea's ability to shine."[40] "Henceforth the essence
of truth does not, as the essence of unhiddenness, *unfold from its proper and
essential fullness* but rather shifts to the essence of the ἰδέα. The essence of truth
gives up its fundamental trait of Unhiddenness."[41] "If our comportment with
beings is always and everywhere a matter of the ἰδεῖν of the ἰδέα, the seeing
of the 'visible form,' then all our efforts must be concentrated above all on
making such seeing possible. And that requires the correct vision. . . . Everything depends on the ὀρθότης, the correctness of the gaze."[42] Heidegger sees
this continuing in Aristotle's *Metaphysics*, where "unhiddenness already stands

---

2, ch. 1, 227–330, at 284: "The understanding of being already moves in a horizon that
is everywhere illuminated, giving luminous brightness. It is not an accident that *Plato, or
Socrates in the dialogue*, explains the context to Glaucon by a simile" (emphasis added).

39. "Plato's Doctrine of Truth," 167.

40. "Plato's Doctrine of Truth," 173.

41. "Plato's Doctrine of Truth," 176.

42. "Plato's Doctrine of Truth," 176–77.

under the yoke of the ἰδέα," where "the false and the true are not in things (themselves)] . . . but in the intellect." "From now on mischaracterization of the essence of truth as the correctness of both representation and assertion becomes normative for the whole of Western thinking" ("Plato's Doctrine of Truth," 178). He sees it "sharpened" in the works of Thomas Aquinas, where "truth is properly discovered encountered in the divine or human intellect." He sees it sharpened further "at the beginning of modern times," in Descartes, in *Rules for the Direction of the Mind*: " 'Truth or falsehood in the proper sense can be nowhere else but in the intellect alone."[43] Finally, he sees it "in the age when the modern era reaches its fulfillment, Nietzsche": "Nietzsche's concept of truth displays the last glimmer of the most extreme consequence of the change of truth from the unhiddenness of beings to the correctness of the gaze. The change itself is brought about in the determination of the being of beings (in Greek: the being present of what is present) as ἰδέα."[44] The "most extreme consequence" of this notion of truth as correctness—of the dominance of Platonic metaphysics—which Nietzsche inherited, is that "life" ceases to be possible, or nihilism.

Strauss actually undertook the examination of all of Plato's dialogues that Heidegger dismissed, at the start of this interpretation, as impossible. In *The City and Man* (50–62), for example, before launching into his interpretation of the *Republic*, he presents a rich, insightful, detailed, cautious, and comprehensive reflection on the Platonic dialogues as a whole and their literary character. A number of the conclusions to which he leads his readers include an implicit critique of Heidegger's approach to the Platonic texts in search of a Platonic theory of truth:

---

43. See also *Being and Time*, secs. 19–21 (pp. 84–94; *Sein und Zeit*, pp. 89–101) and sec. 43 (pp. 186–91; *Sein und Zeit*, pp. 200–206). In contrast to Strauss, Heidegger is deafeningly silent on the *theological* concern behind Descartes's retreat into consciousness. He says nothing of the *deus deceptor*, and instead attributes the turn to the *ego cogitans* to the fall into entanglement with *das Man*.

44. "Plato's Doctrine of Truth," 178–79. See also Heidegger, *Introduction to Metaphysics*, 111 (80 of the German): "Only with the sophists and Plato was seeming explained as, and thus reduced to, mere seeming. At the same time, Being as idea was elevated to a supersensory realm. The chasm, *khorismos*, was torn open between the merely apparent beings here below and the real Being somewhere up there. Christian doctrine then established itself in this chasm, while at the same time reinterpreting the Below as the created and the Above as the Creator, and with weapons thus reforged, it set itself against antiquity [as paganism] and distorted it. And so Nietzsche is right to say that Christianity is Platonism for the people."

Whereas in reading the *Politics* we hear Aristotle all the time, in reading the *Republic* we hear Plato never. In none of his dialogues does Plato ever say anything. . . . One cannot understand Plato's teaching as he meant it if one does not know what the Platonic dialogue is. One cannot separate the understanding of Plato's teaching from the understanding of the form in which it is presented. One must pay as much attention to the How as to the What. . . . The literary question properly understood is the question of the relation between society and philosophy . . . the proper work of a writing is truly to talk, or to reveal the truth, to some while leading others to salutary opinions; the proper work of a writing is to arouse to thinking those who are by nature fit for it. . . . While everything said in the Platonic dialogues is said by Plato's characters, Plato himself takes full responsibility for the titles of the dialogues. There are only four dialogues whose titles designate the subject matter: the *Republic*, the *Laws*, the *Sophist*, and the *Statesman*. There is no Platonic *Nature* or *Truth*. The subject matter of the dialogues as it is revealed by the titles is preponderantly political. . . . Plato conceals his opinions. We may draw the further conclusion that the Platonic dialogues are dramas, if dramas in prose. They must then be read like dramas. We cannot ascribe to Plato any utterance of any of his characters without having taken great precautions. . . . To understand the speeches in the light of the deeds means to see how the philosophic treatment of the philosophic theme is modified by the particular or individual or transformed into a rhetorical or poetic treatment or to recover the implicit philosophic treatment from the explicit rhetorical or poetic treatment. . . . The Socratic conversation and hence the Platonic dialogue is slightly more akin to comedy than to tragedy. This kinship is noticeable also in Plato's *Republic* which is manifestly akin to Aristophanes's *Assembly of Women*. . . . Plato's work consists of many dialogues because it imitates the manyness, the variety, the heterogeneity of being. The many dialogues form a *kosmos* which mysteriously imitates the mysterious *kosmos*. The Platonic *kosmos* imitates or reproduces its model in order to awaken us to the mystery of the model and to assist us in articulating that mystery. There are many dialogues because the whole consists of many parts. But the individual dialogue is not a chapter from an encyclopaedia of the philosophic sciences or from a system of philosophy, and still less a relic of a stage of Plato's development. Each dialogue deals with one part; it reveals the truth about that part. But the truth about a part is a partial truth, a half truth. Each dialogue, we venture to say, abstracts from something that is most important to the subject matter of the dialogue. If this is so, the subject matter as presented in the dialogue is strictly speaking impossible. But the impossible—or a certain kind of the impossible—if treated as possible is in the highest sense ridiculous or, as we are in the habit of saying, comical. The core of every Aristophanean comedy is something impossible of the kind indicated. The Platonic dialogue brings to its completion what could be thought to have been completed by Aristophanes.

On the absence of the comical in particular in Heidegger, Strauss speaks elsewhere of "Heidegger's obstinate silence about love or charity, on the one hand, and the things that deserve to be laughed at, on the other."[45] On the ideas as presented in the allegory of the cave, Strauss says the following: "The whole political scheme of the *Republic* as presented there is based on the premise that knowledge of the highest theme, what is called the good or the idea of the good, is available. It is possible, I think, to show that Plato did not believe this is true. The description in the *Republic* of philosophy at its peak is in its way as utopian as the description given in the *Republic* of the polis at its best."[46] And on Heidegger's understanding of the ideas as "shining," Strauss raises a doubt of Heidegger's derivation of *phusis*: "Heidegger tries to understand *phusis* as related, not to *phuein* (to grow) but to *phaosphos* (light)—'to grow' is for him above all man's being rooted in a human past, in a tradition, and creatively transforming that tradition."[47]

---

45. See "Kurt Riezler, 1882–1955," 33–34.

46. "On Plato's *Republic*" (1958), in "Leo Strauss on Thomas Hobbes and Plato," 239–256, at 248.

47. Strauss, "The Problem of Socrates," 326. See Heidegger, *Introduction to Metaphysics*, 75 (54 of the German): "Until now, *bhu* has been interpreted according to the usual superficial conception of *phusis* and *phuein* as nature and as 'growing.' According to the more originary interpretation, which stems from the confrontation with the inception of Greek philosophy, this 'growing' proves to be an emerging which in turn is determined by coming to presence and appearing. Recently, the radical phu- has been connected with pha-, *phainesthai* to show itself. *Phusis* would then be that which emerges into the

A fundamental difference between Strauss and Heidegger here emerges, namely, that while the moderns indeed sought to have philosophy affect the everyday life of human beings, Heidegger is in oblivion of the *private* character of the philosophic life for the ancients and to some extent even for the medieval (especially with the Arabs and Maimonides), and hence the altogether novel character of the *politicization* of philosophy within modernity, up to and including Heidegger himself. Heidegger mistakenly attributes to *Plato* and his influence the demand, found in contemporary political life as in *all* moral life, for universal moral standards. After all, Glaucon did not take the position he took with regard to justice—that it was something permanent and universal and something that needed to be praised as good in itself—*after* he had heard Socrates declaim about the ideas; he took that position already in book 2 of the *Republic*. Heidegger fails to reckon with the possibility that the ideas are presented to Socrates's interlocutors, especially Glaucon, as something that accords with their own moral opinions and as part of Socrates's effort to make philosophy acceptable to them, an effort that requires a false ("utopian") account of philosophy.

Finally, Strauss ties Nietzsche's doctrine of the Will to Power, and hence its connection with technology, to the moderns (specifically to the British), not to Plato—over and against both Nietzsche and Heidegger:

> Nietzsche, who abhorred the modern ideas, saw very clearly that those ideas are of British origin. The admirer of Schopenhauer thought it equitable to look down with contempt on the British philosophers, in particular on Bacon and on Hobbes. Yet Bacon

---

light, *phuein*, to illuminate, to shine forth and therefore to appear. (See *Zeitschrift für vergleichende Sprachforschung*, vol. 59.)"

In his account of the discovery of nature, Strauss stresses its emergence in opposition to what is authoritative by law or convention, especially divine law: *NRH* 82–95. Contrast Heidegger, *Introduction to Metaphysics*, 16 (11 of the German): "Thus *phusis* originally means both heaven and earth, both the stone and the plant, both the animal and the human, and human history as the work of humans and gods; and finally and first of all, it means the gods who themselves stand under destiny." Heidegger even appears to think that the notion of nature *precedes* that of law: "We oppose to the physical the 'psychical,' the mind or soul, what is ensouled, what is alive. But all this, for the Greeks, continues even later to belong to *phusis*. As a counterphenomenon there arose what the Greeks call thesis, positing, ordinance, or nomos, law, rule in the sense of mores. But this is not what is moral but instead what concerns mores, that which rests on the commitment of freedom and the assignment of tradition."

and Hobbes were the first philosophers of power, and Nietzsche's own philosophy is a philosophy of power. Was not "the will to power" so appealing because its true ancestry was ignored? Only Nietzsche's successors restored the connection, which he had blurred, between the will to power and technology. But this connection is clearly visible in the origins of that philosophic tradition, which Nietzsche continued or completed: the British tradition.[48]

To return to Havelock: he appears to be on firmer ground in his survey of the work of Diodorus Siculus, who after all, as Strauss points out, was an "authority for Machiavelli and Hobbes," and gave a coherent, naturalistic account of the origin of the universe and of man, one that accords with what Havelock considers a "philosophy of history." Havelock's error in this case is one of omission: he mentions that according to Diodorus "the universe and man have come into being," but Strauss points out that for Diodorus it is "equally important" (and deadly to the thesis of a progressive history) "that they will perish," a fact from which Havelock seems again to have averted his eyes. Havelock claims among other things that Diodorus's following of an Egyptian account according to which the arts are gifts of certain gods is "an Egyptian fairy tale" that should be regarded as "a sort of parody." We again are presented with an apparent "Straussian" reading by Havelock, and with a rebuff of it by Strauss. He notes that Havelock raises the question of "why in antiquity it was so difficult for [the scientific] anthropologies to survive in their own stark scientific honesty"—or why Diodorus would in the present case use a "fairy tale" instead of speaking the truth—but "we are not aware that he even tried to answer this question, although Diodorus is not silent about the usefulness of myths of untrue stories of a certain kind" (*LAM* 44). Strauss, that is, does not question Havelock's description of Diodorus's account of the rise of the divine origin of the arts as a "fairy tale," or as something Diodorus knew to be untrue. He simply notes that Havelock shows no serious reflection on this practice of not telling the truth, and even ignores an author's own statements on the matter. The practice

---

48. Strauss, "On the Basis of Hobbes' Political Philosophy," in *What Is Political Philosophy*, 172.

in question *changed*, Strauss notes, with the rise of modern over ancient "naturalism." The former is allied with "popular enlightenment," the latter conceives of the relation between science and society on "entirely different terms" (44–45). Strauss's second section confirms, that is, what we had found to be the case in the first section.

Strauss concludes this second section with a broad judgment of Havelock's procedure: the existence of the alleged scientific sources of the tragedians' words has never been established, so Havelock's claim that there were such sources for Plato (against which Plato allegedly fought mightily and contradicted himself) and such sources for the tragedians, has been left as an unproven assumption, justified in Havelock's opinion, Strauss speculates, by "some" unknown "people." Strauss thus concludes that Havelock has provided an "involuntary satire on the scientific method and on scientific progress."

Reconstructing the Anthropologists' Teaching: *Protagoras* and *Republic*

As important as the arguments thus far have been, Strauss indicates that the heart of his case against Havelock's thesis appears in the long third section, on Plato's *Protagoras* (*LAM* 45–59). Following others, Havelock finds in this dialogue both "the anthropology and the political theory of the Greek liberals," and Havelock's "whole thesis depends" on his reading of this dialogue. Strauss does not, however, devote this third section exclusively to Havelock's analysis of the *Protagoras*. Instead, after indicating its importance, he devotes the opening portion (45–49, top) to Havelock's initial examination of the *Protagoras* and to Havelock's account of the city of sows in the *Republic* (49–50), both of which are a continuation of Havelock's attempt to prove the existence of "naturalistic sources" in Plato's work. This is followed by a look at Havelock's turn to the fragments of the alleged progressivist philosophers, or proponents of a "philosophy of history": Anaximander, Xenophanes, Archelaus, and Democritus. This is followed in turn by Havelock's account of his Greek liberals' political doctrine as disclosed in the writings of Democritus, undocumented utterances, and Antiphon (*LAM* 51, bottom–53). Finally, Strauss returns in this third section to Havelock's direct and full interpretation of the *Protagoras*, which Havelock undertakes when he confronts the fact that the political theory of his Greek liberals known chiefly through Plato are described by Plato as "sophists." Strauss goes out of his way to make this third section a section on "Protagoras" and to highlight its importance.

Havelock faces the initial problem that Protagoras is a character in a Platonic dialogue, his speech a creation of Plato. How can one distinguish what belongs authentically to Protagoras from what is a Platonic import? To Havelock, though, who is confident that he knows "which teachings are peculiarly Platonic (or Socratic)," this poses little difficulty; he easily subtracts the obvious Platonic import in order to produce the Protagorean original. At the outset, then, Strauss calls attention to Havelock's innocent assumption that he knows the thought of Plato. How mistaken this is comes to light immediately: Havelock takes Protagoras's commonsense account of the differences between species of animals, especially between humans and brutes, as "Platonic" and "wholly incompatible with 'previous Greek science,'" which emphasized "process" over essential distinctions. But as Strauss points out, Protagoras, telling a myth—a popular tale—simply makes use of popular or everyday distinctions of "races or tribes of living beings," distinctions made moreover by the biblical redactors and by Empedocles and Democritus, who certainly were not under Platonic or Socratic influence (*LAM* 46–47). The Platonic Protagoras himself even uses later on in the dialogue the doctrine of essential differences between and within species and parts of living beings *against* Socrates, in order to "show the relativity or the 'multi-colored' character of the good." Havelock attempts to explain away this Protagorean use by claiming that Protagoras refers only to classification of acts or performances by men in different situations, which draws Strauss to point out that classifications require classes, and the Platonic Protagoras in the passage in question classifies "useful things" according to a classification of beings or parts of beings to which they are useful. (Protagoras argues that manure, for example, is good for the roots of trees, but not for their branches.) Moreover, even the famous Protagorean teaching that "man is the measure of all things" (cf. *Theatetus* 152a–c, 161b–c, 169d–172b) assumes a difference in kind between man and the brutes. Finally, Strauss makes what we might call the case that Havelock, had he known what he was looking for, could have made: the "species" of mortal beings to which the Platonic Protagoras refers (in his myth), as primarily mixtures of earth and fire, do not possess "natures" or essential properties. Their natures are, rather, the "powers" they have, which "are secondary and derivative," and hence "naturalistic" in Havelock's desired sense. On this "crucial point" Socratic thinking, Strauss suggests, considers by contrast the nature of the thing to be visible and primary, and in contrast to the sophist, does *not* claim to know the primary things or principles out of which things are mixed. Socratic *political* philosophy, we may say, is brought into and sustained in being by recognition of precisely this ignorance.

Havelock likewise considers the references to the gods made by the "complete agnostic" Protagoras to be a Platonic element of his speech, made manifest as such by the "contradiction" in it between saying that all animals were molded by the gods and saying that man (alone) has kinship with the gods. Strauss points out that this kinship is said to be with "the god" (singular), and comes about according to Protagoras "not through Zeus' gift of right, but through Prometheus' theft of fire and technical wisdom from Hephaestus and Athena." That is, the kinship is related to a technical wisdom obtained through a theft, or a rebellion against the gods (and perhaps in favor of intelligence). Had Havelock again merely interpreted the myth, he would easily have arrived at the expression of the "naturalistic," nontheistic doctrine or "creed" he was seeking (*LAM* 47).

But why did Protagoras use a myth at all in addition to using prosaic speech? The context of the myth's use suggests, Strauss argues, that Plato's Protagoras was "aware that he was in some danger in Athens since he was engaged in an unpopular activity, in the activity of a sophist." Or as Strauss will later say, Socrates succeeded in making him fully aware of this danger and hence in making him more cautious. Strauss even suggests that the Platonic Protagoras's "keen sense of danger" makes concealment and frankness a central theme of the dialogue. Protagoras announces that he is the first open or uncloseted sophist because he did not think his closeted sophistic predecessors were in fact cautious in their attempt at concealment. That is, his openness is driven by or in the service of caution; caution is the principle. He will therefore be less than open when he considers it prudent to be so. Strauss draws our attention to one of these precautionary measures: the professed "agnostic" (who had famously begun a book declaring that he did not know whether the gods were or not) declares that "under God, I shall not suffer anything terrible on account of my professing to be a sophist" (*LAM* 47).

In the course of elaborating what he calls the "third clue" concerning the reason Protagoras speaks in myth, Strauss not only points to the deepest reason for this Protagorean caution, but also to a commonality between Plato and Protagoras in this matter, and to a corresponding fundamental difference between the two ancients and Havelock. It concerns the status of the moral life. The "fundamental difference" that Plato's Protagoras presents between "the arts and reverence or right" is mythically presented in the following way: the various arts, practiced variously by individuals, are the result of Prometheus's necessary theft, whereas reverence and right are the "gift of Zeus" and to some extent practiced—that is, at least claimed to be—by everyone, universally. The nonmythical version of this account of the "origin and validity of morality" that is given by Plato's Protagoras is that reverence and right are "taught" by punishment and praise, or by what Havelock would call "social compulsion" or "conditioning." Unlike the arts, they are not taught by any appeal to reason. Havelock himself appears to be content with this, except that he fails to see the radical conclusion to be drawn from it: all right is conventional, or as Strauss puts it here, it produces in thinking men no more than "conformism or lip service." That Havelock is insensitive to the ramifications of this Strauss makes clear by the "few touches of his own" that Havelock adds to Protagoras's argument: Plato's Protagoras says "that the man who does not pretend to be just, whether he is unjust or not, is insane," to which Havelock adds "unless, it is surely implied, in temporary repentance" (*LAM* 48). Yet nothing of the sort is implied by Plato's Protagoras. Like Freud, in other words, whom he sometimes cites (see 36 bottom with 63), Havelock is unable to accept the consequence of conventionalism. His confusion in this regard is made the more evident when Strauss cites Havelock's "remarkable . . . enthusiasm" for the Platonic Protagoras's teaching that punishment makes sense only "as a corrective or as a deterrent," that is, not as vengeance or retribution. Havelock appears to be unaware that this is the view also of "the illiberal Plato," or is what Strauss calls "the rational view of punishment," resting, we might add, in the case of Plato on the Socratic claim, made toward the end of the *Protagoras*, that virtue is knowledge and hence vice ignorance. As we will soon see, Strauss traces Havelock's disposition to the loss, through the modern liberal's faith in "history," of the distinction between what is by nature and what is by convention. But this will entail the (post-Hegelian) modern liberal's acceptance of the law as in effect natural.

Strauss finds a similar difficulty in Havelock's interpretation of the city of sows in book 2 of the *Republic*: the contradictions one finds in it are the deliberate contradictions of the speaker, and not the result of Plato's struggle with an imaginary naturalistic source. The first of a series of cities in speech imagined by the interlocutors is sufficient according to nature to satisfy bodily needs or the noncompetitive society of humans but one that "cannot produce human excellence: it is a city of pigs" (*LAM* 50).

This completes Strauss's look at Havelock's attempt to show the *existence* of progressivist Greek philosophers by examining their alleged "use or adulteration by the tragedians, Diodorus of Siculus, and Plato."[49] It does not quite complete his look at Havelock's account of the "philosophy of history" allegedly held by such progressivists. For this, Strauss turns to Havelock's case made on the basis of late reports on Anaximander, fragments from Xenophanes, Anaxagoras, Archelaus, and Democritus (*LAM* 50–51). In all cases Havelock is shown to establish his points by selectively choosing fragments that seem to support his thesis and suppressing others that refute it, by avoiding reference to key parts of the thinkers' doctrines (such as Xenophanes's denial of any coming into being, or Anaxagoras's reference to the ordering Intelligence), by diluting the distinction (in Archelaus) between nature and convention (according to which the just and the base are by convention and not by nature), by ignoring the same concern (in Democritus) with what is by nature and what is merely by law or convention (such as the benefits of rearing of children), and by the use of amusingly tendentious translations.

Strauss then turns to Havelock's account of the alleged Greek liberals' *political* doctrine, which Havelock finds in Democritus, in undocumented utterances, and in Antiphon. Strauss limits himself here to arguments about Democritus's political teaching (leaving Havelock's examination of Antiphon's political teaching for the fourth and final section of his essay). Havelock would turn Democritus into a value-free, descriptive scientist; to do so, he ignores statements that show clearly that Democritus was not a relativist but thought the good and the true (whatever they are) were the same for all men. Havelock likewise assumes a knowledge of context that we do not possess. Finally, he grants over-the-top praise to a statement about the good that is said to follow when the powerful take heart to help the poor, a statement that he considers without parallel in "better-known classical thinkers," not remembering, as Strauss puts it, similar passages from Plato's *Laws* or Aristotle's *Politics* and moved by "inordinately strong prejudices and the ferocity that goes with such prejudices" to make an assertion that exhibits "the complete absence of a sense of proportion," just as Democritus's arguments in favor of natural rulers do not lead Havelock to consider

---

49. Strauss signals, that is, that he might well have introduced his section break here rather than with the introduction of Havelock's look at the *Protagoras*. He appears thereby to signal the importance of the *Protagoras* not only for Havelock's thesis but for his refutation of it.

that Democritus might have held laws to be a "bad afterthought" (*LAM* 52–53). The fury and incapacity of the many to understand arguments, which had so concerned Protagoras and others, has curiously shifted, in late modernity, to intellectuals, or one could say that modern intellectuals like Havelock actually belong, as Strauss has suggested, to the many (see 47 bottom–48 top).

Having in this way drawn our attention to the issue of the concealment of disconcerting ancient doctrines and their ramifications from a potentially ferocious many, over and against the moral ferocity of their modern proponents, Strauss turns back to the *Protagoras*. For while Havelock "rightly states" or "rightly suggests" or "rightly wonders," and so on (53–54), about the fairness of a number of points in Plato's presentation of the sophists, Havelock must make an effort to understand "by itself" this dialogue, the "Platonic evidence" of liberalism that has permitted him, on the basis of a few fragments of pre-Socratics, to claim that there was indeed a "Greek liberalism."

Strauss's attention to the *Protagoras* shows us in general that Havelock's ax-grinding on behalf of liberalism and against what he takes to be Plato's presentation of the sophists leads him away from the kind of reflection on the text and what it is actually saying that would yield liberating insight. For starters, the second scene of the dialogue (the early morning conversation between Hippocrates and Socrates) and Socrates's introduction of Hippocrates to Protagoras in the opening of the third scene, indicate to the reader that Protagoras has an appeal for a certain type of ambitious young man. By contrast, Hippocrates has Socrates as a comrade yet would never dream of studying with him, and Socrates would similarly never take him on as a student (though he does, philanthropically or justly, protect the poor lad from Protagoras by demonstrating Protagoras's deficiency in good counsel to Hippias [*LAM* 58, bottom]), since Hippocrates lacks the requisite "nature" to philosophize. That philosophic nature—one that craves clarity and awakeness—is, as other Platonic dialogues stress, rare, and there is no "teaching" anyone's way to it. (And this, in truth, is what is meant by Socrates's claim, here in the *Protagoras* and elsewhere, that virtue cannot be taught.) Yet simply because he is wealthy, Hippocrates *is* acceptable to Protagoras. "The place occupied in Socrates' thought by 'nature' is taken in Protagoras' thought by 'wealth'" (which is by convention). Havelock resembles Protagoras in being unaware of this difference between Socrates and Protagoras. He is too busy justifying Protagoras's charging of a fee to notice what Strauss calls "the decisive point" (54–55). If Protagoras is any indication, the sophists, unlike their closeted pre-Socratic forebears, are guided less by nature than by convention.

Havelock likewise complains that Plato has transferred Protagoras's claim about teaching political virtue into a nonpolitical context. Strauss brings out how deeply political the context remains: Socrates "tactfully draws [Protagoras's] attention to the fact that in Athens 'rich and poor' are supposed to possess the political skill which Protagoras claims to teach." And Protagoras's use of myth and then of *logos*, the first unqualifiedly praising democracy and the second adding a significant qualification, shows the reader that Protagoras took Socrates's hint, or that Protagoras is indeed cautious. Havelock, missing this point altogether, simply declares that the continuity of the *logos* with the myth "is tenuous," thereby suggesting without realizing it that Protagoras "is a very great bungler." Here and only here, in a defense of Protagoras, does Strauss permit himself to be blunt: "This suggestion is wrong."[50] While there is, as Strauss has already brought out, a difficulty that Plato would have us see in Protagoras's understanding, only a "very great bungler" would fail to recognize the need, in this political situation, for mythologizing to complement his *logos*. Protagoras's nonmythological or qualified praise of democracy brings out that there are wealthy people in it who can afford the expensive education of a Protagoras and so, Strauss pointedly adds, the "education in that political art which he claims to supply." That education is not universal but only for the wealthy; it is quite distinct from the training in the universal reverence and justice supplied by the "gift of Zeus." Despite Havelock's attempts to claim that Protagoras is a "craftsman of democracy," Protagoras is in fact a teacher of would-be oligarchs. "He takes the side of the wealthy, whereas Socrates takes the side of the gentlemen," those whom Strauss had earlier indicated to be the true ancient liberals owing to their perception, however dim, that the highest life is one of understanding for its own sake (28 bottom–29 top).

In the course of his initial long speech Protagoras mentions that laws are or should be not just any laws but "the invention of good and ancient lawgivers" (*Protagoras* 326d5–6). Havelock notices this but according to Strauss does not stress it enough, nor the awareness that it indicates of

---

50. The blunt judgment is all the more remarkable in that, as the unpublished transcript to Strauss's 1956 class on the *Protagoras* shows, Strauss considered Protagoras's myth and even his very choosing of a myth to have been "inept," since it leaves Protagoras claiming that the political art or virtue is universally taught (by the "gift of Zeus") and hence leaves no need for Protagoras's own teaching of the political art.

the need for reverence for antiquity. He suggests that the reason is that Havelock is preoccupied with why, according to Protagoras, there is such a need: original man, prior to the civilizing work of those lawgivers, were or are savages. Plato finally "here lets the liberals have their say undiluted," Havelock remarks, taking Protagoras's statement as "almost like a piece of Plato's own self-criticism." Was Plato or his Socrates, then, as this suggests, unaware that "in the beginning human beings were worse than the worst criminals living in civilized society"? Strauss has already indicated to us, toward the end of his initial look at the *Protagoras* (*LAM* 48–49 top), that this was not at all the case. Is there then another reason why Socrates, as Protagoras has come to realize, looks down on "that political art which Protagoras claims to teach and of which he claims that every man possess it"?—that is, the "socialization" in pain and praise, mythologically called "the gift of Zeus," through which human beings have become concerned with justice and that Protagoras's oligarchic teachings, no less than the democratic ones, assume? According to Strauss, there is: Protagoras and the modern liberal Havelock share an unawareness "of the existence of a problem of civilization, although to different degrees" (56). But having thus mentioned this problem of civilization, Strauss does not immediately spell it out. He even conspicuously fails to do so, declaring instead that it would be "painful and in no way helpful" to "follow Havelock's analysis of the conversation between Socrates and Protagoras." As Socrates backs off in the end from further questioning of Protagoras, it seems, so does Strauss back off from Havelock's look at the *Protagoras*, allowing "two examples" to suffice to show Havelock's failure to listen "patiently to what Socrates actually says in the context" (57). The examples will, Strauss promises, "shed some light on present-day liberalism." Will they do so by also showing us more concerning present-day liberalism's unawareness of the "problem of civilization," which it shares with Protagoras?

The question that Socrates asks Protagoras after his long speech is whether virtue is one or many. The importance of this apparently academic question becomes clear when we consider that Protagoras has claimed that someone can be courageous but unjust, or of bad counsel but just: the suggestion is that wisdom is or can be compatible with injustice, that the wise (*sophos*) are unjust, or that Protagoras teaches injustice. Moreover, Protagoras had emphasized as "political virtue" justice, moderation, and piety (the "gift of Zeus") in his long speech, but in the exchange with Socrates he adds and emphasizes instead wisdom and courage. Strauss suggests that Protagoras may agree with the Platonic distinction between political (or vulgar) virtue and genuine virtue, the latter consisting (in Plato's case) of wisdom or (in Protagoras's case) of "the gift of Prometheus." This is what is being examined.

Yet there proves to be a difference between the two men. When Socrates directly puts to Protagoras the question of whether one who acts unjustly acts soundly or with good counsel, Protagoras at first claims, coyly, that he would be ashamed to say so (*Protagoras* 333b–c), and then admits that one might say so, but finally, when pressed by Socrates, instead of answering delivers the relatively long statement (which we referred to earlier) concerning the fact that the good varies from species to species and even within living things from part to part. Socrates requests at this point that Protagoras not give long (and it is implied, evasive) speeches but instead answer his questions directly, with short statements. Havelock, who as Strauss had said earlier makes an infinite amount of Protagoras's long statement of what Strauss calls an "obvious but not unimportant truth," takes Protagoras's statement as representing a "pragmatic epistemology," "pragmatic classification," and "sophistic economics." Havelock is beside himself with anger that Plato should unfairly cut this "pragmatic programme" down with the Socratic demand for short speeches, and is still more angry, it seems, with the followers of Plato who have "obediently followed the lead of this preposterous propaganda" (*LAM* 57–58). Strauss patiently points out that Socrates, for the benefit not only of young Hippocrates but also of Protagoras, is insisting that Protagoras face something he does not wish to face. For while Havelock may think that Protagoras holds justice and utility always to coincide, Socrates sees otherwise: he would have Protagoras own up to the "wicked proposition" to which the "somewhat chastened" Protagoras now privately ascribes and to which Protagoras's conventionalism moves him—that injustice is sometimes the wise course of action—and take his beneficial "punishment" for doing so, so that he might reject the proposition not only in word but in thought. Yet what is in Socrates's eyes a painful opportunity for Protagoras to face squarely a problem of civilization—that to follow the justice laid down by the revered ancient lawgiver is not simply profitable—represents to Protagoras a painful "humiliation." He appears to be directed not so much by a desire for clarity or wisdom as by a certain manliness or love of victory; he remains wrapped up in the notions of worth induced by the "gift of Zeus." Strauss suggests that had Havelock himself been less of a propagandist for liberalism—the new, fanatical version of the sophists' moralism—he might have been able to begin understanding the movements that take place in this and other Platonic dialogues, rather than approaching the dialogue as propaganda for a "static" doctrine (58).

The second example of Havelock's misreading, with which Strauss concludes his examination of Havelock's interpretation of the *Protagoras*, has to do with the litigation scene (335a–338e), in which Socrates manages to get the assembly of sophists and their followers to agree to compel Protagoras to respond, as he has demanded, with short answers. Hippias, who is perhaps the most boastful fool in all of the Platonic dialogues, appeals to his fellow sophists for a reasonable solution to the present impasse between Protagoras and Socrates concerning the use of short and long speeches, on the ground that "all present" are "by nature, not by law" kindred and fellow citizens, for they all know the nature of things. His proposal that an arbiter therefore be chosen is defeated by Socrates. Havelock sees in this defeat a "not quite forgivable" treatment of Hippias's doctrine of "man's common nature and brotherhood and world citizenship." That is, he takes Hippias's statement the way it is now commonly taken by liberals who are looking for liberals among the ancients, rather than realizing what according to Strauss Hippias is actually teaching: "By nature all wise men are kinsmen and fellow citizens, whereas all other kinship and fellow citizenship rests on law or convention." This is a teaching of another sophist, Strauss concludes, that Plato "does not ridicule"; he ridicules only Hippias's "childish belief that all present know the nature of the things" (*LAM* 59). The incoherent and hidden moralism of the sophist Protagoras becomes in the modern liberal, reared in the doctrine of universal rights, a proud and open but no less incoherent moralism.

The Account of the Fragments of Antiphon

But the teaching about the brotherhood of man that Havelock mistakenly gleans from Hippias's words he finds also in the fragments of Antiphon, and in the short final section of his essay Strauss addresses this part of Havelock's work, which he sees as the book's culmination. Antiphon speaks of all men being alike in all respects, on the ground that what is necessary to them by nature (such as nose and mouth) is the same for all; the failure to recognize this he calls "barbaric." Havelock takes this questioning of the usual distinction between Greek and barbarian to be something "opposed to the view of the classics"; his view is based on a misreading of the first

book of Aristotle's *Politics* and a disregard of the statements about the superiority of the African city of Carthage found in the *Politics*' second book.
A similar false opposition is present in Havelock's discussion of Antiphon's
counsel to observe the laws of the city when with others and the laws of
nature when alone. Havelock is certain that despite this counsel Antiphon
is "not an immoralist"; Strauss finds no evidence for this view (and, we
may add, the only consistent rule of Antiphon stated prior to this is the
rule to avoid damage to oneself). Havelock does not deny that Antiphon is
advocating "a flexible behavior pattern that involves a double standard," or
is sympathetic to hypocrisy or paying "lip service" to the laws of the city,
evading them when they cannot be fought. Havelock is happy to admit it,
since, he claims, "idealists" like Plato "would object" to such flexibility or
double standards, "as if," replies Strauss, "Plato had never recommended the
noble lie," or indeed as if Socrates had not ended the discussion with Protagoras with two obvious lies. A third false opposition appears in Havelock's
claim that Antiphon, but not Plato, presents an antithesis between law and
nature, which Strauss reminds the reader is present, "although differently
understood," in Plato's own questioning of law, especially in the *Statesman*
(*LAM* 60–61). His discussion of that antithesis will take up the remainder
of his argument concerning Antiphon. If the sophist Protagoras had, unlike
Socrates, failed to grasp sufficiently the antithesis between law and nature
and so failed in truth to take his bearings by the latter, the same is not
true of Antiphon, and yet there remains a difference between Antiphon and
Socrates concerning this antithesis.

   Yet having detailed these false oppositions, and thereby suggested how
close the thoughts of Plato and Aristotle were to some crucial sayings found
in the fragments of Antiphon's work, Strauss digresses for a paragraph, one
that starts with a praise of Havelock for a discovery which, Strauss playfully
suggests, redeems all of Havelock's "lapses." Havelock notices Antiphon's
explicit statement that the law determines for the ears what they are to
hear, for the eyes what they are to see, and for the tongue what it ought
to say. And so it dawns on Havelock that the ancient city "had its totalitarian aspects," or as Strauss puts it, "was not liberal or limited by a First
Amendment." Noting that the frankness of Antiphon's statement is at odds
with both its content and with the previously quoted sayings concerning
the need for dissimulation and caution, Strauss suggests that the shocking
statement against law made as it were "in the presence of witnesses" (because
written down) likely appeared in its original context "hidden away in the

middle of an innocent exposition or not presented by the author in his own name but entrusted to other people." He wishes that Havelock had reflected on this possibility both in Antiphon's fragments and in the work of other writers, who could easily have had the same insight and need for caution. As we have seen, he means of course Plato and Aristotle above all, but he also seems to be including himself in this.

Returning, then, to Havelock's discussion of Antiphon's antithesis of law and nature (61 bottom), Strauss finds Havelock to "unintentionally reveal" the "fundamental difference between the modern liberal and the so-called Greek liberal." Havelock notes that according to Antiphon, not the virtue of an inspired lawgiver but a social compact of society's members is what frames the law. Havelock bases this conjecture on Antiphon's claim that the laws stem from agreement (and not from nature), a statement which, Strauss points out, is not at all incompatible with the possibility that the laws "are the work of an outstanding man regarded as endowed with superhuman virtue whose proposals were accepted by human beings." Nonetheless Havelock's blunder this time drives him to ask a revealing question: "If law is a compact reached historically by human beings, why is it not natural and organic as are other items in man's progress?" In Havelock's puzzlement, Strauss indicates, is disclosed the fundamental difference between the so-called Greek liberal and the modern liberal: for the latter, "'natural' is not a term of distinction." The cause of this difference appears in the word "historically." As Strauss argues in the first chapter of *Natural Right and History*, from the time of Hegel and in the wake of the German historical school that was strengthened in reaction against his thought, the understanding of nature and all that it entailed for philosophy came to be lost, through the adoption of the notion of an organic historical process or processes. As Strauss puts it at the end of this paragraph, "the term 'historical' . . . which is almost the modern equivalent for conventional, serves no other function than to obscure a very obscure event in the development of modern thought." That event is connected to the failure of modernity to satisfy, as it had expected it could, all of humanity through a progressive movement toward a rational, atheistic society. It arose as an effort to supply moral guidance in the face of the Enlightenment's perceived degradation of man.

In Strauss's final elaboration of the ancient antithesis between what is by law or convention and what is by nature we receive not only a better sense of the fundamental difference between ancient and modern liberals, but also the answer to our question of what Strauss means by the "problem of civilization" recognized by ancient philosophers, which now comes to sight as a problem with the laws that make civilization possible. To the modern liberal's Greek predecessors, "not everything that is, is 'natural.'"

> Zeus "is," for otherwise one could not speak about him, distinguish him from Kronos, Hera, and so on; but in what sense "is" he? He is by virtue of opinion or establishment or agreement or law (cf. *Laws* 904a 9–b1 with Antiphon B 44A 2 lines 27–28), whereas man, for instance, is not by virtue of law or opinion, but by nature or in truth. If the liberal rejoins, "But at any rate the law or opinion by virtue of which Zeus is, is not merely by law or opinion but is necessary for the people who adopted it or cling to it," his Greek predecessors would ask him how he knows this: is there no arbitrariness and hence in particular no arbitrary freezing, wise or unwise, of errors salutary or otherwise? (62)

The ancients found law more problematic than do the modern liberals—who have moved toward historicism—because they saw that laws are not necessarily or even likely a reflection of the *genuine* needs of humanity, but instead are determined by "their *opinions* about their needs, or by the opinion of the ruling groups about their needs, and hence above all by their opinions about God, world and man."[51] Putting this into the language of Husserlian phenomenology, as he had in the second and third chapters of *Natural Right and History*, Strauss here declares, "In other words, man fashions a 'state within a state': the man-made 'worlds' have a fundamentally different status from 'the world' and its parts." As we have seen, awareness of this difference is common to both pre-Platonic and Platonic philosophy. But the great advantage Platonic philosophy enjoys over the former is its recognition of the need to establish that the prephilosophic or prescientific "world," the human "world" given its shape above all by divine law, is one that, given the unknowability of first things, cannot be lightly dismissed but must instead be shown to find its true fulfillment in the philosophic life.

With a view to the existentialist alternative, we recall that the doctrine of historical development, through which the crucial antithesis of nature and law or convention came to be lost, is not a doctrine limited to the modern liberal or to progressivist philosophy, but was (uncritically) also taken up by Heidegger. The efforts of those who looked to "history" to supply moral

---

51. "Natural Right" (1946), at 7 (Patard, 390).

guidance in the face of the Enlightenment and its perceived degradation of man finds its most radical expression in the thought of Heidegger, whose analytics of *existenz* is meant to provide the fundamental ontology on which the authentic decisions of the conscientious individual against that degradation will rest. It is true that Heidegger's existentialism recognizes the difficulty entailed in the claim that law reflects the true needs of humanity or of a people, and so frankly abandons any claim to the rationality or naturalness of our moral direction by presenting it as the result of our "decision." But it none the less presents one's historical situation or fate or particular political, legal, or historical situation—or what to the ancients, including the pre-Socratics, is convention—as that which must be freely embraced by anyone who would live a "resolute," actively engaged existence.[52] "Being "in the Moment for 'it's time,'" or the resolution into the world-historical situation, is required.[53] By contrast, the ancients sought what is by nature over and against an embrace of such convention, and as we have seen, the more thoughtful among them were, unlike Protagoras, prepared to accept the moral ramifications of their findings.

In his final elaboration on Havelock's understanding of the meaning of the antithesis between nature and law Strauss reminds us of another key aspect of the pre-Socratics that they shared with Plato and that has a direct bearing on the question of what it means to direct one's life by nature and not law. He notes Havelock's "belief" that Antiphon "had 'a deep feeling for the inviolability of the human organism,'" and that Havelock supports this belief by misquoting a saying of Antiphon: "To be alive is a natural condition." What Antiphon actually says, Strauss points out, is "To live and to die is from nature." As Strauss amusingly puts it, the human organism is "most violable," that is, violable by nature, which Havelock has come, through the conflation of nature and law or convention, to endow with a sacred status in Antiphon's eyes; he even declares Antiphon to have a "reverence for life" instead of realizing that for Antiphon the good is whatever

---

52. Heidegger, *Being and Time* (Stambaugh translation), 275; *Sein und Zeit*, 299. As Strauss puts it in "The Intellectual Situation of the Present," "The free decision of the person 'does not come about in an empty space.' It is conditioned by the history in which the person concerned stands." "The Intellectual Situation of the Present," trans. Anna Schmidt and Martin D. Yaffe, in *Reorientation: Leo Strauss in the 1930s*, ed. Richard S. Ruderman and Martin D. Yaffe (New York: Palgrave, 2014), appendix C, 243.

53. Heidegger, *Being and Time* (Stambaugh translation), 352; *Sein und Zeit* 385; cf. *Sein und Zeit* 383–84, 299–300, 391.

is conducive to life and therefore "the good by nature is ultimately the pleasant," as indeed Socrates proved it to be also for Protagoras (though, in Protagoras's case, the pleasant nobly understood). Law claims to protect innocent lives from violation, especially by other humans, but Antiphon doubts this claim, just as he doubts the natural character of the sacred institution of marriage, that is, its beneficial character. We see, then, why Strauss has called Havelock's account of Antiphon's political doctrine the "culmination" of Havelock's thesis: the modern liberal's political doctrine, having commenced with a doctrine of "natural right" that is absent from the ancient conventionalists, culminates, through the adoption of "History" as a meaningful dimension of human life, in a (hoped-for) resacralization of that which to the ancients was by law or convention. Something similar is true, *mutatis mutandis*, for Heideggerian existentialism.

As we have seen, Strauss's procedure allows him to state as if incidentally what Socratics had in common with the pre-Socratics. This proves to be a great deal: it includes the recognition of the need for esotericism; the recognition of the need to show that first things (whatever they might be) are not gods; recognition of the antithesis of nature and *nomos*; recognition of the deceptive character of the "world" of *nomos*; and recognition of the crucial philosophic need to accept one's mortality and that of all human accomplishment. The modern liberal, by contrast, has lost sight of all of these things. He is closest in thinking indeed to the sophist, with whom he proves to share an incoherent moralism, but lacks even the sophist's liberation from the rage of the many that moves in the direction of barbarism. The modern liberal manifests thereby evidence not of the progress that is ever on his lips, but of a regress. With his essay on Havelock Strauss points the way to a recovery of the insights that had been threatened to be permanently obscured by the victory of modern liberalism and further obscured by Heidegger, who sought to provide a way out of the deeply dissatisfying moral situation of modern man.

CHAPTER FIVE

Concluding Reflections on Moral-Political Reasoning in Contemporary Liberal Democracy

Our look at Strauss's understanding of modern democracy and of ancient and modern liberalism has led us to the beginning of a confrontation between the thought of Strauss and the thought of Heidegger. Both thinkers encourage the recognition of human greatness and the preservation of a humanity perceived to be threatened by the mass society that technological science has produced. Over and against Heidegger and his historicist followers, however, Strauss calls for a sustained recovery of an older political thinking, one that can be broadened and deepened by a liberal education in friendly confrontation with Socratic political philosophy. Yet that is a political thinking whose rootedness in an ancestral tradition is in most cases deepened and enriched, rather than replaced or redirected, by that confrontation. The confrontation is not intended to bring about in most cases a turning toward the philosophic life.[1] Still, there appears to be some agreement between Strauss and Heidegger on the need, for the sustaining of humanity and of human greatness or excellence among human beings generally, for "rootedness," over and against the "mass democracy" that the modern technological enterprise has brought into being. How are we to understand this rootedness in tradition, in the case of Strauss's recommendation, in contrast to that of Heidegger, and what would the political reasoning within a rooted tradition look like in contemporary liberal democracy?

---

1. *LAM* 9–10.

The most visible difference between Strauss and Heidegger concerns precisely a difference in understanding of the philosophic life of contemplation in its relation toward the "rooted" moral life of tradition. Heidegger sees Western philosophy (metaphysics) since Plato as leading in a catastrophic trajectory toward rootlessness, one merely accelerated by modern technology, a rootlessness synonymous with nihilism, the oblivion of being, or the "night of the world." He sees in the deep peril to humanity an equally deep possibility of a salvific transformation of human thinking. While agreeing with Heidegger on the need to face the present, "uprooted" situation squarely, Strauss sees its emergence and its relation to classical philosophy quite differently, and hence sees what is called for in that situation quite differently. He sees our situation as having emerged in the technological thinking of Enlightenment science, in a conscious, novel effort by modern philosophers to replace belief in divine providence and divine law of a creator God with human providence, by means of the human "conquest of nature." And he uncovers in ancient political philosophy not a neglect of the everyday world of Da-sein's care and hence of the manner in which Being uncovers itself, nor a (corresponding) taking for granted of the goodness or rightness of the theoretical life. He uncovers instead a recognition by Socrates and his students of the need to answer the question "Why science?" or "Why philosophy?" through the preliminary activity of dialectic, or "practical science." The prephilosophic or nonphilosophic life is deliberately presented and preserved, he found, in the writings of classical political philosophy, and the ascent from that life to the theoretical or philosophic way of life is quietly shown therein. Simultaneously those writings show how and why an understanding of the needs of the nonphilosophers must be met by and in a thoughtful life guided by their ancestral traditions, thoughtfully renewed to meet new circumstances and political challenges. Accordingly, while arguing for a "broadening and deepening" liberal education of democracy's citizens in the Great Books, Strauss's concrete proposal for contemporary political life goes very little beyond this; it is quite modest, and its watchword is "moderation." It includes a call for staunch defense of constitutionalism and prudence, over and against contemporary tyrannies, but no attempt to guide a political-moral transformation or revolution, by philosophic thought; in fact, he warns against attempts at such guidance, which Heidegger had attempted.

Strauss espied the intention of Heidegger's philosophizing to guide moral-political life fairly early.[2] He saw it as an effort to lead a radical

---

2. See "A Giving of Accounts" [1970], in *Jewish Philosophy and the Crisis of Modernity*, 461. After stating how impressed he was by Heidegger's courses at Freiburg (starting in

rerooting of human life through free, authentic, resolute decision that would allow those who made it to embrace, over and against the blandishments that global commerce, utilitarian thinking, and entertainment threatened to wipe out, the call of conscience, but of conscience atheistically understood. Heidegger eventually invited his fellow Germans to this radical and radically atheistic task in his rectoral address in 1933. A letter that Strauss wrote to Gerhard Krüger seventeen months before the delivery of that address[3] highlights what he characterizes as the indirectly communicated moral intention of Heidegger's philosophizing in *Being and Time*, and the individual freedom and sense of responsibility (for "our Dasein," as

---

1922), Strauss adds the following: "I disregard again the chronological order and explain in the most simple terms why in my opinion Heidegger won out over Husserl; he radicalized Husserl's critique of the school of Marburg and turned it against Husserl: what is primary is not the object of sense perception but the things which we handle and with which we are concerned, *pragmata*. What I could not stomach was his moral teaching, for despite his disclaimer, he had such a teaching. The key term is resoluteness without any indication as to what are the proper objects of resoluteness. There is a straight line which leads from Heidegger's resoluteness to his siding with the so-called Nazis in 1933."

3. Letter to Krüger, December 12, 1931, in "Leo Strauss: Gerhard Krüger Correspondence 1928–1962," trans. Jerome Veith, Anna Schmidt, and Susan M. Shell, in *The Strauss-Krüger Correspondence: Returning to Plato through Kant*, ed. Susan Meld Shell (New York: Palgrave, 2017), ch. 2, 13–88, at 31. Heidegger's politico-moral intention became quite clear, of course, with the publication of *Einführung in die Metaphysik* in 1933. See *Introduction to Metaphysics*, 40 (29 of the German): "This Europe, in its unholy blindness always on the point of cutting its own throat, lies today in the great pincers between Russia on the one side and America on the other. Russia and America, seen metaphysically, are both the same: the same hopeless frenzy of unchained technology and of the rootless organization of the average age man. . . . We lie in the pincers. Our people, as standing in the center, suffers the most intense pressure—our people, the people richest in neighbors and hence the most endangered people, and for all that, the metaphysical people. We are sure of this vocation; but this people will gain a fate from its vocation only when it creates in itself a resonance, a possibility of resonance for this vocation, and grasps its tradition creatively. All this implies that this people, as a historical people, must transpose itself—and with it the history of the West—from the center of their future happening into the originary realm of the powers of Being. Precisely if the great decision regarding Europe is not to go down the path of annihilation—precisely then can this decision come about only through the development of new, historically spiritual forces from the center." And see 52 (38 of the German): "Asking about beings as such and as a whole, asking the question of Being, is then one of the essential fundamental conditions for awakening the spirit, and thus for an originary world of historical Dasein, and thus for subduing the danger of the darkening of the world, and thus for taking over the historical mission of our people, the people of the center of the West."

Heidegger puts it) for which Heidegger intended that work to serve as the foundation:

> In the meantime, I have read a bit in *Being and Time*. Whatever you wish to say about the book *sub specie veritatis*, it expresses the essence of modernity in the purest manner, i.e. *the* modern reservation against Greeks, Jews, and Christians. By the way, nothing appears to depict the inner difficulty of the book more clearly than the passages about Yorck: the latter's words on the moral intention of all philosophy seem to me to be cited with the intention of "communicating indirectly" what is also decisive for Heidegger. In your reading, one must apparently interpret in favor of the defendant [pro reo] Heidegger's direct statements about philosophy not being able to make any authoritative pronouncement [Machtspruch] and other such things. Because the passages from Yorck are not just cited for fun.

The "modern reservation" to which Strauss alludes is a reservation against doctrines that entail a divine being or beings as the cause of both beings and of the knowledge of beings, which Heidegger took to have its origin in Plato yet to have taken place under the sheltering Greek "guard" of belief in gods.[4] Heidegger's presentation of "being-toward-death" and his atheistic analysis of the phenomenon of the conscience is, Strauss is suggesting, meant to prepare the new conscientiousness, in moral-political action, of which Yorck speaks in the quotations. Strauss would appear especially to have in mind this quotation of Yorck:

---

4. The passage Strauss has in mind with regard to Yorck appears somewhere in section 77 of *Being and Time* (Stambaugh translation, 364–368; 398–403 of *Sein und Zeit*), which has long quotes of letters from Yorck to Dilthey. See also "The Living Issues of Postwar German Philosophy," 125: "Historical studies are necessary because of the bankruptcy of modern man. That bankruptcy was asserted by a large number of people—it implied a less fatalistic view of the same facts which had given birth to the title 'Decline of the West.' To mention one example only: Yorck von Wartenburg in his correspondence with Dilthey which was published in 1926, had said: modern man is finished and just fit to be buried; the movement which had begun in the Renaissance or earlier, has come to its close; enthusiastic pupils of Heidegger said that Martin Heidegger marks the end of the epoch which was opened by another Martin, Martin Luther."

To dissolve elemental public opinion and, if possible, to make possible the shaping of individuality in seeing and regarding, would be a pedagogical task for the state. Then instead of a so-called public conscience—instead of this radical external-ization—individual conscience, i.e., conscience, would again become powerful.[5]

This moral intention of Heidegger's philosophizing was arguably visible already in the memorial address for Paul Natorp with which Heidegger begins his 1924–25 lecture course at Marburg on Plato's *Sophist*. (Natorp, a member of the Marburg School of neo-Kantians, had died over the holidays.) Close to the end of that memorial, Heidegger says the following:

Natorp was one of the few and one of the first, indeed perhaps the only one among German professors, who more than ten years ago understood what the young people of Germany wanted when in the fall of 1913 they gathered at Hohen Meifsner and pledged to form their lives out of inner truthfulness and self-responsibility. Many of these best have fallen. But whoever has eyes to see knows that today our Dasein is slowly being transposed upon new foundations and that young people have their part to play in this task. Natorp understood them, and so they are the best ones to preserve his memory.[6]

The difference between the two thinkers concerning the relation of philosophy and moral-political rootedness comes into clearer focus by con-trasting this memorial for Natorp with Strauss's "Memorial Remarks for Jason Aronson"[7] (1961), which contain the following, strikingly different, remarks on one of his recently deceased students:

We are struck by the awesome, unfathomable experience of death, of the death of one near and dear to us. We are grieved particularly because our friend died so young—when he was

---

5. *Being and Time*, trans. Stambaugh, 369 (*Sein und Zeit*, 403).

6. Heidegger, *Platon: Sophistes*; *Plato's Sophist*, 3–4.

7. Published as appendix 3 of *Jewish Philosophy and the Crisis of Modernity*, 475–76.

about to come into his own, to enter on a career which would have made him esteemed beyond the circle of his friends here and elsewhere and his pupils in the Liberal Arts Program. It is not given to me to say words of comfort of my own. I can only try to say what, I believe, Jason Aronson had come to know. I saw him for the last time about three weeks ago in my office. He knew where he stood. He jokingly reminded me of an old joke: all men are mortal but some more than others. He decided bravely and wisely to continue his study of Shaftesbury. At his suggestion we agreed that we would read the Bible together, starting from the beginning.

Death is terrible, terrifying, but we cannot live as human beings if this terror grips us to the point of corroding our core. Jason Aronson had two experiences which protected him against this corrosive as well as its kin. The one is to come to grips with the corrosives, to face them, to think them through, to understand the ineluctable necessities, and to understand that without them no life, no human life, no good life, is possible. Slowly, step by step, but with ever greater sureness and awakeness did he begin to become a philosopher. I do not know whether he knew the word of a man of old: may my soul die the death of the philosophers, but young as he was he died that death.

The other experience which gave him strength and depth was his realizing ever more clearly and profoundly what it means to be a son of the Jewish people—of the 'am 'olam—to have one's roots deep in the oldest past and to be committed to a future beyond all futures. He did not permit his mind to stifle the voice of his heart nor his heart to give commands to his mind.

I apply to his life the daring, gay, and noble motto: *courte et bonne*—his life was short and good. We shall never forget him and for what he stood.

I address to his wife, his mother, and brother, and his sister the traditional Jewish formula: "May God comfort you among the others who mourn for Zion and Jerusalem."

Any observations on this eulogy—which begins with a reflection on death, through the experience of the death of a friend, as awesome and unfathomable—however tentative, run the risk of being indelicate where Strauss is very delicate. But they can help us to understand the differences, which Strauss shows elsewhere a desire to convey, between himself and Heidegger, on the general directions of philosophy and of rootedness. We confine ourselves to the contrast, left implicit, that the eulogy draws between the two anticorrosive experiences in response to death and its "terror" that the young student underwent—neither of which concerns a renewed moral turn to "inner truthfulness and self-responsibility." The first experience he puts in the present tense, "is"; the contrast with the past tense, "was," in which he puts his description of the second experience, indicates the universal and timeless possibility of the first experience. That first experience concerns the knowledge that the student came to have and its effect on him concerning death—his resignation to it as one of the "ineluctable necessities" and his coming to understand that without them "no life, no human life, no good life, is possible." The knowledge led the student, with "ever greater sureness and awakeness" to *begin* to "become a philosopher." Strauss speaks of this path not as part of a movement to determine a new and unprecedented future for a people or for humanity, but as an instance of something attested to by a "word of a man of old," the death of the philosopher, as the type of death to be wished for.[8]

The second experience of which Strauss speaks against the corrosive terror of death is the "strength and depth" that the student acquired through "realizing ever more clearly and profoundly what it means to be a son of the Jewish people," a son of the " *'am 'olam*," or eternal people. The Hebrew term reinforces the shift to the particular. Strauss clarifies what it means for such a one to have "one's roots deep in the oldest past" and being "committed to a future beyond all futures." That the student realized ever more clearly what this means, of course, does not mean that this particular student became a more devout Jew. In fact, nothing suggests clearly that he did. (That on the student's initiative he and Strauss agreed to read the Bible together "from the beginning" tells us nothing of the content of that reading. This information is conveyed, moreover, together with Strauss's offering an

---

8. See also Strauss's letter to Gershom Scholem, November 22, 1960, in *Gesammelte Schriften*, 3:742: "You are a blessed man because you have achieved a harmony of mind and heart on such a high level, and you are a blessing to every Jew now living. As a consequence, you have the right and the duty to speak up. Unfortunately, I am constitutionally unable to follow you—or if you wish, I too have sworn to a flag, the oath to the flag being (in the beautiful Arabic Latin created by some of our ancestors, which to Cicero would appear to be *in ultimate turpitudinis*): *moriatur anima mea mortem philosophorum.*"

example of the student's droll sense of humor even in the face of death, and telling us that the student decided, "bravely and wisely" to continue with his study of *Shaftesbury*.) The student's realization may indicate deepening awareness of the sacrifice of such devotion entailed in his slowly becoming a philosopher. The indications are that he was "deepened," in any event, in the anticorrosive experience of his "realization" about his Jewish root, at the same time that he was becoming a philosopher.

In both cases an experience of and explanation of *time*, as what was and is and will be, is integral to the two anticorrosive experiences in the face of death. It is so in clearly different and even contrary ways. The one who is beginning to become a philosopher, who is engaged in what is a slow and uneasy task, comes eventually to accept death as one of the "ineluctable necessities" that make life, a good life, possible; the good life is in fact one of increasing awakeness to and acceptance of those necessities. As necessities, these must be "the oldest things," by nature, themselves; they cannot not be. They are the object of *theoria*. The "oldest past" in which the Jew as Jew has his "roots" is, by contrast, the lived "past" of a *people*— of a people, moreover, that in this case understands the world as having its origin *not* in necessities but in creation *ex nihilo*,[9] creation followed by the divine choosing of this one people, after having scattered the hitherto homogeneous human race, at Babel, into peoples. And according to this understanding of what has been, as this people's past, the God who created the world has given "commands" to His chosen people. His divine commands are moral commands. Strauss here speaks of "commands" as commands of the student's "heart," and of the student having not permitted such commands to direct his "mind." The heart would impede the mind, while the mind might "stifle" the heart. The contrast between the two directions of life, and their respective guidance by a specific sense of time, is manifest. One may say that Strauss lets them stand in their necessary, implicit, and fruitful tension, while Heidegger, intent on overcoming the problem of global dominion of technology, wishes to found, through the elaboration of the phenomenological structure of *existenz*, a universal education and new rootedness that would somehow *combine* the two.

Having said in his first paragraph that "it is not given to me to say words of comfort of my own," Strauss speaks in conclusion words of comfort to the members of the student's family that are indeed not his own but are rather the "traditional Jewish formula." It is a formula that would transform

---

9. See above, chapter 3, p. 106, note 59.

their mourning for the loss of their son into a mourning for *Jerusalem*—for what Strauss elsewhere (in the opening of "Jerusalem and Athens") calls "the Holy City, the City of Righteousness." The formula is "May God comfort you among the others who mourn for Zion and Jerusalem." It is an expression of comfort for the mourning relatives that calls them to understand their loss in the light of something high or noble of which their husband/son/brother was a part and that guided him—at least until, and as a path to, philosophy—in his particular life.

Judaism and its fundamental source, the Bible, is an exemplary case of the prephilosophic traditions that guide moral life. It, and not a new kind of brave decisionism—the only references to bravery and decision Strauss makes here are with respect to the student's continued study of Shaftesbury—offer the kind of hopeful guidance that the human *heart* desires in the face of death. It is a prime example in the West of the rich traditions guiding those whom political philosophy makes its friendly interlocutors. It speaks to and through the heart, offering comforts to one as a member of a people, not the least of which is immortality, or a "future beyond all futures." A philosopher inevitably grows up in such a tradition and under its care; it initially shields him from the corrosive of death's terror; it affords him his *first* education. But as we have seen, his ascent is to a rare cosmopolitanism that accepts death as a necessity.[10]

It is clear from this and all we have seen that, and why, Strauss, in contrast to Heidegger, does not offer philosophy as providing any morally edifying guidance to political life, even in the present situation. Philosophy does not have available to it, as philosophy, the kind of guidance that political life needs and cannot help but need.[11] The moderns, up to and

---

10. On this cosmopolitanism, see Strauss, "Social Science and Humanism," in *The Rebirth of Classical Political Rationalism*, 7: "By reflecting on what it means to be a human being, one sharpens one's awareness of what is common to all human beings, if in different degrees, and of the goals toward which all human beings are directed by the fact that they are human beings. One transcends the horizon of the mere citizen—of every kind of sectionalism—and becomes a citizen of the world. Humanism as awareness of man's distinctive character as well as of man's distinctive completion, purpose, or duty issues in humaneness: in the earnest concern for both human kindness and the betterment and opening of one's mind—a blend of firm delicacy and hard-won serenity—a last and not merely last freedom from the degradation or hardening effected especially by conceit or pretense." See also "Kurt Riezler, 1882–1955," 5–7, 10–11.

11. See *NRH* 153: "The simply good, which is what is good by nature and which is radically distinct from the ancestral, must be transformed into the politically good, which

including Heidegger, failed to grasp this. As we have seen, toward the end of his talk on liberal education Strauss presents our "awesome situation," in which "we have lost all simply authoritative traditions in which we could trust," as caused by the fact that "our immediate teachers and teachers' teachers believed in the possibility of a simply rational society." "Each of us here," he states frankly, "is compelled to find his bearings by his own powers, however defective they may be." But as we have seen, he immediately warns that "we have no comfort other than that inherent in this activity. Philosophy, we have learned, must be on its guard against the wish to be edifying—philosophy can only be intrinsically edifying."[12] The needed edification is to be found not in philosophy, but rather in whatever remnants of rooted, authoritative traditions remain and are capable of being gathered up and renewed. For the fact that "all simply authoritative traditions" have been lost does not rule out the possibility that traditions may again come to have a significant role in nonphilosophic lives of excellence or greatness, and more broadly in the older political reasoning required for democracy.

What, then, would the role of tradition, on one hand, and of the study of political philosophy, on the other, have in the preparation of those citizens who might come to set the tone of democracy and thereby sustain and improve it?

Certainly presenting examples of greatness, including the ability to articulate the cause of genuine greatness over and against the rule of a powerful tyrant—and examples of greatness in the modern world are not lacking since Churchill[13]—important as they are, can only begin the required liberal

---

is, as it were, the quotient of the simply good and the ancestral: the politically good is what 'removes a vast mass of evil without shocking a vast mass of prejudice.' It is in this necessity that the need for inexactness in political or moral matters is partly founded."

12. *LAM* 8.

13. See especially the work of Daniel Mahoney and F. Flagg Taylor. Greatness has lately become a theme of the Republican Party in America, but the greatness Strauss had in mind is not the preserve of any particular political party. It is manifest, for example in the first part of Washington's Farewell Address, in Lincoln's Second Inaugural, and in Kennedy's Inaugural, and in an episode from Lyndon Johnson's presidency. In 1966 France's President Charles de Gaulle had ordered that American forces all be removed from France. Johnson ordered Secretary of State Dean Rusk to ask de Gaulle whether

education of citizens that democracy needs. Strauss indicates as much with his statement that Churchill's *Marlborough* is "not a whit less important" than the defeat of the Nazi tyranny.[14] For—in addition to what we have noted in chapter 3—he therein seriously qualifies his praise of the singular greatness of Churchill's defeat of Nazi tyranny. It makes perfect sense to do so, of course, if even the noblest deeds of war are a means to peace—if, that is, not the cultivation of "blood and soil" but the "cultivation of the mind," and the serious reflection that is its peak, is the end of civilized life.[15] And we citizens of liberal democracy, facing an unprecedented situation, are especially in need of such cultivation of the mind. On one hand, it is the regime in which both philosophy and decent political life, and even human greatness, have been preserved. Yet the modern attempt to bring about a society based on a rational ethics has resulted in a mass society whose characteristics are repulsive to those whose deeply human longing for a moral life find little support for it in public life, and who for that very reason have been, and remain, attracted to the destruction of Western civilization.

No serious student of Strauss would think that the situation that he limned in the works we have examined can be answered if it and its deepest causes are ignored or not fully understood, and if serious moral thinking is not devoted to responding to it. Such thinking must now entail not

---

this included the removal of American soldiers *buried* in France. When Rusk demurred, Johnson ordered him: "*Ask him about the cemeteries, Dean.*" Recounted in Thomas J. Schoenbaum, *Waging Peace and War: Dean Rusk in the Truman, Kennedy, and Johnson Years* (Ann Arbor, MI: Simon and Schuster, 1988), 421. Johnson had served as a lieutenant commander and received the Silver Star and the Presidential Medal of Freedom. The deep sense of devotion to the fallen that he was expressing is well captured in this video montage: " 'Hymn to the Fallen' by John Williams," RemySwiss YouTube channel, uploaded August 5, 2011, https://www.youtube.com/watch?v=Omd9_FJnerY.

14. Harry V. Jaffa, in his otherwise helpful discussion of Strauss's encomium of Churchill, omits this astonishing statement; he limits himself to saying that "Strauss also paid tribute to Churchill's writings, 'above all his *Marlborough*,' for "their inexhaustible mine of political wisdom and understanding." See Jaffa, "The Legacy of Leo Strauss: A Review of *Studies in Platonic Political Philosophy*, by Leo Strauss," *Claremont Review of Books* 3, no. 3 (1984).

15. See "German Nihilism," 365: "The term civilisation designates at once the process of making man a citizen, and not a slave; an inhabitant of cities, and not a rustic; a lover of peace, and not of war; a polite being, and not a ruffian." See also *The City and Man*, 147, 156, 159, 235–36; *The Argument and Action of Plato's "Laws,"* 6, 105–106, 117; and Xenophon, *Anabasis* 2.6.4–7 (on Clearchus).

only an attempt to understand the ends and means that have informed the West, and a (much-needed) recognition of the West's relative successes and accomplishments, especially in constitutional government, but also an attempt to understand the modern West's genuine shortcomings, and how they might best be addressed. Even to begin to understand the changes that have taken place, since the advent of modernity, in our lives in the West requires now an education in the texts of the Western tradition. Strauss presents the means to these ends as genuine liberal education—education that aims to understand, through reasoned thought and debate, the human condition and our particular situation within liberal democracy. And as everything we have seen indicates, Strauss considers that education to be, not in just any tradition, but of a unique tradition, one that has within it two poles, "Jerusalem and Athens," East and West, existing in uneasy but fruitful tension with one another. For he recognized within the biblical tradition a serious, most reflective, and therefore most radical, alternative to rationalism—not of the modern variety but of the true, classical variety. We therefore conclude with some considerations that may help thoughtful proponents of the Western "tradition" understand both parts of the "fruitful tension."

As we have seen, what made the support that classical philosophy offered to classical aristocracy desirable is something that may still be cultivated by the "aristocracy within democracy" that Strauss recommends: the gentlemen's justification of their leisured activity rested on a dim perception of what is best simply for a human being, the life that deserves to be called best, or that constitutes human perfection, and hence their perception of a high or noble human activity that is good in itself rather than instrumentally good. This does not mean that the philosopher found the moral life of the gentleman to be the natural perfection of man.[16] But it does mean that the gentleman could see in the philosophic life the noble leisure for which he longed and sensed as his own goal. It can thereby offer a sufficient common ground to be able to afford philosophy the dialectical activity that it needs to justify itself, and a political defense of philosophy that allowed it to find

---

16. See the 1946 general seminar on Natural Right (Patard, 404); Strauss, letter to Klein, 25 July 1939, in Leo Strauss, *Gesammelte Schriften*, bd. 3, ed. Heinrich Meier (Stuttgart: J. B. Metzler, 2001), 574 (Patard, 29). See also Strauss's letter to Kojève, April 22, 1957, in *On Tyranny*, 275. And see "A Giving of Accounts," in *Jewish Philosophy and the Crisis of Modernity*, 463–64. See also Aristotle, *Nichomachean Ethics* 1177b31–32, 1178a10, 1178a13–14, 1178a21–22.

a home within the city—from Greece to Rome to the cities of medieval Christendom. And the example of the activity of philosophizing could, in turn, humanize the gentleman's political life.

Strauss found in the deeds and speeches of not only aristocratic gentlemen but of *all* serious prephilosophic life the same awareness of *sacred* restraints, explicit or implicit reliance on revelation of providential gods,[17] and deference to divine law, that he found, in a more thoughtfully

---

17. See *NRH*, 130: "Man's freedom is accompanied by a sacred awe, by a kind of divination that not everything is permitted. We may call this awe-inspired fear 'man's natural conscience.' Restraint is therefore as natural or as primeval as freedom." See also *On Tyranny*, 192: "Kojève knows as well as anyone living that Hegel's fundamental teaching regarding master and slave is based on Hobbes' doctrine of the state of nature. If Hobbes' doctrine of the state of nature is abandoned *en pleine connaissance de cause* (as indeed it should be abandoned), Hegel's fundamental teaching will lose the evidence which it apparently still possesses for Kojève. Hegel's teaching is much more sophisticated than Hobbes', but it is as much a construction as the latter. Both doctrines construct human society by starting from the untrue assumption that man as man is thinkable as a being that lacks awareness of sacred restraints or as a being that is guided by nothing but a desire for recognition." A lack of awareness of sacred restraints would seem, however, to characterize those "noble" but decidedly impious Athenians to whom Strauss refers in *The City and Man* (212–13) when he tells us that "Thucydides presents to us a galaxy of outstanding Athenians—outstanding by intelligence or sheer cleverness and efficiency, by nobility of character or *hubris*." Yet this statement occurs in a section of Strauss's essay subtitled "The Athenian Tragedy," a section that Strauss later tells us is misleading: "The agreement between Thucydides and Pericles is less complete than the argument of the preceding section assumed. In a word, that argument is too 'poetic' in Thucydides' sense to be in ultimate agreement with his thought" (227). As he then goes on to say, "in a language which is not that of Thucydides, there is something reminding of religion in Athenian imperialism" (229). And a bit later, he adds that the "universalism" of Periclean Athens, which aims at everlasting glory, and the "universalism" of Thucydides, which aims at "understanding the universal and sempiternal things, seeing through the delusions by which the healthy city stands or falls," even if the latter suffuses the former, cannot be synthesized: "The 'synthesis' of the two universalisms is indeed impossible. It is of the utmost importance that this impossibility be understood" (230). Finally, see *The City and Man*, 240:

> Neither according to the classical philosophers nor according to Thucydides is the concern with the divine simply the primary concern of the city, but the fact that it is primary "for us," from the point of view of the city, is brought out more clearly by Thucydides than by the philosophers. It suffices to remember what Thucydides tells us about oracles, earthquakes,

and eclipses, Nicias' deeds and sufferings, the Spartans' compunctions, the affair of Cylon, the aftermath of the battle of Delium, and the purification of Delos, in brief, all these things for which the modern scientific historian has no use or which annoy him, and to which classical political philosophy barely alludes because for it the concern with the divine has become identical with philosophy. We would have great difficulty in doing justice to this remote or dark side of the city but for the work of men like Fustel de Coulanges above all others who have made us see the city as it primarily understood itself as distinguished from the manner in which it was exhibited by classical political philosophy: the holy city in contradistinction to the natural city. Our gratitude is hardly diminished by the fact that Fustel De Coulanges, his illustrious predecessors, Hegel above all, and his numerous successors, have failed to pay proper attention to the philosophic concept of the city as exhibited in classical political philosophy. For what is "first for us" is not the philosophic understanding of the city but that understanding which is inherent in the city as such, in the pre-philosophic city in accordance with which the city sees itself as subject and subservient to the divine in the ordinary understanding of the divine or looks up to it.

It is nonetheless fair to ask whether men of Churchill's greatness of soul spoke and acted within such sacred restraints. The evidence strongly suggests that Churchill himself not only did so, but called for such restraints over and against the fruits of technology. In "Fifty Years Hence," (*Thoughts and Adventures,* ed. by James W. Muller [Wilmington: ISI Books, 2009], 292), after describing inventions of technological science that he (presciently) foresaw, Churchill expresses the hope that "the laws of a Christian civilization will prevent" their sinister use. And a bit later (at 295) he argues that "there was never a time when the inherent virtue of human beings required more strong and confident expression in daily life; there never was a time when the hope of immortality and the disdain of earthly power and achievement were more necessary for the safety of the children of men." For an illustration of Churchill's use of the older reasoning, recommended by Strauss, in political oratory, one need look no further than his speech in Fulton Missouri ("The Sinews of Peace," or the "Iron Curtain" speech), to which Strauss refers in his classroom praise of Churchill quoted in chapter 1 above. Toward the beginning of that speech, Churchill says the following: "What, then, is the over-all strategic concept which we should inscribe today? It is nothing less than the safety and welfare, the freedom and progress, of all the homes and families of all the men and women in all the lands. And here I speak particularly of the myriad cottage or apartment homes where the wage-earner strives amid the accidents and difficulties of life to guard his wife and children from privation and bring the family up in the fear of the Lord, or upon ethical conceptions which often play their potent part." A bit later, again, Churchill addresses the matter of famine in the aftermath of World War II: "If the dangers of war and tyranny are removed, there is no doubt that science and co-operation

anti-philosophic and hence consistent version, in the Bible.[18] Yet given the prevalence of the alternative thesis according to which modernity represents a secularization of a postclassical, Christian morality, it is reasonable to ask: Is the non-biblical morality of the ancient gentlemanly political actors and interlocutors really such as to retain any relevance for the two philosophic ends for which they are worthy partners, or for the much-needed moral reasoning of contemporary citizens and statesmen? In its moral form, as Strauss himself has noted, the realm of political reasoning, the serious erotic call from within awareness of mortality surely takes two distinct paths: what we may call a deprecation of human achievement and hence the overthrow

---

can bring in the next few years to the world, certainly in the next few decades newly taught in the sharpening school of war, an expansion of material well-being beyond anything that has yet occurred in human experience." He then quotes his friend Bourke Cockran. "There is enough for all. The earth is a generous mother; she will provide in plentiful abundance food for all her children if they will but cultivate her soil in justice and in peace." He leaves his listeners to note or not to note the difference between the earth as a "generous mother" and the need for "science" to bring about the unheard-of prosperity that he anticipates.

18. See Leo Strauss, "The Frame of Reference in the Social Sciences," the New School, 1945, box 14, folder 10, Leo Strauss Papers; edited by Svetozar Minkov as part 1 of Colen and Minkov, "Leo Strauss on Social and Natural Science," 627:

> Yet the two radically different ways, the Greek way and the Hebrew way, have a common basis. This common basis shows itself if we go back from the peaks to the roots: from Plato's dialogues to Lycurgus as the Spartans saw him, from Jesyah or Paul to Moses as the Hebrews saw him. Provisionally expressed, the common basis is the notion of a divine law, a notion that can be shown to be a necessary consequence or a more thoughtful expression of what all peoples originally mean when they speak of their way. For "our way" is the ancestral way, the way of our ancestors, but it doesn't make sense to cling to the way of our ancestors if our ancestors were not superior to us. And superiority to us ultimately means superiority to human beings as such, that is to say, divinity.
>
> The notion of divine law became questionable in the moment when man became sufficiently familiar with the variety of ancestral or divine ways, or with the contradiction between these ways. Out of this experience, there arose the idea of nature and the idea of science.

See also NRH, ch. 3, "Origin of the Idea of Natural Right."

of the mighty, on one hand, and the exaltation of human greatness, on the other. The first, which is dominant in democracies, ancient and modern, entails humility and repentance for reliance on human prudence, and a focus on human weakness and the obligation to redeem oneself by attending to the weak. The latter, more dominant in aristocracies, focuses on human greatness in moral matters, and human admiration of that greatness. Strauss must then have found the genuine virtues of the former sort, later elevated by Christianity, to be fully present in the ancient city. And indeed, Strauss found them there.[19] We have already noted the deep and crucial agreement that he found between the love of the noble and the love of justice, in their self-sacrificial character. He thus found the two paths to share considerable common ground within the classical city. But beyond this, he found that its inhabitants were fully aware of the fact that the promotion of the arts, or of human prudence in general, were a means of ameliorating their situation and pursuing good things that tended against the claimed sufficiency of obedience to divine law.

But it may be helpful to note other aspects of the ancient morality of which Strauss speaks that one would expect to flow from such fundamental agreement. Of particular interest is the fact that Strauss moves from Aristotle to Plato to Thucydides in his *The City and Man* in order to uncover the prephilosophic reasoning that he had, since studying with Husserl, been attempting to uncover.[20] That uncovering includes careful attention to Thucydides's presentation of the gods and of the memorials of the perfect beginning preserved in high political life—the sacred—and of the poets who attempted to provide comprehensive, powerful, moving articulations of the world that support the belief in a past when human beings were not at all compelled to attend to their interests by evildoing, an articulation that would ensure that devotion to the common good, and hence free sacrifice

---

19. Perception of them, it must be noted, is obstructed in our day by the Nietzschean tendency to stress the differences between the "master morality" and "slave morality," the better to make the case against modernity's leveling efforts to abolish suffering—a case made the more plausible by the widespread thesis that modernity is a "secularization" of Christianity.

20. See *The City and Man*, 240: "The quest for that 'common sense' understanding of political things which led us first to Aristotle's *Politics*, leads us eventually to Thucydides' *War of the Peloponnesians and the Athenians*."

of one's own good for the good of others, is possible and worthwhile.[21] He points especially to Thucydides's focus on Nicias,[22] who held that the gods punish in accord with desert, and, having punished, can reasonably be hoped to show pity, not only to the soldiers under him but to himself, who had practiced piety to gods and justice to men, or had, as Thucydides puts it, spent his entire life practicing what is held by law to be virtue.[23]

He finds that the Socratic Xenophon, similarly, in his account of the 10,000 Greeks who followed the younger Cyrus in an effort to overthrow his brother, not only presents the Spartan Clearchus attempting to teach the Persian Tissaphernes the effects of a troubled conscience on those who are conscious in themselves they have violated a sacred oath, but later presents himself (Xenophon), as the new leader of the Greeks, suggesting to his men that they can understand a particular failure suffered by a group of noble-loving Greeks on the ground that "the god" wishes both to humble

---

21. This is not to suggest that Strauss finds Thucydides to present these poets—as opposed, for example, to the Biblical redactors—attempting or intending to present *all* human vice, much less all evil, as due to human fault, or to make human beings infinitely responsible. They tend rather to trace its existence to an inscrutable divine wisdom. The poets nevertheless sustain or uphold the understanding of prephilosophic men according to which the first or immortal things are caring gods, an understanding which explains the prescriptions given by a community's authority in a manner consistent with moral obligation or responsibility, or which makes the human race responsible for evil. The difference between the poets and the Biblical redactors may be said to be this: the latter make an attempt (through, e.g., the account of the fall, the deprecation of cities, the presentation of God as unknowable or altogether mysterious, and the consistent abstention from terms like "nature," "necessity," and "doubt") to preclude the search for truth that characterizes Thucydides's activity, an attempt which, however, demonstrates an awareness of that activity; the Bible is deliberately consistent with the prephilosophic understanding, or deliberately opposed to philosophy. See "Progress or Return?," in *The Rebirth of Classical Political Rationalism*, especially 256.

22. *The City and Man*, 202n68.

23. Thucydides 7.77.1–4 with 7.86.5. Nor is Nicias's virtue by any means unique to him or the Athenians. His understanding of things belongs also to the Spartans (7.18.2–4), and the virtue of the very Syracusans against whom he was fighting included the practice of mercy toward enemies, as, for example, Diodorus Siculus shows in the speech of Nicolaüs the Syracusan calling for mercy for the vanquished Athenian invaders, who had killed all of his living sons: see Diodorus Siculus, *Bibliotheca historica*, ed. Immanuel Bekker, Ludwig Dindorf, Friedrich Vogel, Theodor Fischer (Leipzig: B.G. Teubneri, 1893), 13.2.19–27.

those who speak "big" or haughtily, with mere human prudence, and to honor those who, like himself, "begin with the gods" in all things. Nor did Xenophon, whose own awareness was permeated by attention to necessities, think it wise to omit from his rule the sharp and immediate punishment of a mule driver who, tasked with the duty of carrying a sick and dying fellow soldier, "one of us," had attempted cynically to use the sacred law of burial to dispose of the burden by burying the man alive. The estate that Xenophon later built for himself at Scillus even has as its peak a temple to Artemis, and while the inscription on it contains a reminder of the decay of all things, including the decay of the sacred temple itself, that reminder is conveyed as part of the goddess's command to keep up the temple's repair. Xenophon could, similarly, easily become the guest-friend of the pious and compassionate Spartan Cleander, and have as a murderous enemy the ruthless "Machiavellian" Spartan Aristarchus.[24]

Aristocratic virtue would similarly include, in our day, a recognition of weakness and of the role of fortune in human affairs, and an attempt, not indeed to overcome fortune, but to mitigate its effects. As it includes "crushing the arrogant," it includes "sparing the vanquished." As it recognizes the need to fight just wars, it does not consider war anything good in itself.[25] And such virtue will in our day include a much more heightened awareness of the arbitrary character of claims to superiority made by entrenched classes, especially of those with no evidence of concern for genuine human excellence. Finally, it will be marked by a devotion to divine law and by a corresponding freedom from "ideology"—from the guidance of its moral reasoning by any claims, of left or right, to have access to a scientifically or philosophically grounded morality.

Yet if Strauss's concern is to preserve a relation between philosophy and the moral-religious life and its traditions, his Christian readers may find it odd that he omits from his account of liberal education the medieval Christian understanding of it; one hears nothing from him, for example, of the trivium or quadrivium, whose roots may even be said to be traceable to book 7 of Plato's *Republic* and the peak of which is the contemplative life. But Strauss understood that version of contemplation to be an attempted synthesis of the West's biblical and philosophic roots, rather than an example of their fruitful tension. The original source of this synthesis is what

---

24. Xenophon, *Anabasis* 2.5.7; 6.3.8; 5.8.8–12; 5.3.13; 6.6.34–37, 7.2.5–6, and 7.12.12–16. See Strauss, "Xenophon's *Anabasis*," in *Studies in Platonic Political Philosophy*, ch. 5.

25. "German Nihilism," 373, 369.

Strauss describes as the political defense of philosophy; the home that Plato had made for philosophy by such efforts as that of book 10 of his *Laws* had been very successful in the Christian West, but, as Strauss said, with reference to the recent recovery of the question "Why philosophy?" those efforts were "perhaps too successful." That is, he found it necessary, in light of the present assault on reason, to return to the source and to indicate what he understood their true relation to be. His work on the thought of medieval Arab and Jewish philosophers, motivated by his search for a premodern rationalism, uncovered a tradition in which philosophy or the contemplative life was not taken for granted, but had undergone the same subjection to the tribunal of the city and its laws that had, he subsequently discovered, characterized the Socratic turn. He found there the question "Is philosophy forbidden, permitted, or commanded by the law?" instead of the opening question in Thomas Aquinas's *Summa Theologicae*, "Whether, besides philosophy, anything further doctrine is necessary?"—a question that takes for granted that philosophy or science ought to be pursued, or overlooks its questionable character.[26] Christians can rightly point with pride to the long tradition of high learning that Christian universities have nourished and sustained, but just as Christians would do well to be cautious of the embrace of modern political philosophy and its doctrines—to become more aware of the anti-biblical origins of modern, technological natural science and modern political philosophy—so too they might take advantage of the shattering of the tradition of philosophy, achieved, in the wake of Heidegger, by Strauss, to recover the original understanding of philosophy, of the original purpose of political philosophy, and of the radically different, deep understanding conveyed by the Bible. Strauss for his part made great efforts to understand the Bible on its own terms, thereby reinvigorating the biblical tradition that offered the East within the West, a tradition that had been confined by various accommodations and concessions to modernity and its "higher" biblical criticism.[27] And his recovery of classical political philosophy permitted him to see the great alternative to philosophy that is present in

---

26. See *Persecution and the Art of Writing*, 19–20.

27. See "On the Interpretation of Genesis," in *Jewish Philosophy and the Crisis of Modernity*, 359–76, and "Jerusalem and Athens: Some Preliminary Reflections," in *Jewish Philosophy and the Crisis of Modernity*, 377–405. For outstanding examples of serious engagement with the Bible by Strauss's students, see especially Thomas L. Pangle, *Political Philosophy and the God of Abraham* (Baltimore: Johns Hopkins University Press, 2003), and Leon R. Kass, *The Beginning of Wisdom: Reading Genesis* (New York: Simon and Schuster, 2003).

the Bible, rather than assuming, as do our contemporary postmodernists, that the biblical God is the "God of reason" who must be rejected together with reason. Instead of awaiting, in a new thinking, a new god to "save us"—the god that lies behind Heidegger's claim that *ex nihilo et a nihilo omnia fiunt*[28]—doubting Christians might instead return to that God whose call they have hitherto neglected. Strauss's liberation from the historicism that had appeared to make possible a "new thinking" within religious orthodoxy, as attempted by his friend Franz Rosensweig,[29] likewise strengthens the case of those who seek a genuine return to the beliefs of their tradition rather than a return that in fact does not take seriously the fundamental truths of that tradition, such as creation, revelation, and all other miracles. And it allows them to resist the related temptation to think that, without further ado, they can adopt the metaphysics of Aristotle or Thomas Aquinas or Dun Scotus as they wish; as a kind of perspectivalism, such adoption is a version of historicism, at the bottom of which is human constructivism or "aesthetic" creativity of the will.

Finally, the critique Strauss offers of German nihilist youth is one that applies to contemporary postmodernist critics of liberal democracy, who likewise oppose science, reason, the notion of a single truth—in however apparently tame or academic a manner. Nihilism opposes science or reason

---

28. Strauss, "The Problem of Socrates," 327–29.

29. Strauss's first book, *Spinoza's Critique of Religion,* is dedicated to the memory of Rosenzweig. Between 1922 and 1925 Strauss worked at the *Freies Jüdisches Lehrhaus* in Frankfurt-am-Main, founded by Rosenzweig, and published articles in *Der Jude* and the *Jüdische Rundschau.* English translations of these are available in part 2 of *Leo Strauss: The Early Writings, 1921–1932,* trans. and ed. Michael Zank (Albany: State University of New York Press, 2002), 63–137. On the relation between Rosenzweig and Heidegger, Strauss recommends (in note 14 of his 1965 preface to *Spinoza's Critique of Religion*) Karl Löwith's *Gesammelte Abhandlungen: Zur Kritik der geschichtlichen Existenz* (Stuttgart: Kohlhammer, 1960), 68–92. The German title of the essay to which Strauss is referring is "M. Heidegger und F. Rosenzweig, ein Nachtrag zu 'Sein und Zeit.'" An English translation of this essay appeared as "M. Heidegger and F. Rosenzweig, or Temporality and Eternity," in *Philosophy and Phenomenological Research* 3, no. 1 (September 1942), 53–77. It also appeared as "M. Heidegger and F. Rosenzweig: A Postscript to *Being and Time*," in *Nature, History, and Existentialism,* ed. Arnold Levison (Evanston, IL: Northwestern University Press, 1966), 51–78. For Strauss's critique of Rosenzweig, see the preface to *Spinoza's Critique of Religion,* 9–15, and three talks, "Conspectivism" (1929), "Religious Situation of the Present" (1930), and "The Intellectual Situation of the Present" (1932), all trans. Anna Schmidt and Martin D. Yaffe, in *Reorientation: Leo Strauss in the 1930s,* 217–54. See also Timothy W. Burns, "Strauss on the Religious and Intellectual Situation of the Present," in *Reorientation: Leo Strauss in the* 1930s, 79–114.

by speaking of *cultures*, or as it is put today, of "social construction." It thereby denies the possibility of science.[30] The most common form that nihilism now takes is an untenable amalgam of Marxist and Heideggerian opposition to the West, in what has come to be called "identity politics." It takes from Marxism a concern for structural oppression, and from Heideggerian postmodernism a contempt for the claims of universal truth (and hence, contempt for claims of error) and turns it into a demand for respect of any and all perspectives, mores, and "values," but especially a demand for respect of the "other." It still couches its demands in the liberal idiom of "rights," but attempts to enforce by shame and law strict prohibitions against "hate" speech, which signals its opposition to any deep devotional attachments. It argues, that is, for prior restraint against speech, public or private, that manifests an allegedly "bad" disposition of the soul or the (constructed) self—of any speech that does not honor an individual's or group's authentic choices or decisions. It thus comes to oppose freedom of speech, of the press, of religion, of parental authority, and of science that does not conform to the fierce moral demands of groups that claim to be offended or made unsafe by the thoughts and words of others. In short, it stands against modern constitutionalism and moves in the direction of a new, secular despotism. When its proponents carry out social science, that science tends to be politicized science, a fight on behalf of alleged victims, just as its public analyses tend to take the form of advocacy journalism. Its proponents seek not to grasp the truth—an attempt they claim to be both futile and oppressive—but to bring about "social justice," a term that implies structural oppression and the universal guilt of hegemonic participants in the reigning social and economic order. The older moral thinking to which Strauss points us, by contrast, while attentive to the need to correct genuine injustice, is firmly rooted in the prudence of tradition, and hence, today, in the need to defend decent democratic constitutionalism and its spiritual and religious traditions.

---

30. "German Nihilism," 366: "Nihilism is the rejection of the principles of civilization as such, and if civilization is based on recognition of the fact that the subject of civilization is man as man, every interpretation of science and morals in terms of races, or of nations, or of cultures, is strictly speaking nihilistic. Whoever accepts the idea of a Nordic or German or Faustic science, e.g., rejects *eo ipso* the idea of science. Different 'cultures' may have produced different types of 'science'; but only one of them can be true, can be science."

Index

Aaronson, Jason, 169–73
Adams, Henry, 72n45
Aeschylus, 133–42
Ahrensdorf, Peter, ix
ancestral, 15–16, 29–33, 48–49, 74,
    91–112, 128–32, 140, 165–66,
    173–74n11, 179n18
aristocracy, 17–20, 22, 26
    classical, 5, 17–20, 26, 37–47, 52,
        56, 119–20, 176
    within democracy, 15, 22, 24–28,
        37–72, 91–92, 108, 176
Aristophanes, 44n9, 134n22, 146–47
Aristotle, 3–4, 30, 33, 40n3, 42n5,
    47n13, 49–50n16, 51–52n18, 71,
    89, 98, 105n58, 113, 118–21,
    125, 132–33n31, 146, 155,
    160–61, 177n16, 180, 184
    technology and, 3–4, 33–34n24,
        66–67n38, 103–104, 127–28,
        139–41, 144–45

Bacon, Francis, 33–34n24, 42n5,
    56–57, 58n23, 60n29, 62n32,
    66n38, 68–69n40, 75, 86n26,
    92n37, 97n44, 148–49
Bancroft, George, 26n13
Bartlett, Gabriel, 9n15

Baumann, Fred, 66n38, 112n70
Benardete, Seth, 116
Berlin, Isaiah, 90
Bloom, Allan, 57n24
Bolotin, David, 13n22, 48n15,
    89–90n31
Bruell, Christopher, 13n22, 48n15,
    58n25
Burke, Edmund, 53–54n20, 54–55,
    85, 107–108n60

cave, allegory of the, 45–46,
    47–48n15, 50–51n16, 125,
    130n19, 143–48
Chambers, Whittaker, 24
charity, see "mercy"
Churchill, Winston S., ix, 16, 22–28,
    35, 73–108, 174–78
civil religion/theology, 27n13, 55,
    60n29, 61n30, 64n34, 119, 140
Colen, J. A., 4n8, 6n9, 7nn10,11,
    42n5, 179n18
compassion, see "mercy"
conscience, 51, 61, 64n33, 71, 97n43,
    99, 101n49, 120–21n11, 167–69,
    177n17, 181–82
constitutionalism, 12, 16, 70, 166,
    185